Michael Veitch comes from a [obscured by sticker] although known mainly as a performer in television and theatre, has contributed to newspapers and publications for a number of years. He has had a lifelong interest in aviation, particularly during the Second World War, and studied history at the University of Melbourne. He lives and works in Melbourne and is currently the host of *Sunday Arts* on ABC television.

True stories from the men who flew in World War II

MICHAEL VEITCH

PAN
Pan Macmillan Australia

Imperial measurements have been used in some chapters of this book as they would have been during World War Two.

1 inch	25.4 millimetres	1 centimetre	0.394 inches
1 foot	30.5 centimetres	1 metre	3.28 feet
1 yard	0.914 metres	1 metre	1.09 yards
1 mile	1.61 kilometres	1 kilometre	0.621 miles

First published 2006 in Macmillan by Pan Macmillan Australia Pty Limited
This Pan edition published 2008 by Pan Macmillan Australia Pty Ltd
1 Market Street, Sydney

Reprinted 2009

National Library of Australia
cataloguing-in-publication data:

Veitch, Michael.

Flak: true stories from the men who flew in World War Two/author, Michael Veitch.

Sydney: Pan Macmillan, 2008.

ISBN 978 0 330 42408 0 (pbk).

Australia. Royal Australian Air Force - Airmen.
World War, 1939-1945 - Aerial operations, Australian.
World War, 1939-1945 - Personal narratives, Australian.

940.544994

Main cover image: Gunners J Venning of Gympie, Queensland (left) and C W Harris, RAF, demonstrate night fighter damage to the elevator of their 460 Squadron RAAF Lancaster the morning after a big raid on Peenemunde, August 8, 1943.
Both cover images from the Australian War Memorial, Negative Numbers UK0393 and 072930.

Typeset in Sabon by Midland Typesetters, Australia
Printed in Australia by McPherson's Printing Group

Papers used by Pan Macmillan Australia Pty Ltd are natural, recyclable products made from wood grown in sustainable forests. The manufacturing processes conform to the environmental regulations of the country of origin.

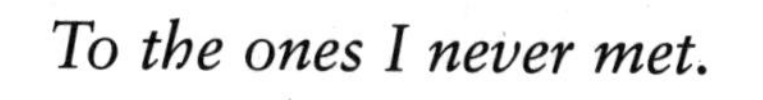

To the ones I never met.

Contents

Foreword

Michael Veitch has done a fine job of getting those of us who were shot at a lot in the skies of World War II to talk about things we seldom discussed in great detail – anywhere. Though I had many friends in heavy bombers I was never in one myself. My Mosquito navigator had been shot down on his first tour in a Beaufighter – then came to me. I had friends on long range Coastal Command aircraft, on medium bombers, on fighter squadrons and low-level ground attack. Not many survived.

The accurate descriptions in this book taught me so much, almost for the first time. I may have been frightened on several occasions in my job as a photographic reconnaissance pilot but I have often wondered if I could have done what other air crews had to do. That any of us survived at all, regardless of what our duties were, is sometimes hard to believe. Thank you, Michael, for illuminating so much about so many.

Charles 'Bud' Tingwell, 2006

Introduction

An obsession

Inside the head of every pilot, navigator or gunner who flew during the Second World War is at least one extraordinary story.

One of the best I heard was from a bloke I never got to meet. He was a rear-gunner in a Lancaster bomber and as such, sat away from his six fellow crew members at the back of the plane, shut inside a tiny perspex and aluminium cage right under the tail. A hydraulic motor powered by a relay in one of the bomber's four engines allowed him to swivel back and forth through slightly more than 90 degrees while the four mounted machine guns tracked vertically, protruding rearwards through the turret, controlled by a small hand grip. The trick was to coordinate the sideways movement of the turret with the vertical movement of the guns and bead in on a moving target, usually an enemy night fighter, in an instant. In 1943 this was brilliant technology. Indeed, the aircraft itself symbolised the absolute upper limit of what was achievable both technologically and industrially at the time, and required a massive – some have argued disproportionate – investment of Britain's wartime resources.

Inside the turret there was virtually no room, not even for the gunner's parachute, which had to be stowed on a shelf inside the fuselage and separated from the turret itself. So, if the moment came to jump, he would need to open the two small rear doors, climb back into the fuselage, locate the 'chute, strap it on, then make his way forward and leave the aircraft via the main door, presumably while being thrown about as the mortally wounded aeroplane went into its death spin from 20,000 feet. Easier said than done.

As the story goes, this fellow was directly over the target on a big night raid into Germany, his aircraft right above one of the large doomed cities being systematically wrecked by fleets of up to a thousand RAF heavy bombers at night, and possibly the Americans by day. Peering into the black sky, he swept his guns up and down, back and forth, watching for enemy fighters. Some of them reckoned that by just looking busy you appeared more alert to the German pilots and were less likely to be attacked. Suddenly he saw something – a dark shape moving fast – possibly another bomber, possibly a German night fighter passing underneath. As he leaned forward over his guns to gain a better view he felt two mighty almost instantaneous bangs and something slither quickly down his back. The turret instantly stopped working, making the guns inoperable, but both he and the aircraft seemed otherwise undamaged. He looked up. Inches above his head he saw a baseball sized hole in the top of the turret and underneath it, a matching one in the floor. It took only a moment for him to work out what had happened. An incendiary bomb – a small aluminium pipe crammed with magnesium and dropped in their hundreds – had fallen from another bomber above and passed clean through the turret before continuing on its way.

At night, with inexperienced pilots and up to a thousand four-engined aircraft passing over the same target in roughly 20 minutes, being bombed by your own side, not to mention mid-air collisions, were just a couple of the occupational hazards of flying with Bomber Command during the Second World War. Were it not for the fact that this fellow just happened, in that very instant, to be looking out for something he wasn't even sure was there, he would have certainly been killed. As it was, his turret was useless and he could only hope a night fighter didn't decide to pick on him on the way home. This night he was lucky.

As this was being told to me in the living room of a modest unit in a suburb in Perth, my jaw was agape and a cup of undrunk tea sat cooling in my hand. In the coming months, as I collected similar stories from the men, now in their eighties, who flew the aircraft of the Second World War, I would assume a similar position many times.

'So what got you interested in this stuff?', people ask me when the subject comes up unexpectedly, wearing a look on their face as if they've just digested something unsavoury. Dwelling on the awfulness of war is hardly the healthiest of mental occupations I admit, so I don't talk about it much. I usually just mumble, a little embarrassed and skirt the topic. Because in reality, I have no idea, and I've often asked myself the same question: how *did* I get interested in this stuff? I'm not particularly aggressive, am a complete coward when it comes to any form of confrontation and being involved in a war is just about the most appalling thing I can imagine. But I can't deny that the fascination is there, lodged deep inside me, and I'm not expecting it to go away anytime soon. I conveniently put it down to the unavoidable effects of growing up virtually as an only child in a semi-dysfunctional family. I was the youngest of four by about ten years, and an accident. Apparently, I owe my existence to a noisy and persistent mosquito buzzing around my parents' bedroom late one summer night, 'The night of the mosquito!', as my mother would spontaneously announce to anyone who would listen, amusing herself enormously at my expense.

My siblings wisely left home as soon as they could in their teens, so I was left to ferment in the eccentricities that most only children tend to develop. Mine happened to be aeroplanes. Model aeroplanes. I made hundreds of them and by the time I was ten could identify everything that flew between about 1937 and 1945. I spent every cent I had in hobby shops and made up the plastic kits of Spitfires, Typhoons, Blenheims and Lancasters. But it was never enough just to have them on a shelf. In my bedroom I constructed a complicated overhead mesh of string and fuse wire and arranged them in simulated combat, even building several of the same types to make up the numbers for realism. I developed a rudimentary light show using torches and standard lamps to simulate an air raid, and those planes for which I had no further use would end their days in fiery backyard dioramas of firecrackers and melted plastic. My fingers became permanently dried and wrinkled from the glue and my mother, fed up with the permeating odour of turpentine and enamel paint, exiled me to a corner of an upstairs balcony where, it now seems looking back, I spent the larger part of my childhood, summer and winter.

Many boys of that age go through a similar stage, but then grow out of it. I just never did. Failing that, one could reasonably have expected me to evolve into the jet age but that never really took off either. Although one year I did try to force myself, and put together the Airfix Hawker Hunter, perhaps the most elegant jet aircraft ever built, and even the mighty Vietnam-era Phantom (more like an airborne truck). But I could never come to terms with jet propulsion and soon regressed once again to propellers.

I have no military tradition to fall back on. My father thought about enlisting in World War Two but was too young; I did have an uncle in the army but bad feet prevented him from ever leaving the country, and a grandfather (I barely knew him) who spent some time on minesweepers in the navy. I still keep his medals in the same old Sheaffer pen case in which they were given to me, and that, I'm afraid, is where the Veitch military heritage begins and ends.

Well, not quite. In order to avoid the call-up for Vietnam, older brother Simon spent some time at Puckapunyal, north of Melbourne, in something called the Citizens Military Force, and I remember being enormously impressed by his uniform during weekend family visits.

Then in the mid 1970s, the landmark British documentary series *The World at War* screened on television at a time coinciding with a particularly hideous period in my parents' often strained relationship. In front of a small grey plastic AWA television set, I sat mesmerised by the black and white images of a distant and terrible conflict, which had the effect of blotting out that other war raging around me in my own world, the relentless set-piece battles played out on the field of my father's affairs and my mother's depression and drinking. For hours I would shut my eyes, try to ignore the shoutings in the night, and concentrate hard on what it must have been like to have actually *been there*, not in black and white but in real, living colour. It was my perfect mental escape hatch. One particularly gruesome evening I lay in bed for hours pondering the bakelite light switch on the wall I used every day. In a moment of revelation, it occurred to me that someone must have made and installed the thing before the great conflagration had even started.

I watched every episode of that series, my head spinning with the sounds and images for days afterwards. One part on the Russian war featured the recollections of four or five men and women, all veterans of the slaughter on the Eastern Front, recounting the tragedy in stupefying detail. At the end of the episode, the camera re-visited each one of them in turn in a kind of recapitulation, as they simply gazed into some middle distance behind the camera, pondering the scale of what they had seen and done in agonising, eloquent silence.

But it was the air force stuff that *really* fired off the the synapses of my early adolescent imagination. Then, on a Sunday afternoon in 1976, aged thirteen, I made an expedition to a small museum, which was, and still is, attached to Melbourne's light aircraft airport, Moorabbin. I fervently refused my father's offer to drive me (he loved an excuse to get out of the house) and eagerly plotted the complicated Sunday afternoon timetable myself. This was one childhood expedition I wanted to savour entirely alone.

After a train ride and some interminable waiting at suburban bus stops, I eventually got there. Entering the museum was like walking into a kind of paradise. Bits of old aeroplanes were scattered all over a vast yard that I was permitted – welcomed even – to crawl all over. The nose section of a Beaufort here, the wing of a Fairey Battle there. And then there were the complete types, including one of the meanest aircraft of the war, the magnificent Bristol Beaufighter – twin engined with a tall single tail fin, four evil-looking slits under the nose to house its 20-millimetre cannons and two enormous Bristol Hercules radial motors extending slightly beyond the nose, further exaggerating its immense power. Used by Australia in the Pacific, its dark grey livery gave it the appearance of an immense marauding shark.

I walked around it awe-struck. It seemed almost alive. But there was more. Up the back stood a single seat fighter, a P-40 Kittyhawk, used by the RAAF in the Middle East and in the early stages of the Pacific war. About the best thing that can be said about this machine was that it could take a lot of punishment, which was just as well, because it was frequently required to do so. Although well armed, it was big, slow and heavy – inferior to just about everything it went up against. Built by the

Americans in the late 1930s, it was outdated even on the drawing board but times were desperate and it was rushed into production. The only way it could make an impact on the nimble Japanese planes was fall on them from a great height, blast away hopefully and just keep on going downwards, ably assisted by gravity. Those Kittyhawk pilots foolish enough to take on a Zero were often living their last moments. But despite its shortcomings, I was in a forgiving mood and delighted to make its acquaintance nonetheless.

This particular Kittyhawk had not only survived the war but had been given a new lease of life by enthusiastic volunteers who had restored its Allison engine (an appropriately underwhelming name) to a point where it was very occasionally started up. As luck would have it, this Sunday afternoon was one of those occasions. I stood back and watched as a couple of devotees attached a large and ancient trolley accumulator (an antiquated portable battery) to a socket in the fuselage. The enormous propeller then jolted and then roared into life for ten glorious minutes. Suddenly this dilapidated museum piece, outmoded even in its day and half decayed in a scrapyard was, before my eyes, resurrected into the very essence of power. It was like seeing a dinosaur come back to life and start roaring.

The other aspect of that day, I remember, was a total solar eclipse that eerily blotted out the daylight during the bus trip on the way home. But for me, it was by far the minor event of the day!

Around this time came another strange and seminal event. At home one night, instead of doing my homework, I was, as usual, working diligently on the Airfix 1/72 scale Avro Lancaster, the big black four engined backbone of Bomber Command and primary ravager of western European cities throughout the second half of the war. This particular kit came with the markings of a famous Australian aircraft known by its individual letter coding as ‘S for Sugar’, which flew with number 467 Squadron from its base at Waddington in Lincolnshire.

My mother had arranged to go to a theatre restaurant show and for some reason insisted on dragging me along. At our table sat an older bloke, vaguely connected to the party of drunken adults I was forced to endure. He was quiet, sober, and slightly aloof. Somehow we got chatting. I'll never know how the subject came up, but he revealed he'd been in the air force during the war, flying in Lancasters.

He seemed happy to talk, apparently stimulated by my interest, and further questioning revealed that he had been the navigator on the very same aircraft I'd been constructing in model form a couple of hours earlier. I was thrilled, stunned and tried to impart my amazement to my mother. Then he offered to show me some of his memorabilia including, to my wide-eyed amazement, his Distinguished Flying Cross, a medal awarded solely to officers for extended or exceptional service in the face of the enemy (although some disgruntled sergeants I've met claim they were handed out like yo-yos).

I jumped at the chance to see one up close. My mother arranged the meeting. At school the next day I raved about the seemingly unbelievable coincidence of the night before, to be met with almost complete boredom by my school friends. But I pitied them. They weren't going to see a DFC!

A couple of weeks later I spent most of a wet winter's afternoon with my new, but old friend Arnold in his living room surrounded by old photographs, his log book and a real live Distinguished Flying Cross, still in its original presentation box. It was a magnificent liquid-looking silver cross struck in the shape of a propeller, mounted on a ribbon of diagonal purple and silver stripes and, to me, quite the loveliest thing I'd ever seen. He talked and I listened, listened like never before. I looked at his hands as he spoke about his tour flying into the night skies over Germany: the cold, the flak, the friendships, the loss and the fear. Despite the violent events he'd been a part of, he was a gentle man, and spoke quietly with a slight stammer, which I later learned was a legacy from the stress of flying. As he went on, he obviously found the dredging of the memories difficult and by the early evening when I was picked up, he seemed utterly drained. I shook his hand, and watched his eyes, those same eyes that had seen it all.

Cast-iron and life-long, my obsession had been set.

I seriously contemplated joining the air force myself, a laughable idea now, but at fourteen, one which I took very seriously. But to discover just how unsuited to such a career I in fact was, I would need to join up.

At the expensive private school to which my parents somehow found the resources to send me, some form of after-class physical activity was compulsory. I loathed the idea of stomping around an oval in badly fitting dungarees with the army cadets and my natural indolence left me pathologically terrified of sport. Then, at the nadir of my despair, an older boy told me of an antiquated clause in the school's constitution (it was that kind of place) that allowed certain outside activities to be taken in lieu of their own. Upon further investigation, I discovered that one of those sanctioned was the air force cadets, the Air Training Corps.

I'd hit the jackpot. Or so I thought. Twice a week after school I donned my snappy dark blue uniform and headed off on the train. Rough boys on the platform sniggered but what did I care? The headquarters of number 14 Flight, ATC was a big, drafty wooden drill hall sandwiched between an industrial air conditioning factory and North Melbourne railway station. I naturally assumed that with my profound knowledge of the history and heritage of the air force, I'd be running the place within a few weeks.

I hated it from the very start, and it didn't much like me either. The drill, the constant yelling of orders, having to address the smarmy part-time officers as 'sir' and attending lectures comprised of reading out slabs from textbooks all combined to alienate me. The officers sneered at anyone displaying any knowledge beyond their own and my attitude probably didn't help. I was a smartarse, and the other boys, all from tough suburbs, pounced on my private school mannerisms immediately. The one and only camp ('bivouac') I attended was misery from start to finish: a cross between a southern chain gang and *The Lord of the Flies*.

Perhaps if I'd stuck at it I would have eventually got near an aeroplane and maybe even some rudimentary instruction in flying, but it was not to be. In eight months, it was all over. I handed back the uniform – much to the joy of the other cadets – and tried tennis, at which I was also appalling.

My passion, however, was undiminished and as I got older, grew into an obsession with every aspect of the Second World War. I collected uniforms and medals and books and badges, totally oblivious to the passion-deadening effect it had on the opposite sex, explaining why my youth was spent in a state of extended sexual frustration.

About ten years ago, having exhausted all other means of throwing away my money, I had a go at learning to fly. Another disappointment. The flight manuals were incomprehensible and I was airsick every time I went up. But I persisted. To no avail. In a fitting end to the experiment, my instructor was involved in a non-fatal air crash, came under investigation by the Civil Aviation Safety Authority and the school went bankrupt. I hadn't even learned to land. It did, however, equip me for my moment of glory.

On the redeye flight from Perth to Sydney one night to promote a less-than-successful sit-com in which I was given the poisoned chalice of the title role, I found myself seated at the front end of a Qantas A-300 Airbus.

The show, *Bligh*, a less-than-hilarious romp through early colonial New South Wales (fertile comic ground in anyone's eyes) has since faded into TV oblivion. At the time, it was quite a big deal and Channel Seven had me criss-crossing the country on a two week publicity blitz before everyone cottoned onto the fact that the show was a dog. Half an hour into the long flight, the first officer emerged from the cockpit and sauntered aimlessly down the aisle, an activity no doubt riveting compared to his normal occupation of watching the plane fly itself and praying that chicken was not, yet again, on the menu. He was a genial fellow and catching sight of me, started to chat about comedy, a subject I usually find about as exciting as he does his own job.

It was pre 9-11, so a mention of flying lessons produced an instant invitation up to the cockpit. I did my best to charm the pilot (also a comedy fan) and gradually steered the conversation around to flying. What happened next still today makes me shudder to think about it. The first officer said something I couldn't quite hear to the captain, which made him look a little uneasy. But then he nodded, turned to me and uttered the words, 'Would you like to sit in?'

I looked at him blankly but suddenly his seat made a whirring sound and moved back on a motorised track. He got up and indicated I should take his place. Without thinking, I did just that. I sat there for a moment, motionless and a little stunned. The pilot meanwhile had lost his initial apprehension and chatted some more, pleased to be showing an interested observer the controls. What happened next is, I swear, true.

The first officer leaned over me and hit a button on the console, producing a tinny American-accented electronic voice that warned, 'Auto-pilot disengaged' to the accompaniment of a whooping siren.

'Handing over,' he said.

'Er, t-taking over,' I stuttered, giving the prescribed flying school response. Modern airliners have dispensed with a control column as such. Instead, the pilot steers the aircraft with his left hand clutching a small plastic grip. Gingerly I held it. I was now in complete control of a real live passenger aircraft, flying at night, somewhere over the West Australian desert with sixty or so unsuspecting souls on board. A bead of perspiration emerged at my hairline. Just to see if I really did have control of the thing, I eased the stick a fraction to the left. Out the window, the port wing dipped ever so slightly. I corrected and did the same on the right. After about a minute, the nature of the situation began to dawn on me, and a voice in my head said something like, 'Right, that's enough. This is too weird'. I thanked the gentlemen for their hospitality and made my way back to my seat, not quite believing what had just happened. It was so odd I told no one about it for months.

A few years ago, an excellent Australian documentary series, *Wings of the Storm*, was screened, telling the story of the Australians in Bomber Command during World War Two and the losses they endured over Europe. One of the people featured was my navigator friend, Arnold, looking pale and nervous, an older, sicker version of the man I had spoken to several years earlier. Seeing him like this shocked me. He didn't look like he had long to go, and in fact died soon after being interviewed for the program. It gave me the germ of an idea.

Many fellows completely clammed up after the war, and who can blame them? Returning servicemen believed the best way to get over their trauma was to shut up about it. This was after all, a generation born in the shadow of one mind-numbingly dreadful world conflict, only to have to grow up and fight the next, with an economic depression in between. People were traumatised even before it got started. It's easy to see why boys were told not to cry – how would you ever get them to stop? People back home, weary after six years of grief, stress and deprivation, would not, indeed could not understand what their fighting men had been through.

Over the last few years, however, to 'He never spoke about it' has often been added the rejoinder 'until now'. It's not hard to understand the reason. The youngest age a participant of the Second World War can be in the year 2006 is eighty years old. All of them have now seen most of their contemporaries pass on, often taking their experiences to the grave. They were witnesses to, and participants in, one of the most dramatic, darkest and most vitally important chapters in our history, at a time when the stakes have rarely been higher or less ambiguous. And as I discovered, most of the people I met were more than happy to discuss what they'd been through, provided they were being asked the right questions.

I found the best way to get a man of that generation to clam up was to ask 'What was it like?' or 'How did you feel?' So I've stuck to the facts to let the drama speak for itself.

A word of warning: I have never believed there to have been anything inherently special about the Second World War generation as a whole. The people who fought it were brave, certainly, and responded when their country was in need, but were never, and have never claimed to be, the breed of righteous demi-gods the mantra of resurgent jingoism would have us believe. All that Aussie Anzac legend stuff quite frankly bores me rigid. I have no reason to believe that either my own, my children's or any other generation would not perform as well, or as badly, as they did given the circumstances, and most of the men I met during this project agreed. As far as they were concerned, they were ordinary people who, in extraordinary times were called upon to perform extraordinary actions. These they spoke of with frankness, humility, and in remarkable good humour. In this, perhaps, they are indeed special.

1

Gordon Dalton

Bomb-aimer

I've always been a lazy bugger. I like to go into battle lying down.

Gordon was my first cab off the rank and in a way, my most memorable. It was one of Gordon's neighbours who contacted me with a simple email: *Call Gordon Dalton. I think he was in bombers* and a phone number. Later that afternoon, I stared at the telephone like a teenager calling a girl for a first date, overwhelmed with an irrational bout of nerves that was to grip me whenever making a new contact. I put the receiver down several times before dialling, finding distractions in the garden or kitchen for hours at a time. Pulling weeds out of the cracks in between brick paving (the most fiddly and time consuming task I could find), various uncomfortable scenarios played in my head. What would these people say to me? What if they told me to get lost, to stop prying into their dim, distant and traumatic past? I heard a scratchy, irascible old voice lecturing me in my head: 'Do you know what war is? Do you know the sorts of things that happen in war? The scars people carry with them? Do you have feelings?' Now I came to think of it, I'd never known anyone in their eighties. What would they be like? Doddery? Deaf? What if they all had Alzheimer's and thought I was their uncle Stan? How much would I have to explain? Wouldn't my lefty, middle-class leanings clash with everything they stood for? What if, as usual, I was unable to keep my mouth shut and get asked to leave in a hurry?

At last, I dialled. A man sounding as if he were in his fifties answered. I fell into a chaotic tumbling explanation of who I was and what I was doing.

'Someone gave me your number . . . I'm doing this book . . . thing . . . about aircrew . . . and . . . the planes . . .' I sounded like an idiot. Why on earth was I so nervous? The voice on the other end was calm and patient. Was he a son? Perhaps a brother? I needed to speak to Gordon. Could he put me onto Gordon?

'I'm Gordon,' he said. 'Come over tomorrow if you like. Two o'clock OK?'

Gordon was sharp. Just like he'd sounded on the phone. He lived in a stylish 1950s ground floor apartment-style house with his equally charming wife Jo, a woman of great style who punctuated much of what she had to say with a big, earthy laugh, emitted between lusty draws on a cigarette.

I walked into the living room and a beer was placed in my hand, the first of several for the afternoon. I glanced around briefly at the random objects that signify a long, shared life: pictures of children and grandchildren, exotic wall-hangings and small statuettes from what used to be called the Far East, some books on cricket and near the door, a large framed print of a Lancaster bomber in flight.

'How long have you been married?' I asked.

'Fifty-seven years,' guffawed Jo, 'forever!'

I sat in a large comfortable armchair on a parquetry floor. Instead of the judgemental patriarch I had anticipated, I found myself sitting opposite a man so laid back that I was completely thrown. His tone was quiet, low-key and terribly, terribly dry. I pulled out the tape recorder. 'OK if I switch this on?'

'Go for your life,' he said.

When it came to the business end of a bombing raid, it all came down to the bomb-aimer. Lying on his stomach in the cramped nose compartment of the aircraft, it was the bomb-aimer who identified the target (or coloured target indicator flares), called 'bomb doors open' over the intercom, then lined it up along an illuminated 'sword' in the Mark VII bombsight, guiding the pilot over the intercom with precise directions of 'left, left a bit . . . steady' etc. The rest of the crew could only listen to this seemingly interminable exchange as the big bomber flew straight and level into the cauldron of the target, through flak and, at night, search-lights. (Gordon's navigator, the only fellow Australian on his crew, would often interject with an exasperated 'Just drop the bloody things!') At the right moment, when the target crossed the hilt of the sword, the bomb-aimer pressed a button or 'tit' on the end of an electric lead clutched in his hand, called 'bombs gone', and several tons of explosives fell away from the aircraft, making it surge upwards as if gasping with relief. Then it was 'Bomb doors closed – let's get the hell out of here!' But not until the photoflash, a flare timed to go off at the moment of impact to visually record the accuracy (or otherwise) of the drop. It must have seemed the longest 20 seconds of their lives.

While the bomb-aimer's job was crucial, out of all the crew, he usually had the least to do. While the pilot was busy flying, the navigator constantly working out where they were and where they had to get to, the gunners on vigilant look-out for fighters, the bomb-aimer often had to find things to occupy himself. Occasionally he was required to drop bundles of cut aluminium strips, known as 'window', out of a small chute in the nose to confuse the German radar, or man the rarely used front gun turret, but on a long trip, he could sometimes go to sleep (the padding on the bomb-aimer's mat was, after all, relatively comfortable). But on the run up to the target, it was time for the bomb-aimer to remind the rest of the crew why they were there.

After joining up, Gordon had a go at being a pilot but was scrubbed early and trained as a navigator and wireless operator instead.

'A flying arsehole,' he said in a dry drawl, referring to the winged 'O' for Observer he wore on his tunic. He hated it. 'Too much work.' So, when arriving in England as part of the bombing offensive over Europe, and an opportunity arose to volunteer as a bomb-aimer, his hand shot up the highest.

Gordon did his entire tour of thirty operations in Lancasters, and most of those in daylight with 622 Heavy Bomber Squadron operating out of Mildenhall in Suffolk. Along with the rest of the crew of seven, the bomb-aimer would undergo the pre-flight ritual, that dramatic moment when, in the briefing room, a curtain was drawn back and the target revealed on a big map of western Europe covered in spidery coloured lines of tape indicating routes to and from the target, searchlight and flak batteries and known enemy fighter stations along the way.

He would be issued with a green canvass bag containing maps and information about the target, and an escape kit containing a silk map and currency of the countries overflown in the event of being shot down and lucky enough to survive. Just before take-off, in a wonderful piece of English bureaucratic absurdity, he would be required to sign a form taking possession of the several thousand pounds of bombs he was about to deliver, as if flogging them off somewhere en route was a possibility.

Gordon's first operation was in some ways his most memorable, a trip (all bomber crews called operations 'trips') to Walcheren Island, a chunk of Dutch marshland reclaimed from the sea opposite the Scheldt estuary, remarkable only for its proximity to the Belgian port of Antwerp. Antwerp was desperately needed to enable supplies to reach the Allied armies pushing into Europe, and to shorten the ever lengthening supply route which wound its way up from the original D-Day beaches 300 miles (nearly 500 kilometres) away in Normandy. The port itself had been captured largely intact in a lightning thrust by the British and Canadian armies, but the approaches were defended from the sea by the Germans manning the guns of Walcheren.

On 3 October 1944, Gordon's target for his first trip was the sea wall on the westernmost point of the island, but even at the astonishingly low altitude of 5,300 feet, he couldn't see a thing through all the smoke from the bombs of some of the other 252 Lancasters detailed to attack the same target. However, a direct hit was essential to breach the sea wall and flood the German gun batteries, the object of the exercise. The famous 617 'Dam Buster' squadron had eight of their Lancasters circling with special 'Tallboy' deep penetration bombs ready to come in if the conventional attack was unsuccessful. Peering through a gap in some of the smoke, Gordon saw the sea wall emerge and gave an impromptu order to the pilot: 'Turn 30 degrees, Skip.' Part of the bomb-aimer's office equipment was the bomb selector panel on his immediate right – sixteen switches enabling him to select which bombs were to be dropped in what order and a primitive 1940s style computer (it was the first time Gordon ever heard the word) to calculate air speed and wind direction and then make the appropriate corrections, all by means of an ingenious mechanism based on gyros and compressed air. One of the switches was 'salvo' by which the entire load could be dropped at once, rather than in sequence. Gordon chose this as the most effective way to attack a small target and let them go in one big bang. Meanwhile, at the other end of the aircraft, the rear-gunner was firing his four machine guns at the ground below, emptying his entire stock of 12,000 rounds into anything that moved.

'I claim to have sunk the island,' he told me sixty years later, and had the evidence to prove it, handing me automatic target shots, souvenired courtesy of a friend in the Intelligence lab on the base. They are square black and white stills taken at the moment of impact, the large format film yielding extraordinary detail. Underneath the image, the Intelligence officer has written time and place, height, squadron, film run number and the individual aircraft which took it. Rocks, broken concrete and the disintegrating sea wall can clearly be seen. The sea rushed in, inundating the German gun positions and allowing amphibious operations to mop up and open the port of Antwerp. The circling Lancasters from 617 took their Tallboys home, possibly a bit miffed. The headlines in the papers the next day said it all: RAF SINKS AN ISLAND.

A couple of months later, Gordon reckoned he was nearly witness to a historical, indeed mysterious event. On 15 December his Lancaster was one of 138 planes detailed to attack the railway yards in the German city of Siegen. They were recalled due to the bad weather that prevented their escorting fighters from taking off. It was considered too dangerous to land with bombs still onboard, so the standard procedure was to drop them safely in one of two designated jettison areas, one south of the English Channel and another in the North Sea. The 500-pound general purpose bombs splashed down harmlessly without exploding (one of the features of the selector panel being the ability to drop them unarmed) but the 4,000-pound 'Cookie' was a different matter. Most Lancasters carried this monstrous and highly sensitive weapon loaded dead centre of the enormous bomb bay. The Cookie blast bomb was simply a huge canister filled with high explosive, like a couple of 44-gallon drums stuck end-to-end and packed with TNT. In fact, there were three sizes, the largest of which weighed a massive 6 tons and took up the entire bomb bay. It was a crude but highly effective weapon, and could not be dropped harmlessly. Even in the sea, the blast rose up 5,000 feet.

Late that afternoon, the Lancasters were over the jettison zone, releasing their payloads into the sea. As Gordon said, 'Cookies were going off everywhere' in great plumes rising out of the Channel. Amidst the chaos, someone in the squadron (Gordon was never quite sure who) reckoned he saw, unbelieveably, a small single engined aircraft flying through the explosions thousands of feet below. This sighting was confirmed by several others back at the base, amazed that anything at all was flying in this designated 'no-go' area. Later that evening, the BBC news bulletin reported that band leader Glenn Miller had been reported missing en route to France on his way to begin a series of concerts to entertain the troops. Officially, the fate of Miller's plane has always remained a mystery.

Siegen was given a 24-hour reprieve until the next day. This trip saw the most dramatic incident in Gordon's flying career.

On the way to the target at 16,000 feet, the pilot of Gordon's aircraft started behaving strangely. The navigator noticed it first as the aircraft began wandering off course.

'You alright, Skip?' he called over the intercom, but received no reply. Suspecting he was beginning to black out, the navigator asked Gordon to check the pilot's oxygen tube in case it had become tangled and cut off the supply. Gordon clambered out of the nose to the cockpit, but found the tube to be operating correctly. Then, at 24,000 feet, the pilot passed out, slumping over the controls. Gordon stood behind his seat and flew the aircraft with one hand, while the navigator, wireless operator and flight engineer tried to pull the man's dead weight out the seat in a hurry. I myself have inspected the inside of a Lancaster cockpit – roomy it isn't. At high altitude over occupied Europe lifting an unconscious man out of his seat and onto a small rest stretcher to the rear would have been extremely difficult. Oxygen hoses and intercom leads became twisted and tangled, and as the only crew member with any flying experience, Gordon climbed into the pilot's seat to keep the thing straight and level. All this would have been tricky enough, except that on this day, their aircraft happened to be leading the entire formation of over one hundred Lancasters, which were now flying in formation directly behind them. They were being led by a bomb-aimer whose only flying experience had been a few hours on a single engine Tiger Moth biplane back at Initial Training School, a task to which he admits to being singularly unsuited and to which the authorities apparently concurred.

Reaching the target was now out of the question and the most sensible option was to head for home but strict radio silence had to be maintained. The problem was that every time they attempted to turn and break out of formation, the entire force started to turn with them. Gordon told the navigator to fire off red Very flares to signal the other aircraft that something was wrong, and the mid-upper gunner had a go at signalling with an Aldis lamp. All to no avail. Whenever they veered away, the great black fleet of Lancasters followed.

The consequences of being responsible for an entire force returning to base still with their bombs were apparently too ghastly to contemplate so Gordon needed to think of something. With his right hand he dragged back one of the four throttles and feathered the outer starboard engine, bringing the big propeller to a halt. Finally sensing something was awry with the lead aircraft, the others at last stopped playing Follow the Leader and let them break away and head for home.

The wireless operator tapped out the signal by morse in plain, uncoded language: *Skipper unfit. Returning to base.* Two hours later, the Cookie was jettisoned in the North Sea and Gordon who was becoming quite relaxed in his role of impromptu pilot, began warming to the prospect of a landing, but thought he'd give the crew the option to bail out. One by one, they all chose to take their chances and stay put. It was only in the circuit area with the undercarriage lowered that Gordon felt a tap on his shoulder and there was his pilot, suddenly awake and ready to take over, apparently none the worse for wear. Gordon duly vacated the seat, quietly disappointed.

The pilot spent a fortnight in hospital, the episode put down to 'operational fatigue'. These days, we'd call it stress. In Bomber Command, an operational tour usually comprised at least thirty trips before an individual could be taken off flying duties. At various stages of the war, the loss rate was so high that the chances of completing that tour were one in three. That is, a one in three chance of survival. How any of them could do it night after night without completely falling to pieces is beyond me.

After taxying, Gordon and the rest of the crew were met by a welcoming committee, and a fuss was made of the bomb-aimer whose cool headedness and quick thinking probably saved an aircraft and its crew. But that's where it ended. The station commander greeted Gordon with a hearty, 'Very well done, Dalton. I'll see you get an award for this.' It's been sixty years. He's still waiting.

Postscript: Gordon's pilot, who he described as a 'quiet Englishman', spent four years after the war with what was then termed 'war neurosis', no doubt endlessly re-living the days and nights of his tour.

2

Dick Levy

Pilot, B-25 Mitchells

Levy, you're the worst bloody pupil I've ever had.
Go and kill yourself.

I met Dick and his wife, Barbara, in the foyer of a theatre in a town in central Victoria. We had been in contact by phone and by chance I was to perform there in a scratched together production about the joys and foibles of contemporary fatherhood. To my surprise (horror really), he expressed interest in coming along to see it so I duly arranged some tickets. What on earth would he make of all this touchy-feely stuff about modern parenthood and the fears that confront men of my generation? 'Don't give me this "life is so hard these days" crap,' I could hear him saying. 'You think *you've* got it hard? I watched my best friends vapourised over the target!'

But of course he wasn't like that at all. In fact, he was utterly charming and found the show highly entertaining, so much so that he invited me to lunch the next day at his house for our interview.

Our meeting took place on a clear, cool spring afternoon. Books on art and theatre and classical music adorned the walls of the post-war brick house they'd lived in since the late forties. We lunched on a formally set dining table of dark polished wood with a string quartet playing softly on the stereo in the background and several excellent glasses of wine. This did nothing for the quality of my questions, a fact borne out months later when listening back to my voice.

After completing his training, Dick headed off for overseas in the middle of the night. Sailing down the Brisbane River in 1943, people in the flats and houses along the bank waved towels out the window to say goodbye.

Two weeks later, they were under the Golden Gate Bridge and for four days, wartime San Francisco opened its doors to these strangers in their odd dark-blue uniforms and even odder accents.

'They'd never even heard of Australia,' he recounts. 'They wanted to know how our English was so good!' (In sixty years, I assured him, little had changed.)

Thousands of Australian airmen and service personnel made this eye-opening journey across the United States on their way to the European war. They travelled across the continent by train in luxurious Pullman sleeping-cars, being frowned upon by fellow whites for striking up friendly conversations with the black porters.

Dick boarded the massive liner *Queen Elizabeth* and, with 17,000 others, sailed off across the Atlantic at 35 knots, too fast for any U-boat and so did without the company of a convoy. They were crammed eight to a cabin which normally held four, and six more piled up in makeshift bunks in the bathroom. Up above, the Americans walked the decks in shifts, waiting for their turn to sleep.

After months of waiting, clay pigeon shooting on Brighton beach and visits to the English countryside, Dick was finally sent to an Operational Training Unit at the delightfully named

Leighton Buzzard in Bedfordshire to train on Wellingtons. The Vickers Wellington had been the workhorse of Bomber Command for the first couple of years of the war and were still in service in the Mediterranean but by 1944 most examples were well and truly past their prime. Dick remembers everything in them rattling and creaking like an old truck. It was easy to sustain injuries while being jolted around the rough interior so he and his crew took to wearing gloves at all times to stop burring their hands.

Wellingtons were remarkable for their unique construction. Instead of a nice even skin made up of metal sheets riveted together in sections, the body was built around a peculiar lattice frame of criss-crossing or 'geodetic' aluminium, which was wrapped in an outer skin of painted cloth. It made for a light, strong airframe but burned like blazes if in trouble. The rear gunner also had to navigate a hazardous narrow walkway to the tail section which, should he slip off, risked putting his foot through the bottom of the fuselage. As a kid, I thought their long, rather slender wings resembled the old Fokker Friendship turbo prop airliners that TAA used to operate. But there was nothing friendly about the Wellington's early experiences over Europe in daylight without fighter escort. The first versions even lacked proper gun turrets and were slaughtered by the German fighters.

While at Leighton Buzzard, Dick also experienced the phenomenon of 'crewing up', whereby the various pilots, navigators, bomb-aimers and gunners would form into individual fighting units by means of a remarkably democratic, even organic process. Instead of the powers-that-be dictating which pilot would fly with which navigator, gunner, etc, it was left to the trainee crew members to get together in a large hanger and sort it out for themselves. There they would mingle, size each other up from a distance, trying to glean some quality or talent or spark, some indication that this person was a good sort to risk one's life with. Sixty-five pilots, sixty-five navigators, the same number of wireless operators and about double the number of gunners mingled like shy teenagers at a dance, all hoping not be the last one picked. It was often the pilot who made the first move to a navigator, then the two of them would size up the rest, based entirely on instinct and first impressions. It was an ingenious system: brilliantly simple and circumventing a whole realm of resentment towards senior officers should someone end up in a crew not to their liking. It was also successful. Barely anyone I spoke to complained about the men they ended up completing a tour with. It would seem the cauldron of experience was a highly effective leveller.

Upon completion of training, Dick and his crew fully expected to be sent to Bomber Command to train up on the Lancaster. One day, however, a call went out for crews to volunteer for what was ominously described as 'special duties'. 'Could be interesting,' said Dick to his new crew. 'What about it?' On leave a couple of weeks later, they all received telegrams to report to yet another Operational Training Unit, not in Bomber Command, but as part of the Second Tactical Air Force to train on the twin engined B-25 North American Mitchell medium bomber.

The Tactical Air Force was about as close as you could get to being a fighter pilot while flying in bombers and was formed out of a need to provide close support to the fighting troops with a mobile air strike force that could operate from temporary airfields close to the front line, a role in which the heavier aircraft had failed spectacularly. On D-Day, the beaches were supposed to have been peppered by the heavies with bomb craters in order to provide the troops with some shelter. They missed, and on some beaches, the casualties were enormous. Later, in Operation Cobra, the breakout from Normandy, American aircraft bombed their own men when hitting the wrong side of a road. The highest ranking American general of the war, a certain Lieutenant General Lesley McNair, was also killed in a similar 'friendly fire' incident.

It was thus decided that the Tactical Air Force was to be used for close and rapid response, constantly on the move to bases just behind the advancing armies and to be called upon at short notice. The catch for the crews was that a tour in the TAF constituted not thirty, but fifty operations. Flying shorter missions, sometimes several in a day was considered less risky. Others might disagree.

Dick had never even heard of a B-25, but was impressed from the moment he saw one. Compared to the old Wellington, the American-built Mitchell was a thoroughbred. Fast, sleek, easy to handle and with an unusual tricycle undercarriage (a wheel in the nose instead of the tail) it took off and landed at about 130 miles an hour, disconcertingly faster than the old Wellington.

A few weeks later on a cold night in November 1944, he and his crew of three boarded an aircraft at Blackbush airfield north of London to join number 180 Squadron, Second Tactical Air Force, British Liberation Army at their base at Melsbroek near Brussels. As a squadron emblem, 180 sported a medieval mailed fist, an object as the crews were wont to point out, 'not much use on the ground and fuck-all use in the air'.

Almost as soon as they arrived, their names were placed on the battle order for their first operation. The theatre of the briefing room provided an apprehensive Dick with his first look at the big target map. To his astonishment, instead of the coloured route markers leading east into Germany, they headed west, to the French port of Dunkirk, still in German hands and isolated six months after D-Day.

Flying largely over friendly territory was an easy introduction to his tour but the target itself gave Dick his first close-up view of flak. It was not to be his last. From a distance it was unnerving, up close it was terrifying, a dark red flash at the heart of black explosion. You could feel it, hear it, even smell it. A near-miss would pelt the aircraft with white-hot fragments of shrapnel as if from a gigantic shotgun. Anything closer could tear a hole in the wing or fuselage.

The word 'Flak' is an acronym for Fliegerabwehrkanonen or aircraft defence guns and the Germans were masterful in its use. Guns coordinating with radar would predict the course and direction of an individual aircraft and catch it as it flew into a tight box barrage of exploding shells. The pilots in Dick's squadron never liked flying in the same direction for more than ten seconds but running up to the target when the flak was often heaviest, they weren't always afforded that luxury.

Among a pile of photographs, documents and assorted memorabilia, Dick showed me a photograph of his training course at Mallala in South Australia – row upon row of young male faces, smiling in uniform and wearing the distinctive white flash denoting a student aircrew. In a matter of fact way he mentioned that 25 per cent of them did not come home.

'There I am in the middle,' he told me, pointing to his younger face. 'This is Bob Chalmers – he was from Footscray – he didn't survive . . .' For a few minutes Dick's gaze travelled across the faces, some forgotten but many others remembered. 'Jamie Cameron – a stock and station agent – survived with terrible burns after an engine failure at take-off . . .'

Dick flew his entire tour in daylight, usually in formations of six aircraft. The flight commander was number one, two and three were close on the left or right, four was close under number one, five and six with positions of their own, the entire formation stacked in a tight box providing not only mutually supportive defensive fire from its guns, but concentrating its bombing power as well. Much of Dick's tour was completed in early 1945 when the German air force was severely weakened and often did not put up much of an appearance or fight. Number 180 Squadron was not so lucky.

Coming back from a trip to Wesel, Dick's plane was flying low under the clouds when three Messerschmitt 109s suddenly appeared. Dick didn't even see them, hearing only an unusual 'ratt-a-tattat' and instinctively drawing his elbows into his sides for protection from the armour plate at the back of his seat, only realising what they were when they roared past him and peeled away. 'It was like seeing the grey underbelly of a shark,' he told me. Jock Maher, new to the squadron and flying number six, was just out of the formation, about six or seven lengths over to the right, isolated from the protection of the others and a sitting target. The gunners saw it all, just one pass by the German fighters and then they were gone. Jock's Mitchell went straight down, flames pouring out of the starboard engine and in a steep dive, too low for parachutes. There were no survivors.

Among his pictures was a photograph of Jock's grave, taken just after the war in June 1945.

March 8 was another terrible day. Detailed to attack railway marshalling yards in Haltern, the flak over the target was dreadful. With bomb doors open, the Mitchells in Dick's squadron attacked as one. Dick got his bombs away but then the flak found him in a box barrage and began exploding in violent grey puffs within a few feet of the aircraft, holing him several times. Barely two lengths away and slightly ahead, he remembers seeing a red flash in the aircraft next to him, then a massive bang. A burst had exploded directly inside the bomb bay of the adjacent aircraft as its bombs released, detonating the entire payload and destroying it and its crew in an instant. The close range blast made his aircraft momentarily uncontrollable but it kept flying, pelted by debris. One by one, he called the roll. All answered, shaken but unhurt. All but Tony Kendrick, one of the gunners who was hit in the knee and bleeding badly. Another crew member jabbed him with a morphine stick from the medical pack and the aircraft passed safely over the target. Then Dick noticed that all the hydraulic pressure gauges on the instrument panel were registering zero. Shrapnel had cut the lines and the entire fuselage floor was awash in the distinctive blood-red colour of hydraulic fluid, vital for the control of flaps, brakes and undercarriage.

Even before the advice from base came over the radio, the navigator was hard at work, pumping the manual under-carriage lever back and forth to lower the wheels by hand.

I asked Dick what the atmosphere was like among the crew, heading in for a potential crash-land in a stricken aircraft. Was there panic? Tears? Hysteria? He looked thoughtful for a moment.

'Calm,' he told me. 'It was all very calm. Everyone knew what they had to do. Everyone had been trained. We all spoke calmly and clearly to one another and communication was good.' At last a reassuring *clunk* indicated the wheels were in position.

Dick was given a priority landing and brought the aircraft in as slowly as he could without flaps, and as close as he could to the beginning of the runway. It touched down, still at a dangerous speed, and he managed to prevent it from skewing off the side of the tarmac and to an eventual halt. Immediately they were surrounded by crash tenders and ambulances. A medical officer handed him a tot of rum.

'Give it to Tony. He needs it more than I do.'

Dick's instructor back in Mallala would surely have been impressed.

Later, walking around the aircraft, Dick counted no less than thirty-nine holes in every part of the machine.

'I've said it before and I'll say it now: I knew I'd make it home in one piece, I knew it. I believe some power beyond human understanding was protecting me. That, and the prayers of my mother,' said Dick with the assurance of a man safe with his convictions.

3

Allen Tyson

Air-gunner

The pilot and bomb-aimer both got the DFC. We just got the pants scared off us.

Allen got into the air force because he already had the uniform. It wasn't quite the right uniform but it was close enough. Originally from Broken Hill, Allen had been in the Air Training Corps cadets since he was sixteen and decided to tag along one night in 1943 with a bunch of new recruits to a draughty hall in Perth on the off chance that some other bloke hadn't turned up. He was in luck. Although the youngest, he was taken straight in without having to wait the usual six months in the reserve between sign up and call up. He was, as they say, a keen type. He still is.

I met Allen in an aircraft museum in Perth where he works as a volunteer and as soon as he sat down he was eager to talk, delighting in recalling the events of sixty years ago as if they'd happened on the way in that morning. He reacted to my specific line of questioning as if it were a game of mental gymnastics and actually became more enthusiastic as we progressed, answering quickly, fixing me with alert, pale eyes and applying minute elaborations to his stories such as sitting in the Nullabor next to the troop train on the way over from South Australia and opening a tin of sausages in the red dust.

To train as an air-gunner, Allen, along with most air-gunners, was forced to endure one of aviation's great misnomers, the infamous Fairey Battle light bomber. The British made some wonderful aircraft during the Second World War, but the Battle was not one of them. The biggest battle this lemon ever had was staying in the air, and at that it was usually hopeless. It's a shame, because visually speaking, it's always been one of my favourite aeroplanes: a low-wing monoplane with sleek lines, a single aerodynamically handsome liquid-cooled engine and long glasshouse canopy to accommodate its two occupants. It looked like a large-ish fighter, but that's where any similarity ended. Conceived in 1932, the Battle was completely out-dated from the beginning of the war and by 1940, despite a Rolls-Royce engine, it was dreadfully underpowered, heavy, and lacked manoeuvrability. It plodded its way through the skies like grandma's old Austin, which was in fact the factory where it was built. Add to this its lack of self-sealing fuel tanks and subsequent habit of catching fire with ease, the only thing it had going for it was the courage of the men who flew it, and this they demonstrated in spades.

The black day, or days, of the Royal Air Force were during the German invasion of France in May 1940 when, utterly overwhelmed by the Luftwaffe, they threw precious men and machines at the problem until realising what they should have known from the start of the campaign, namely that it was over, and time to retreat to fight another day. In the meantime, however, the Battle crews of Bomber Command were called upon to perform one hopeless suicidal task after another, often suffering 60 per cent losses, culminating on 12 May in an infamous low-level attack by number 12 Squadron on two bridges over the Albert Canal near Maastricht, in which the entire attacking force of six Battles was shot down. Even the

Germans were appalled, reprimanding some of the captured airmen on their lack of sense ('Why didn't you attack *before* we got here to defend the bridges?') but admiring their obvious courage. Two Victoria Crosses were awarded to the Battle crews that day, one posthumously, but at least one of the bridges was destroyed. The Germans, however, put up a perfectly effective pontoon bridge the very next day.

Having wasted enough precious industrial muscle on churning out Battles (and some other lame ducks which we'll come to later) the government at last decided to halt production and pull all remaining Battles out of squadron service, relegating them to docile tasks like training and target towing in the far corners of the globe such as Iceland, and somewhere even more remote, Australia.

That's why at the Air Gunnery School in Port Pirie, South Australia, Allen Tyson found himself climbing into the rear cockpit of a well used Fairey Battle to acquaint himself with a World War One vintage Vickers gas-operated machine gun. With this he was expected in four short weeks to master the principles of shooting down an attacking enemy aircraft. After ten hours ten minutes flying time, he was qualified and packed off to Melbourne (via some ignominious nights billeted in the sheep pens at Ascot Vale cattle yards) to prepare for overseas embarkation.

A fast American troop ship – in actual fact a converted luxury liner – took him the first step of the long journey to England via the United States. In New York, his convoy was delayed by the German battleship *Scharnhorst*, which was currently running rampant in the Atlantic, so Allen and his mates were condemned to spend an all-expenses paid three weeks in New York city.

'Must have been hard,' I suggested.

'Yeah. It was,' he said, looking down and bashful, gently shaking his head. 'We were sorry they sunk the *Scharnhorst*.'

Eventually he arrived in comparitively drab England to commence further instruction at an Operational Training Unit at Lichfield in Staffordshire on Wellingtons. These were long-in-the-tooth workhorses as well, but a vast step up from the Battle.

Allen handed me his log book, the same blue cloth-bound volume issued to every aircrew in which is recorded every detail and every minute of training and operational flying. Everything was in ink, entered in the meticulous handwriting of the day. Black for day trips, red for night, green for operations at sea such as mine-laying, or 'gardening' as it was called. It is a prized possession among anyone who flew. Every one of them I examined had been kept lovingly and were in immaculate condition. The few fellows who for various reasons had lost theirs (one had had his destroyed by a vindictive ex-wife) still felt it keenly.

Allen's training consisted of many hours of night flying, bombing practice, fighter affiliation exercises, more bombing and seemingly endless cross-country exercises, some lasting up to five and six hours at a time. Fighter affiliation taught the principles of engaging with an enemy fighter, learning the exact moment to yell to the pilot, 'Corkscrew port, go!' or, 'Corkscrew starboard!' the name given to the manoeuvre of twisting and turning the aircraft, causing it to over-shoot before the enemy had a chance to open fire.

From Lichfield it was on to 1660 Heavy Bomber Conversion Unit at Swinderby in Lincolnshire to train further on four-engined Short Stirlings. He was now getting into the big league. One afternoon, on a training flight just before landing, the aircraft's hydraulics failed and the wheels had to be lowered by means of an emergency system. They were diverted to an emergency runway 3 miles long and the Stirling needed every foot of it to pull up without its brakes. It was a big aircraft.

Then to Lancasters in Syerston in Nottinghamshire for a few short days to acquaint himself with the aircraft that would be his office till the end of the war, at the curiously named Lancaster Finishing School.

'Do you remember your first op?' I asked.

'Yes, vividly,' said Allen.

As mid-upper gunner in a Lancaster, Allen had the best view of the whole crew, including the pilot. Armed with two .303 inch Browning machine guns, Allen, in his clear perspex turret on top of the fuselage could revolve 360 degrees. On his first trip, though, he thought the view looked decidedly unhealthy. Allen and his crew began operating over daylight targets in France when the Allies had begun to push the Germans back home and so the bomber force were taken off the big city targets inside Germany to assist the army and attack special targets such as the flying bomb sites from which the enemy was currently attacking London.

St-Leu-d'Esserent is just north of Paris and Allen's aircraft was one of about five hundred attacking factories set up in caves where the V1 flying bombs were being assembled with slave labour from occupied Europe. It was a beautiful day and the approaches looked peaceful. Maybe operations aren't that hard after all, he thought. Then all of a sudden the target came up and then the flak, a storm of exploding black shellfire concentrated on a very small patch of sky, the same patch they were about to fly through. Looking forward at the barrage, he simply could not conceive how anything could get through it and until the last seconds, was convinced the pilot would go around. He still doesn't understand how he came through. It wasn't going to be as easy as he thought.

On his way back, the pilot gave a wide berth to the French town of Calais, a no-go zone as it had been bypassed by the army, leaving a very active German garrison free to fire at any

Allied aircraft passing overhead. To his amazement, Allen watched a lone American Dakota transport, about 3,000 feet below them heading directly over the town on its way back to England. How could the crew not know about Calais? Were they lost? Or drunk? There was no way of warning the slow-flying plane so Allen simply looked on, helpless, knowing what was about to happen. As he watched safely out of range, a single shell was fired from the ground and the lumbering aircraft went down like a stone.

Soon after, he watched an entire load of bombs fall from one Lancaster directly onto another which had drifted out of its allotted bombing position in the formation. The daytime view was becoming less attractive.

Allen's first night trip was a long flight to Stettin, a seaport on the Baltic, and on this one he reckons they could very easily have 'bought it' – wartime parlance for getting killed. At night, there was no formation to follow, so it was up to the navigator to find the way to the target and back home again. On the way out, the pilot noticed they had been flying along the same leg for quite some time and asked the navigator when he could expect the next turn. Usually a serious, quiet type (as many navigators were), the reply was odd to say the least – a strangely dismissive 'Keep going, you're right'. A while later the pilot asked again. 'Navigator, we've got to turn soon.' This time the reply was almost incoherent, a mumbled 'Nah, we're OK . . .' Allen thought he must be drunk. The wireless operator went to inspect and found the navigator delirious with hypoxia, his oxygen lead unplugged. They were alone and lost somewhere over Germany with a navigator not in a fit state to care. In the distance they could see the glow of a big fire and presuming it to be Stettin, headed for it. But something was not quite right. The closer they got, the bigger the city seemed until the sudden sickening realisation: this wasn't the relatively small city of Stettin, this was Berlin, currently under attack by a force of sleek, fast, twin-engined Mosquitos. To be the sole four-engined bomber over the German capital on such an occasion was an extremely unhealthy place to be. The pilot wrenched the aircraft around just as the navigator, oxygen restored, came good.

'Get us out of here!' demanded the pilot, hurtling home under the radar at low-level, hoping that a German night fighter hadn't spotted them.

'What are they going to think of me back in Nav section?' seemed to be the now fully functioning navigator's primary concern, somewhat to the annoyance of the rest of the crew.

'Stuff Nav section,' remonstrated the pilot, 'just get us home.'

In September 1944, the British decided the German garrison at Calais was due for a visit. Why a low-level daylight force was chosen as the most appropriate method to deal with it was and still is beyond Allen Tyson. They hurtled across the sea so low that he saw the propeller wash churning up the channel just a few feet below. He already had a foreboding, a feeling confirmed when arriving over Calais and hearing 'Leader Two to Master Bomber' called repeatedly over the radio. There was no reply. Allen could see the Master Bomber already lying shot down in the harbour. A short while later it was 'Deputy Leader Two calling Leader'. Again, no reply. Then a message was sent out to the entire formation: 'All main force aircraft return to base'. But eight of the force of nearly two hundred aircraft missed the message, and Allen's was one of them. Light flak opened up. Then the machine guns and everything else that could shoot. Looking out from his turret, he saw a German soldier shooting at him with a rifle. Forbidden to use the guns in his turret on ground targets in case of hitting French civilians, Allen attempted to crouch into a ball for some kind of protection. At that height the target came up quickly. At least they'd be out of there soon.

Then the bomb-aimer (who had, unbeknown to Allen, already been hit by a shell fragment in the upper leg) called over the intercom, 'We've got to go around again!' Allen couldn't believe his ears, but through they went again with two other Lancasters. Both of them were hit and shot down, plunging for barely a second at that height then hitting the ground.

'We managed to get home but it frightened the hell out of me.'

A much longer trip – nine and a half hours in fact – was to the port of Gdynia in Poland to bomb the port and its facilities and a German battleship, the *Lutzow*. It was the middle of December 1944 and Europe was blanketed in white, making the port an un-missable target. The bombs were dropped all around the port and the ship but the results from the photo-reconnaissance next morning were bewildering: no evidence that the bombs had hit anything. An investigation revealed that the bombs they were carrying had been fused at the wrong height.

'They're probably still there under the water in Gdynia,' says Allen.

4

Alec Hurse

Bomb-aimer

For Conspicuous Gallantry

Alec Hurse lived in a tiny rural hamlet several hours' drive from home that I took ages to find. I was late and bad tempered. Arriving at his house at the edge of a large dairy property, I sat in the car for a few minutes letting the stress of the drive seep out of me and trying to adopt a more positive attitude. Inside, I was shown into a living room where a table had been laid with napkins in silver holders and crockery of an old and satisfying vintage and at which I was the guest of honour. Peg, Alec's wife of many years, had prepared a lunch of corned beef and vegetables. The meat was incredible. 'Killed on the farm,' I was assured.

Alec was a farmer, having spent his entire life on the land, minus a brief extraordinary few years in Bomber Command as a bomb-aimer on heavies. He spoke slowly but with the measured, rhythmic meter of one who has never had any use for hurrying. I adjusted my interviewing style accordingly. His powers of recall were astonishing and his considered answers delivered logically and in sequence. His mind was obviously as sharp as a tack.

The first real experience of England for most Australian members of Bomber Command was the resorts of Bournemouth and Brighton on the south coast. Here, in seaside holiday hotels, stripped of everything that hinted of their former peaceful incarnation (including the carpets off the floors), thousands of airmen were housed while the powers-that-be decided what to do with them and where they should go. Eventually, the steady expansion of the war effort and the relentless flow of casualties saw them dispersed to airfields right across the country. But for at least a few weeks, there was often little to do but drink the beer, meet the girls and wait.

Alec's early experience of Bournemouth was slightly more dramatic. The Germans, knowing exactly what the town was being used for had long been planning to attack and one sunny Sunday morning, just as Alec had finished his lunch, they struck.

The first thing he knew about it was a line of cannon shell explosions tearing up the road just in front of him as he emerged into the sunny main street. Thirty-five Focke-Wulf 190 fighter-bombers had swooped in over the Channel and pounced, strafing and bombing everything in sight, including a direct hit on a hotel used by Canadian airmen, eighty of whom were killed. Bombs also fell in the park, killing people enjoying the sunshine.

At Alec's Operational Training Unit in Wescott, near Reading, thirteen bomb-aimers, thirteen navigators, pilots and wireless operators milled around a hanger in the crewing up ritual. Alec heard a pilot mutter in a New Zealand accent, 'I want one of these bloody Australians.' 'You've got one,' he told him and thus became the sole Australian in Bomber Command's only dedicated New Zealand squadron, 75, based at Mepal in Cambridgeshire.

I'd heard about the New Zealanders in Bomber Command. People had told me they were quieter than the Australians, highly professional, often tended to keep to themselves and drank less than the Australians.

'I wouldn't say that,' said Alec, about the last point.

As a young fella off the farm, he was, to begin with, a teetotaller. On nights off, another crew would drag him down to the local pub.

'Come on, Hurse, you'll be dead soon,' they said encouragingly. Soon after that, *they* were the ones that had gone.

'I thought, I'd better start drinking,' said Alec.

Alec began his tour in October 1943 on the Royal Air Force's first four-engined bomber, the Short Stirling. I'd always liked the Stirling, but it somehow reminded me of a brontosaurus: noble, but enormous, ungainly and slow. It was built by Short Brothers to an extremely high mechanical standard and crews and pilots talk glowingly of its handling capabilities, relative comfort and an enormous ability to absorb punishment. One 75 Squadron Stirling even survived a head-on collision with a Messerschmitt 109 over Hamburg, losing 4 feet off its starboard wingtip but making it home with the pilot wrenching the control column as far over as possible and lashing it there with parachute rope.

But not many in 75 were so lucky, especially in the dark months of early and mid-1943. According to Alec, not a single crew on Stirlings completed their tour of thirty trips throughout the entire year. In fact, two crews were taken off operations after just twenty-one. It became known as 'the chop squadron'. I ask Alec if he thought he'd make it through.

'Nah. Not a hope,' he answered without hesitation.

The fatal flaw in the Stirling was its dreadfully low ceiling, a characteristic in-built by a ludicrous act of governmental bureaucracy. When the RAF called for tenders for a four-engined bomber in the late 1930s, they stipulated the wingspan must conform to the existing dimensions of the standard RAF hanger, in an effort designed to save them the expense of building bigger ones. A classic story of 'don't raise the bridge, lower the river'. Hence – the Stirling's wingspan was a mere 99 feet, 1 inch – far shorter than it needed to be – giving it a strange stumpy appearance and limiting its altitude to around 15,000 feet, far lower than its contemporaries such as the Lancaster or Halifax, a fact not lost on Alec when flying over the target.

'You'd be dodging the flak from below, and dodging the bombs coming down from the Lancs above.'

Nor was it lost especially on Alec's first flight engineer, a Scot. Unlike the Americans, the Royal Air Force did away with co-pilots and instead created flight engineers, often a former groundcrew whose job it was to assist the pilot when needed and also monitor the aircraft's various mechanical systems, fuel, hydraulics, etc. On the Stirling, he sat up near the pilot and had roughly the same view. Alec's first trip was a 'gardening' operation, code word for mine-laying in a German harbour or shipping lane. Gardening ops were often given to new crews, as they were regarded as being marginally safer targets than the big cities, especially in a Stirling. Nonetheless, the flak which came up to greet them was enough to make a very deep impression on the flight engineer. Back at the de-briefing, Alec remembers him announcing that flying was too dangerous and that he no longer intended to do it. The de-briefing officer looked at the man to determine whether he was serious, then quietly reached over to the phone. A few minutes later, two military policemen appeared at the door and escorted him to the guardhouse. He was charged with what was caustically described as LMF or Lack of Moral Fibre, a stigma often fierce enough to eclipse the fear of death itself. By the time Alec had returned to his barracks, the man's belongings and gear had already been cleaned out as if he'd never existed. In reality he, like all dubbed 'LMF' would have been stripped of rank and entitlements and given the most humiliating and menial of tasks in an out of the way location – often cleaning toilets.

Unusually, Alec had lost his log book, making the interview a little structureless. Slowly going through a log book, examining the details of dates and places often revealed details hidden for many decades. Without it, I had to rely on Alec's memory, which although excellent, didn't give me some of the detail I was after.

I asked Alec if he had completed his tour of thirty.

'Shot up on the twenty-ninth,' he told me.

My ears pricked up. 'Tell me about the twenty-ninth.'

There was a very long pause and a bit of a chuckle. Something about the pause made the hairs on the back of my neck stand up and I sensed the conversation was about to turn in an entirely new direction. For the next half hour I sat with a cold, half-drunk cup of tea in my hand, listening to the astonishing story of Alec Hurse's last trip.

Log book or no log book, 11 June 1944 is a date Alec has never forgotten. 75 Squadron was part of a larger force attacking the railway junction at Nantes near the French coast on the Loire river. At that time it was a vitally important place for the Germans who were attempting to rush men and equipment north to join the battle in Normandy, still only a few days old. On arriving over the target, it was, contrary to the forecast, solid overcast. Having made it all the way to the target, aborting was something crews hated. Recently they had made their way almost to the Swiss border on a supply drop to the Resistance, only to find the drop zone obscured by snow. The memory of having to bring everything all the way back was a bitter one. A brief discussion among the crew decided that it might be an idea to briefly duck below the clouds and see what was what. After all, the Nantes railway yards were a huge target and not easy to miss, especially as it had already been marked by the Pathfinders. Just head for the flares, drop and sneak back into the clouds. Should be easy.

The Germans also knew the railyards were an easy target and so when a lone Lancaster emerged out of the safety of the clouds, six searchlights fixed it like a moth in a spotlight. Then the flak opened up. They were low, so it was only the lighter stuff. However, from the nose, Alec remembers seeing the tracer coming up to meet them, then two big explosions. Then all hell broke loose. A voice yelled, 'Get out, get out, they've got us!' Then the plane started to climb.

'Push the nose down!' shouted Alec into the intercom, but the pilot could only yell back, 'I can't see, I can't see, we're going to crash.' Alec let all eighteen bombs go in one big salvo to get them away from the aircraft and pulled his way up to the cockpit. There was blood everywhere and the pilot, wounded badly, was pulling the control column towards him, forcing the aircraft upwards. Alec gently restrained the pilot and pushed the stick forward, levelling out the aircraft. An explosion had torn into the side of the cockpit and Alec could see the pilot had been hit badly in the abdomen.

'Get me out of here,' he managed to mumble through the shock.

'Just wait on,' said Alec.

The flight engineer, though not as badly hit, had nonetheless taken a couple of splinters from the explosion and was acting 'like a stunned rabbit'. It was left to Alec to fly the aircraft. He pulled up into the cloud but the flak gunners, sensing a lame duck, were following him.

We're never going to get out of here, he thought to himself when the navigator came in over the intercom.

'Get out of the target area, go south!'

But which way was that?

'Just turn to port!' came the voice, and Alec wheeled the big bomber around to the left.

The wireless operator and navigator managed to pull the pilot out of his seat and take him down the back of the aircraft where they dosed him up with morphine. Alec was now in charge. If they were ever going to get home, he was going to have to get them there.

After an SOS, there was radio silence for an hour, then an instruction from England: 'Land Boscombe Down'. Boscombe Down, near Salisbury was, and still is, the RAF's experimental aerodrome where aircraft and weapons both brilliant and ludicrous were tried and evaluated. Today, it boasts the longest runway in Britain, a runway which during the war, was made of grass, making it ideal as an emergency aerodrome where the chance of crippled aircraft catching alight from sparks was greatly reduced. Ideal, apart from the numerous hills that surrounded Boscombe Down, requiring anyone who landed there, emergency or otherwise, to be on their toes.

Alec's rudimentary understanding of flying an aircraft got them as far as the aerodrome, which they proceeded to circle. But there was another problem. The place they had taken off from, Mepal, was 1,400 feet above sea level, and their altimeter had been set accordingly. Boscombe Down, much nearer the coast, was only 700, so their height reading of 1,000 feet (305 metres) in reality meant that they were a mere 300 feet above the ground, surrounded by hills. Not only that, but they were flying at night with a damaged aircraft, a wounded pilot and a very young bomb-aimer who had never flown before at the controls.

On the ground, Aldis warning lamps flashed red, indicating they were too low. Seeing them, Alec knew he must have been low, but how low? Uncertainly, he increased the aircraft's revs to gain height whereas he should have in reality lifted the nose fast. After three circuits he decided to come in, despite the urgently flashing red lights around him. He landed too fast and the big Lancaster hit the deck at high speed, bounced and immediately took off again.

'Too much pace up,' he said dryly with his soft, punctuating chuckle.

He tried again and managed to get it down about halfway along the runway. Quickly, he applied some brake via a lever on the control column and it immediately swung left, risking the collapse of the undercarriage. Counter-applying some rudder, the aircraft came to a halt.

'Cut the motors. Let's get out,' yelled Alec.

It was 4 am and freezing cold. The rest of the crew emerged, white as sheets, from their crash positions, backs hard up against the main wing spar halfway down the fuselage and praying for dear life. A line of torches from the groundcrew led them away from the aircraft. An ambulance took out the pilot and cut away his clothes there and then.

'The whole of his side was like pulp,' Alec remembered. He didn't think he had a chance but in fact the pilot survived and went home to New Zealand, where he died a couple of years after the war.

It was Alec's twenty-ninth trip, his second last. It was enough. His tour was marked down as completed.

There was a long silence in the room as Alec, smiling slightly, fixed his gaze on the middle distance, remembering. I asked my first question in a long time.

'Were you decorated?'

Almost inaudibly, under his breath, he said, 'Conspicuous Gallantry Medal.'

I felt stunned. The CGM is an extremely rare decoration awarded to non-commissioned officers, an equivalent of the officers-only (and much more common) Distinguished Service Order. Originally a naval decoration, in 1943 it was opened up to the air force. Alec, a warrant officer, was a member of this very exclusive club. The RAF handed out a mere one hundred and three of them during the Second World War, of which only nine went to Australians.

I had never seen one before. Without a word, Alec got up and ushered me towards a table, then pulled back a cloth to reveal his decorations, mounted with the unmistakeable dark and pale blue ribbon and the head of King George VI, engraved with the words *For Conspicuous Gallantry*.

We chatted about other things. I can see that for all Alec's quiet, measured responses, a lot has been stirred up in the old farmer. I'm curious to know what happened to his log book. Peg is clearing up, and provides the answer.

'Burned it,' she says.

I looked at Alec. He just gave me a chuckle.

5

Les Smith

Air-gunner

How come you're still alive?

My interest in Les Smith was twofold. Firstly, he was the only person I have ever met who flew in the Battle of Britain, and secondly, he flew one of the silliest aircraft of the Second World War, the Boulton-Paul Defiant. Somebody, somewhere, deep within His Majesty's Air Ministry back in 1935 had the startling idea that if you stuck a rearward-firing gun turret in a single seat fighter, you would surprise any enemy making a conventional attack from behind. And true enough. For about five minutes, which is about how long the Germans took to cotton on to the Defiant's peculiarity. Add to the equation the enormous weight of the turret and extra man, as well as the resulting loss of speed and manoeuvrability without any additional engine power to compensate, and it's not hard to conclude that the only thing the Defiant actually defied was common sense.

Actually, it was barely five minutes. The Defiant's debut was with number 264 Squadron over the beaches of Dunkirk on 12 May 1940, when they managed to shoot down two German bombers who were probably curious about the thing sticking out of the top of the Defiant's fuselage. The very next day, however, this same squadron lost four of its five aircraft to the German Messerschmitt pilots who found shooting down the cumbersome Defiants pitifully easy.

It was also a death trap. The Defiant's turret was hydraulically powered, so anything which severed the hydraulic power line – like a German bullet, say – rendered it immobile, trapping the poor gunner and condemning him to almost certain oblivion should the aircraft be shot down, which it frequently was.

One of those gunners was Les Smith, though there was nothing particularly poor about him when I visited him in his Melbourne inner-city retirement village early one summer evening. Les was also the first Englishman I interviewed so I was curious to compare his experience to that of the Australians I had already met.

When Les joined the Royal Air Force just before the war (another thing that made him interesting) it was an odd organisation, only twenty years old, but having wasted no time in sycophantically adopting many of the traditions of its senior service partners, the army and Royal Navy. Despite this, it was openly sneered at by both as new-fangled, radical, even dangerous, and not really worthy of displaying the crown on its uniform. To that generation of young men which immediately followed the one which had been slaughtered in the trenches of the First World War, however, the air force was an infinitely preferable option.

Les was a short wiry, highly active man from Gravesend, still with a distinctive London accent and all the energy of a bee in a bottle. He met me at the front entrance of the village and escorted me on a whirlwind tour of the dining room and gaming facilities, proudly showing off the garden and water feature on the way through. Nearly exhausted I sat down and caught my breath in his room.

Like almost all air force volunteers, Les wanted to be a pilot, but as with the vast majority, it was not to be, and he was assigned to the pool of trainee wireless/air-gunners. Soon realising he couldn't achieve the necessary speed on the morse key, he was relegated to 'straight' air-gunner and thus very quickly found himself in action at the height of the Battle of Britain in late 1940.

More has been written about the Battle of Britain than has ever really needed to be, but the idea of it still mesmerises me. Over the years, it's become such a mish-mash of myth and cliché that it's hard to distil the actual drama from the Python-esque images of men with silly accents and even sillier moustaches. Legend has it that the German army wanted to invade England but wouldn't even try until the British air force had been neutralised, so over the course of one particularly glorious summer, the two giant air fleets slogged it out high above the lovely fields of Kent, the only things standing between the victory-drunk Germans and defeat being a few hundred well-spoken Spitfire and Hurricane pilots. In reality, I don't think the Germans could ever have invaded England by sea because they were not properly equipped to do so, and the Royal Navy was still dominant. But the fact that the Germans were defeated for the first time, albeit defensively, makes the Battle of Britain one of history's true turning points.

Prior to the Defiant, Les was condemned to spend time in yet another dreadful old crate, the Bristol Blenheim, a twin-engined jalopy with a few machine-guns stuck in the front and laughingly classified as a 'fighter-bomber'. The fact that it was never fast enough to catch anything didn't seem to impact on its risible classification.

'We called it the Widowmaker,' said Les with a disconcertingly infectious chuckle, and on his first day in action, many widows were made indeed. At the start of the battle, the Germans had three air fleets stationed in France, Denmark and Norway, threatening Britain like the talons of a vast claw. On 15 August 1940, histrionically dubbed by the Germans 'Eagle Day', they unleashed all three in a simultaneous three-pronged aerial assault across the north, south and centre of the United Kingdom.

Just before midday, Les, along with the rest of 219 Squadron in their northern England base at Catterick were busy putting on their best uniforms for a squadron photo and a round of sandwiches, when the urgent clanging of a bell told them they were being scrambled.

'Caused a terrible panic,' said Les. 'We were just about to go to lunch!' Number 219 had been on convoy protection patrols, but not yet in the thick of it and certainly nothing like this. Fifty Junkers 88 bombers had appeared on the radar, sweeping in over the North Sea from their Danish base at Aalborg. Radar was a weapon unappreciated by the Germans at that time, and full warning was given to the defenders.

'It was so big they needed backing up,' he said, still with a slight note of amazement. Number 219 was sent in to join a Spitfire, Hurricane and Defiant squadron already engaging the astonished Germans. Assuming the RAF would have its hands full with the raids further south, the enemy bombers went in without fighter cover and were cut to pieces. The fifty broke into eight sections, panicked, dropped a couple of bombs here and there but mostly just high-tailed it back out to sea, chased by people such as Les, who met them over the seaside town of Bridlington, near York.

'We don't know if we hit anything but we expended all our ammunition,' he said, well aware that had the Germans decided to bring along some fighters, it might have been a different story. As it was, thirty out of the fifty German bombers were shot down or damaged, a result so appalling that never again was an attempt made on Britain using their Scandinavian-based aircraft.

The Royal Air Force soon came to their senses and began relegating the early Blenheims to more appropriate uses such as training, target towing or just sitting on the ground and rusting.

Les meanwhile found himself transferred to 141 Squadron at the height of the Blitz, when towns and cities in southern England were being attacked on a nightly basis. Luckily for him, he was stationed at his home town, Gravesend.

'It was marvellous,' he said. 'If there was nothing on, I'd get on a bike, go around the perimeter track, nip out the back and spend the night in my own room. They called me Lucky Les.'

'Lucky', however, would not exactly have been the word used by the crews to describe themselves upon learning they were to fly the Defiant.

'The pilots hated them,' said Les.

Dreadful by day, the Defiant had by this stage been adapted as a night fighter. Their brown and green camouflage was painted over black, making them look for all the world like enormous bats. Flying at night simply amplified its well-known handling vices. Underpowered and overweight, landing accidents were particularly common, obviating some of the cover afforded by the night. But as Les said, 'At the time, we just didn't have anything else.'

The crews had to be rotated: two days on convoy patrol, two days on nights, then two days off. The strain on the often inexperienced pilots was terrible.

'We could only do it for an hour and a half. You could see it in the pilots. The stress. It really got them down.'

In his rotating turret of four machine-guns, Les flew behind his pilot, hoping to catch the bombers on their way in, or out. Radar, rudimentary as it was, would find a contact, and the voice of a fighter controller somewhere on the ground would guide the pilot as close as he could to the interception. Then it was eyes peeled, watching for the tell-tale glow of the exhaust stubs from the bombers' engines. Down below, Les could see the fires of towns and cities burning.

One night, on a patrol near Canterbury, Les saw his own town of Gravesend being hit. He knew that his mother, father and brother were somewhere down there and all he could do was watch the fires and wonder at their fate. Exasperatingly, there was no sign of the planes that were dropping the bombs, despite peering desperately into the night.

'The sky is a huge void, and one aircraft just a dot,' he said.

He returned home, sick with worry and frustration. Nor was there relief back at the base, strictly closed as it was to outside communication. It was days before Les was to learn of his family's safety. He had discovered the downside of being stationed so close to home.

For sixteen weeks, Les and his pilot patrolled the night skies of southern England, straining his eyes into the darkness, night after night. The Germans weren't their only danger. Barrage balloons – big, gas-filled dirigibles tethered to the ground with a long steel cable presented their own particular obstacle. And then there were their very own, very trigger-happy anti-aircraft gunners, famous for their inability to distinguish friend from foe.

Usually the underpowered Defiant was too slow to catch anything, but eventually, they reckoned, their luck had to turn.

Then one night, a contact: a lone Heinkel 111 bomber, possibly hit already with anti-aircraft fire from the ground and flying slower than usual, thus giving the Defiant a sporting chance. By no means possessing a monopoly on sub-standard aeroplanes, the German He-111 was as atrocious as anything the worst examples of British industry could produce at the time, and as hated by its crews as it was by the bombed-out residents of the East End. A big, ugly twin-engined slug of a thing, it had done well in Poland and France where there was no opposition but was no match for the British fighters, even the Defiant. So lacking was it in adequate defensive armament, some Heinkel crews resorted to hurling tin boxes attached to reels of wire out the window in the hope of it catching in a fighter's propeller. Les and his pilot, guided onto the contact by the voice in the dark, saw it barely illuminated in the fug of the night sky and, hearts pounding, quietly sidled up alongside. Les opened fire from about 700 yards, the four machine-guns tearing the big green fuselage open just behind the mainplane. It was all over in a flash. The Heinkel with its six crew fell to the ground somewhere far below.

Two nights later, it happened again. This time it was a Junkers 88, one of the German's better aircraft. It had already dropped its bombs and was heading back over the coast, oblivious to being stalked by the Defiant. Les watched it. It seemed to him just a bit, well, overconfident.

'It was just cruising along,' he said.

He caught it over the coast and saw it go down in the sea. Les felt he was on a roll.

But that was it. Nothing else but the odd contact that materialised into nothing. By October 1940, Les's patrols were being wound down, and the Defiant was at last put out to pasture.

With his characteristic chuckle, Les digresses for a moment. Until recently, Battle of Britain Race Day was held every year on September 15 at a prominent Melbourne race course. The host read out the names and service history of the guests who participated in the great event. When he came to Les, he paused, looked at his notes again, eyeballed Les and said with astonishment, 'Les Smith. Defiants? How come you're still alive?!'

Les chuckled. He's proud of that one.

Then he shows me something on the wall, a large poster dedicated to his squadron during the Battle which takes up a relatively large space in his small unit. His name appears down the bottom and he points it out to me with considerable pride. He also hands me some photocopied pages, the brief extract from his record of service, complete with a passport-sized photo of himself in uniform, a rather cheeky-looking urchin face and wearing a cap.

Les, a bright bloke by anyone's standards, decided to give the navigators' course a go, found himself in South Africa, then on Wellingtons in the North African campaign supporting the army. He gives me a brief potted history of the next couple of years: training on an obscure aircraft called an Albemarle and towing gliders for D-Day. And Pegasus Bridge.

In the annals of British military history, Pegasus Bridge was one of the truly showcase moments, the first and most spectacular operation of D-Day. This particular bridge over the Orne River in Normandy had to be taken to prevent the Germans getting tanks up to the landing beaches, and then held to be used in turn by the British coming up from those same beaches and fanning out. One of those wonderful old British regiments, the Oxfordshire and Buckinghamshire Light Infantry, led by a former policeman, Major John Howard, landed in gliders and took it. In short, it was very heroic, brilliantly successful, took all of ten minutes with a cost of two dead and fourteen wounded and the Germans never re-took it. Les was navigator in the aircraft which towed the second glider.

A few months later, he was towing gliders again, this time in four-engined Halifaxes for the disastrous Arnhem landings in Holland. On the afternoon of the first day of the ten-day debacle, he towed part of the South Staffordshire Regiment. I asked him if he got to see the soldiers themselves, and what he observed of their demeanour.

'There's one of them living downstairs, you can ask him yourself.'

I could see he wanted to wind up the interview. He was virtually pushing me out the door. What else could he tell me? Just a sec. He thought for a moment. Crossing the Rhine in '45 (he has kept his original flight plan) going into newly liberated Norway right at the end. He went back into his room to show me something, a long list inside a manila folder, which he handed to me with a quizzical expression.

'Some Norwegian bloke sent me this list of every German aircraft captured in Norway at the end or the war.' It went on for pages. Les looked at me, perhaps hoping to understand why someone would have done such a thing.

'Pretty crazy, some of these buffs,' I told him. He wasn't reassured.

6

Gerald McPherson

Air-gunner

If you could see the colour in the flak, you knew it was close.

Gerald had a go at being a pilot, failed and was scrubbed down to wireless/air-gunner. The wireless part just didn't suit him. He hated fiddling around with radios so opted to be a 'straight' air-gunner instead. What you might call a specialist. A little bit later, on the boat going over, he was nevertheless grateful for the smattering of wireless knowledge he'd acquired. When at sea as part of an Atlantic convoy, he was able to interpret the morse signal being sent across the water from their rather famous escorting battleship, America's first 'Super Dreadnought', the World War One vintage USS *Texas*: 'If you do not immediately stop the smoke from your funnel, you will have to drop out of the convoy.' As the crew of the *Texas* knew all too well, U-boats could spot the smoke from a ship's funnel from over the horizon. 'We nearly went and put it out ourselves,' remembered Gerald.

Gerald's brief but highly eventful career in Bomber Command could fill a book on its own, and my brief time with him over tea and biscuits could in no way do it justice. Talking to him was like being on a roller-coaster that hardly ever hit the flat. Like many former fliers, he seemed grateful for the chat, and happy not to have to explain too many of the basics to a novice. Nevertheless, at the end of our meeting, I was the one exhausted. His tone barely wavered from one of quiet, open, matter-of-factness, illustrated with many a soft chuckle and an understated sense of enduring amazement at what he saw, what he did, and how the hell he survived.

Within weeks of arriving in England, he had witnessed two horrific air crashes and had lost both his pilot and his wireless operator, all before starting operational flying.

The worst day in the history of the British Army is 1 July 1916, the opening day of the Battle of the Somme, when twenty thousand soldiers were killed going over the top in a single day. The equivalent catastrophe for the Royal Air Force is undoubtedly 30/31 March 1944, the night of an infamous raid on the German city of Nuremberg. On this brilliantly moonlit night, when everything that could go wrong, did, German fighters pounced on the nearly eight hundred-strong bomber stream and shot down a staggering ninety-six four-engined bombers, almost all on the way in to the target. One squadron, 51, lost six out of the seventeen Halifaxes dispatched.

Gerald, who was based at Silverstone, which straddles Buckinghamshire and Northamptonshire, remembered the night well. Although not yet operational, he recalled one Lancaster, battle-damaged and limping along on three engines coming into Silverstone for an emergency landing but failing to line up properly with the runway. At the last minute the pilot radioed, 'I'll try to come round again. I'll try . . .', then his wing clipped the fire section roof. The bomber keeled over and crashed, tumbling through playing fields for 200 yards, killing all the crew except the tail gunner. For the new trainees on station who hadn't even formed into crews yet, it was a sobering sight.

Later, at a Heavy Conversion Unit, where the new crews got their hands on a four-engined aircraft for the first time, Gerald witnessed another horror. One night, as the crews were practising landings and take-offs in Stirlings, a German intruder aircraft got among them, following one in and shooting it down before vanishing into the night. The bomber careered to the ground, narrowly missing the control tower but ploughed into a hanger, wiping out another couple of aircraft inside. Gerald saw the aftermath the next morning. 'Terrible mess. Terrible,' he said.

Living through such precarious times, some people set great store by lucky charms or treasured possessions. Gerald told me about one of his pilots, Jim Houghton, a New Zealander from Christchurch. Every pilot was required to fly one operation as a 'second dickie' or spare pilot with an experienced crew immediately prior to beginning operations with their own. It was a way of giving the most important crew member, the pilot, some idea of what to expect on a real trip. Jim had actually attempted this introductory trip with this same crew the night before, but their rear gunner had started having convulsions and the aircraft had turned back. So the next night, they had to do it all again. That's when he lost his lucky charm, a New Zealand tiki. He was edgy before take-off and Gerald helped him to look for it, knowing how important it was to Jim. It was a warm night and Gerald remembers frantically going through lockers and kit bags to find the little green talisman, but to no avail.

By the time he had to go to the briefing, Jim still hadn't found it. 'He was in a lather of perspiration,' Gerald told me. 'I think he had a premonition . . .' The crew he was with were all on the last trip of their tour. They flew to Stuttgart, and never returned.

The next morning, a wing commander called them into his office. After delivering the news, he proposed making this now incomplete crew 'spares', for the rest of the squadron, on call to fill the place of a sick gunner or navigator at the last minute. Gerald and his crew, having trained and been through so much together already, would have none of it. Besides, being 'odd man in' with people you'd never flown with before was regarded as a virtual death sentence. In the face of vociferous protests, the officer relented and instead, they picked up another pilot and went back into training.

Another memory Gerald had of a small but significant object concerned his wireless operator and a watch. Despite having known each other for only a month, Gerald and Charlie Smallwood, from Birmingham, had become good friends. One day while still in training, Charlie was asked by another crew to fly with them on a gunnery exercise over the Wash. At the last minute, Charlie came racing up.

'Gerald,' he said, 'I need a watch. Can I borrow yours?'

As wireless op, Charlie would be required to send signals at precise times. It was a nice watch, a farewell gift from his family a few months before, but Gerald had no qualms in lending it to his friend.

That afternoon, Gerald heard that the plane, a Wellington, had made a forced landing in the sea. All the crew got out – except the wireless operator. Later, Gerald asked one of the gunners what had happened.

'I can't understand it,' the man said. 'We were told to take up our ditching positions but just before we hit the water, he got up and raced back to his wireless station.'

Soon after the Wellington hit the water it began to sink. It was too late for Charlie to get out.

'I've always had the feeling his death was caused by going back for my watch,' Gerald told me. Although Gerald wasn't visibly upset, I imagine it's a burden he's carried for over sixty years, and, I sensed, as painful now as the day it happened.

Gerald tried to reconstruct the tragedy in his mind a

thousand times. Wireless operators frequently placed their watch beside them on the table rather than on their wrist for easier reference. Not braced for impact, Charlie was probably knocked unconscious as he tried to retrieve it, mindful of its value to his mate. But he'll never know for sure. As the Wellington was sinking, the Australian gunner dived down to try and find Charlie, but to no avail.

'We'd been out for a drink together in the local town the night before. Next day he was gone.'

I exhaled slowly and made a rather impotent sounding exclamation. 'Gee . . .' There's very little else I could say.

Having picked up a new pilot, new wireless operator and a flight engineer, Gerald was now part of a full crew, ready to convert onto the Lancaster at Feltwell in Norfolk. Gerald hadn't forgotten his first time in a Lanc, and the feeling that he was at last flying in a thoroughbred. The Wellingtons and Stirlings would, as he put it, 'stagger off the ground. You'd say a prayer and hope you made it'. Sitting in the rear turret on that first flight, he heard the pilot say, 'Full power to the engines', in his headphones and immediately felt himself surge up off the ground. 'This will do me,' he thought.

His stop-start period of training at last over, Gerald began operations with number 186 Squadron at Tuddenham in Suffolk. It was a brand new squadron and Gerald was one of the original crews, joining it just a week after it was formed.

'It was dreadful,' he said and laughed softly. Newly formed squadrons often operated out of newly formed bases, which usually meant inadequate accommodation.

'We didn't even have hot water, and this was November.'

The crews protested loudly. It took a few weeks but eventually the hot showers arrived.

A few days after arriving, Gerald was listed on the battle order for his first op. This time his pilot didn't complete his 'second dickie' trip. Instead, it was the boss, the squadron's wing commander who announced, 'Right, I'm taking you lot today.' Perhaps he'd heard about their earlier bad luck. It was only a three hour trip to Flushing on the Scheldt estuary, but Gerald could at last enter his first trip into his log book.

Remembering his rather lonely, dangerous position in the rear turret, Gerald reflected that it was not the gunners' job to go looking for trouble. The Lancaster was a bomber, not a fighter.

'We didn't really have the firepower to take the fighters on,' he says. Gerald spotted German fighters but was never attacked. Occasionally, he would see one that hadn't noticed him and would direct the pilot to quietly slip sideways out of harm's way. In actual fact, by the time Gerald commenced operations in late 1944, the night fighter threat had diminished, but the German anti-aircraft defences remained fierce right up until the end of the war.

'The flak was just as bad and in the daytime they could see you,' he said.

One raid on a synthetic oil plant in early December 1944, at Merseburg near Leipzig, Gerald was told to expect no less than 750 anti-aircraft guns. Over Gelsenkirchen, Gerald heard the voice of his mid-upper gunner over the intercom.

'Hey Gerald, take a look at that starboard tail.' Looking around, he saw a hole the size of a large beach ball had been made in the tailplane a few feet from his head. One another occasion, Gerald's Lancaster was so badly damaged the amazed groundcrew counted nearly sixty holes in her. It was written off and never flew again.

'Did you ever see another plane going down?' I asked.

'Yep. Some of the crew slept in the same hut as me. I didn't like the pilot but I changed my mind about him when I saw what happened.'

It was a daylight raid, somewhere in the Ruhr, and the Lancasters were flying close. The Americans flew exclusively in daylight in an intricate box formation, well rehearsed and rigidly adhered to, allowing the many guns of the formation to target any attacker. The Royal Air Force, flying at night, was much more laissez faire. It's amazing there weren't more collisions but the facts and figures are frightening. On any of the big raids, up to a thousand aircraft were scheduled to be over the target in a twenty minute bombing window, with no lights and all within an altitude of 18 to 20,000 feet. At night, you couldn't see the proximity of the aircraft next to you, and that was probably a good thing. But in daylight, it was unavoidable.

On this raid the Lancaster next to Gerald was hit and caught fire, burning fiercely from the front. He watched it gradually going down, flames pouring out as it accelerated into a dive. All of a sudden it levelled out, the pilot somehow managing to find a way of controlling it for a few moments inside the blazing cockpit. Five of the crew baled out in quick succession. As soon as the last one left the aircraft, down she went in a mass of flames.

'There were other sights, too,' Gerald told me.

The 4,000 pound 'Cookie' had only a thin casing and if it was hit by flak, it simply blew up.

'Nothing even fell from the sky. Nothing. I saw that several times. It's hard to imagine.'

Another problem was hitting the turbulence from the other aircraft.

'Once, it nearly made me bail out.'

Approaching a target one night, he felt his aircraft start to go down.

'What's wrong?' he called over the intercom. No answer. Again, '*What's wrong?*' Still nothing.

Fearing the worst, he grabbed his parachute, stowed just inside the fuselage. The moment before he removed his helmet with attached earphones, he heard the voice of the pilot.

'Hold on.'

The pilot had simply been occupied fighting to regain control of the aircraft in the turbulence. Another moment and Gerald would have been out of the aircraft, and on his way down to land alone in enemy territory.

I turned another page in Gerald's log book and stopped reading at the first entry. I'd been expecting to see it at some stage in these interviews and here it was, written in plain red ink: *February 13/14 1945 – Dresden*. Gerald's voice lowered. Looking at it even gave me a slight shudder, like a door in an old house behind which you know some ghastly event has occurred in the distant past.

Ironically, it was serial Holocaust denier David Irving who first brought the world's attention to the number of civilians killed by the Allies in the Dresden raid in a book written in 1963. Since then, the controversy had raged on, fanned by historical perspective and a refusal to see the Second World War simply in terms of good and bad, black and white.

When the Royal Air Force at last accepted the fact that it was almost impossible to bomb a specific target at night in a blacked-out city, they decided in March 1942 on the policy of 'area bombing'. In other words if you can't destroy the factory in the town, destroy the town itself. This indiscriminate method of destruction largely became the pattern for the next three years, and the speciality of the RAF, who dropped a whopping 45 per cent of their total tonnage of bombs on industrial city targets. The Americans, on the other hand, generally bombed by daylight, using the 'precision bombing' theory. For any city to suffer area bombing was terrible, but the full horror of Dresden can still barely be comprehended today. What cannot be denied is that at the very least, twenty-five thousand people perished in the firestorm that engulfed the beautiful medieval city after a particularly successful air attack by 796 Lancasters and nine Mosquitos.

'Do you remember it?'

'Yep,' he answered definitely. 'It was just like daylight.' The light from the burning city was so bright it even illuminated the other bombers flying with him. On other trips, this would have been a hazard, but one of the salient features of the Dresden controversy is that the city was virtually undefended, with only eight Lancasters lost on the trip, and two of those over France on their way home. If such a target was so undefended, why was it worth obliterating, along with its population? This is just one of the questions that still rage around the subject of Dresden today, and haunting those who took part in it.

'We didn't question what we were told, we were just kids,' said Gerald. And of course, they were.

I asked Gerald whether he thought he'd get through his tour. 'Not when my brother-in-law had got through. Too much luck in the one family.'

I read another entry in Gerald's log book: *Aircraft severely damaged. All tanks holed except one. Port outer hit twice. 6 inch × 12 inch hole in elevator. 40 holes in aircraft.* Another rough trip, but it could have been a lot rougher, as Gerald learned on returning. After inspecting the aircraft, the ground-crew saw something lodged inside the port wing. It was a shell, a German anti-aircraft incendiary of a type as yet unknown to the Air Ministry. It had lodged in the metal spar that separated the two massive fuel tanks inside the wing, burning itself out without incident. A few inches either side and the aircraft would almost certainly have been set ablaze.

Datteln, Recklinghausen – coking plant. Went to target on three engines read another entry.

'Tell me about that one.'

One of the engines had packed up soon after taking off. A quick conference between the pilot and flight engineer decided that it was still possible to make it to the target, a benzol plant, bomb on time and make it home in one piece. By cutting corners of the original flight plan, they reckoned they could do it, but off course they would have to risk being alone and unprotected for certain periods along the route. They did, and they made it back safely.

Gerald's log book gets busier and busier the longer the war goes on. In the last few weeks, he seemed to have been up almost every night. I picked another at random. The city of Munster.

'Yeah, I remember that one. We had to dodge our own bombs.'

Attacking railway yards and a viaduct in Munster, Gerald's squadron was slated to lead the attack at a height of 21,000 feet. Suddenly, over the target, another squadron of Lancasters appeared, ahead of schedule, 500 feet above. Gerald and the mid-upper gunner watched with trepidation and then horror as the bomb doors opened and the 500-pounders began falling less than 100 feet away.

'Left! Right!' came the frantic shouts to the pilot to avoid the falling bombs.

'[There was] nothing more terrifying than seeing [those] bombs coming down.'

Then came their last trip. It was their worst, and one they later discovered they weren't obliged to go on. By mid-March 1945, Gerald and his crew had completed thirty-eight, and were regarded as highly experienced. The battle order went up early at Stradishall in Cambridgeshire, where he was now based. Their names were on it for that night's raid to Kiel. Unbeknown to Gerald, that same day a signal had come down from Bomber Command Headquarters, reducing the maximum amount of missions in a tour from forty to thirty-five. The CO of the squadron at the time was an Englishman and Gerald didn't like him.

'And he obviously didn't like us,' he reflected. He later

heard that one of the flight commanders pointed out that Gerald and his crew had, according to the order, completed their tour and could be stood down. The commanding officer paused, then muttered, 'They're on the list. Let them go.'

Over the target, Gerald was blinded by searing light as the aircraft was 'coned' – caught like a moth in the beams of between twenty and thirty German searchlights which beckoned every surrounding gunner to get a bearing and open fire.

'It was like day,' he remembered. The pilot threw the Lancaster around like a toy in the surf. Later, the flight engineer told Gerald that at one point, they were actually upside down.

'Gosh . . .' I heard myself exhale again.

Through the pilot's skill and experience, they eventually extricated themselves from the searchlights and even managed to bomb. But if they'd been attacked by fighters, Gerald, his eyes still blinded, would have been useless.

Their return flight path took them back over the Danish coast, where the plan was to descend to 7,000 feet and come home across the North Sea. Shaken, Gerald and the crew were anxious to get home. As soon as the Danish coast had been reached, the pilot elected to seek the relative safety of the lower altitude sooner rather than later, and put the Lancaster's nose down into a steep dive.

Hurtling downwards, the flight engineer, sitting next to the pilot saw something loom up out of the blackness. It was another Lancaster directly in front. He didn't have time to say a word. Instead, he hit the pilot across the chest and grabbed the control column himself. In the rear turret, Gerald felt the sudden surge of the G-force and startled, looked up to see this aircraft that had appeared out of the night, close enough for him to spot the faces of the two gunners in their turrets. For a moment, he was convinced of the imminent collision.

'We skidded across the top,' he said.

I don't quite know what he means and ask him again, but for a moment, I have lost Gerald and he was back out over the North Sea.

'We just skidded over the top of them.'

It was the middle of the night. The disappearance without trace of two aircraft and their crews was avoided by luck, and mere inches.

Strangely, it was the image of a near-miss that still seemed to haunt him, the faces of the fellows in another aircraft whom he never met – his own mirror image in a picture of near-catastrophe. This time, it was his turn to let out a sigh. It was the only time I saw him rattled.

'What a finale,' I offered after a little while.

'Yes. Yes, it was,' he said.

His amazing tour of operations was over. He had completed thirty-eight trips, thirty-one of them in daylight. He and his crew went down to London, and celebrated having survived. By the end of the war, in August, he was back in Australia working in a bank. And all this happened before his twenty-first birthday.

Postscript: Gerald later made contact with Charlie's surviving brother, now in his eighties and still living in Birmingham, explaining what he knew of Charlie's death.

'Don't blame yourself,' he told Gerald. 'If it had been his watch, he would have gone back for it just the same.'

7

Tom Hall

Pilot

I said to myself, this game is for keeps.

One very cold afternoon, my mobile phone rang. I was in the car, in traffic, stationary, running late. The call was crackly. I could just make out a male voice saying something about flying.

'. . . the book . . . would like to . . . Tom . . . Typhoons . . .' he said and then dropped out.

My heart bounced. I pulled over and checked my 'received calls' list. A private number. I hoped he would ring back soon because the Typhoon is my unequivocally favourite aircraft of all time.

Just looking at a picture of one is enough to make me happy. Silly, I know. Nevertheless, the Hawker Typhoon is my unchallenged number one pin-up of Second World War aviation.

And yet the Typhoon was a brute and had one of the dodgiest beginnings of any aeroplane. It was a great mother of a thing, like an aeroplane version of a V8 ute developed before the war as a single-engined fighter to succeed the famous Hurricane, but bigger and more powerful. Sadly, its construction was all too rushed. Its chief designer was Sydney Camm, a workaholic genius, already father to several famous military aircraft (as well as the man who gave his name to the camshaft). I imagined him saying to himself one day before the drawing board, 'I'm going to make the biggest, scariest thing I can think of.'

But initially, no-one was more scared of the Typhoon than the pilots who had to fly it. Fast tracked with wartime urgency from drawing board to production without realistic flight trials, the early Typhoons were plagued with faults. Small things really, such as the tendency of its tail to er, fall off. One of the Typhoon's early debuts was the disastrous Dieppe raid in August 1942 where a squadron of them swooped out of the sun onto a formation of Focke-Wulf 190 fighters. Three of the Germans were damaged, but two of the Typhoons failed to pull out of the dive due to the tail section deciding to part company with the rest of the fuselage. This and other structural faults became almost endemic to the Typhoon. It wasn't until well into its service that the rear fuselage was strengthened and this particular nasty rectified. And then there was the engine, a 1-ton, twenty-four-cylinder monster, the Napier Sabre. Immensely powerful, the early Sabres had some unpleasant habits as well, such as suddenly stopping, shattering its cylinders, spewing out oil and blinding the unfortunate pilot, or just blowing up. Then there was its tendency to leak carbon monoxide into the cockpit, quietly asphyxiating the pilot (this was never completely solved so Typhoon pilots used oxygen at all times, even at low level). But when they finally got it right, the Typhoon was magnificent. While it was found to be simply too cumbersome to be a successful fighter, as a ground-attack army support machine, it was to have no equal.

It looked magnificent, with a big round nose spinner from which protruded three enormous propeller blades and a distinctive open 'chin' radiator that made it look like a gaping monster (though it has to be said, this same feature made it impossible to ditch safely in the sea). Its wings were thick and strong, balanced by the high, strengthened tail. Seven tons in weight, it could carry a big payload of bombs, and four 20-millimetre cannons protruded from the leading edge of its wings. But the weapon with which the Typhoon was to become synonymous, as the Germans in Normandy were to find out to their utter dismay, was the rocket.

So I was looking forward to hearing from my unknown caller about Typhoons. But he didn't ring back. I waited, and I waited. Weeks went by. Damn. I had never met a Typhoon pilot, and my project would not feel complete without doing so.

A month or so went by. A colleague who knew someone who worked at a radio station mentioned to a mutual friend that someone had tried to contact me about 'some old bloke who was a pilot' and who had talked about it on the radio. I tracked down a name. Apparently a man by the name of Tom Hall had called up a few weeks earlier and had talked about flying Typhoons on D-Day.

A week later I was standing in front of a modest suburban unit on another dismal, overcast day.

'Have you read my book?' was Tom's opening remark.

I hadn't. He seemed unimpressed and a paperback was placed in my hands. *Typhoon Warfare – Reminiscences of a rocket-firing Typhoon pilot*. 'Twenty dollars,' he said.

Over the past few years, Tom had become something of a celebrity as one of the last surviving Typhoon pilots of the Normandy campaign. In 2004, he was offered a trip to France by the government to take part in the D-Day sixtieth anniversary, an offer he declined. There were also tributes from the French embassy, radio appearances and, of course, his book.

Tom came from Port Melbourne, an iconic working class suburb.

Being young and possessing outstanding natural aptitude, he had qualified for nearly every volunteer's dream, single-engined pilot training. But Tom's ambitions were not typical.

'I didn't want to stooge around at 30,000 feet never meeting the enemy', he said, and so when asked to state his flying preference, Tom was one of a mere two per cent who nominated 'army cooperation'. His flying career would be much closer to the ground, supporting the needs of the advancing army.

After qualifying, Tom had the melancholy experience of departing overseas from the heart of his very own neighbourhood at Station Pier. I had an image of him being seen off by his family, watching his home recede into the distance, wondering if he would ever see it again. But it wasn't nearly so romantic. He left at night and in secret, having farewelled his family long before. Perhaps that's even sadder.

Even before he left the country it was dangerous. Memorials all over Australia at aerodromes past and present attest to the numbers killed in training accidents. It's not hard to see why.

'We used to practise dogfights at low-level over the lake at Mildura. One bloke would try to strafe the surface shadow of the plane in front of him! We lost so many. It was wicked.'

Take-off in the Typhoon was a matter of timing and correction, using the rudder to compensate for the big torque swing as the tail wheel left the ground, generated by the Sabre's enormous 2200 horsepower. Even starting up was an issue, with a groundcrew required to stand by, fire extinguisher at the ready, in case the pilot over-primed the engine and started a fire in the radiator. Tom's friend and fellow pilot Bill Speedie wasn't deft enough on his first flight and narrowly missed collecting a hut situated a considerable distance off the runway. I flipped through Tom's book as he talked and came across a photo of Bill Speedie in Normandy, an impish looking lad with a mop of wavy hair.

Sometimes the air force was a rigid, highly organised machine, at other times it was the opposite. In May 1944, Tom arrived at Number 83 Group Support unit at Redhill in Surrey to complete training on the Typhoon before being assigned to an operational squadron. It was not what he expected. There was no training schedule and hardly anyone there to teach. Eventually, a bloke he assumed must be an instructor mumbled, 'Um, what would you like to do?' Tom had to think.

'Well we could, maybe, practise?'

'Yes. Alright then.'

And off they went, flying at 20 feet above the paddocks, blowing the hats off the farmers working the tractors and roaring away before their identifying numbers could be read.

Tom was assigned to number 175 Squadron, earmarked to join the impending invasion of Europe, supporting the army in ground-attack operations.

He exchanged his air force uniform for the khaki battle dress of the army, on account of its dangerous resemblance to the blue grey of the Germans, and was made to get used to living in tents, as they would soon have to do on the Continent. White lines were drawn on the runway to the reduced dimensions of their forward bases within which they were made to practise landings and take-offs. Big thick, black and white stripes were painted on the underside of the Typhoon's wings for extra recognition, the so-called 'invasion stripes'.

On the morning of 6 June 1944, D-Day, Tom was in the air at 7 am, heading towards France to attack a gun battery on the coast near Cabourg on his first operation. It was all he could do to concentrate on the job. Below him was stretched the awesome, never-to-be-repeated sight of 5,000 ships carpeting the ocean – the great Allied invasion armada. Sixty years later, his eyes still misted over at the image.

'Staggering,' is all he could say.

He'd been told to use his cannon on the way into the target, and to fire his rockets in a salvo. Out of a formation of twelve Typhoons, Tom was lucky last.

He lined up his aircraft at the biggest gun he could see and fired his rockets. In Typhoons, these are slung on rails, four on each wing, and operated by a switch on the throttle. In effect, they were the world's first air-to-surface missiles. There was a bang behind his head as a 20-millimetre cannon shell hit his aircraft on the starboard side just behind him, then passed out through the other side before exploding, taking a large chunk of the fuselage with it. Immediately the port wing dipped and started to drag. Gingerly, Tom tested the control surfaces and found all to be functioning. By compensating with opposite rudder, he made it back to England.

On the ground, his fitter looked at the hole in astonishment.

'What was it like?' he enquired of his first trip.

'Draughty,' said Tom.

The next day he was on again, flying alongside a more experienced pilot, Kelly Kelsic, swooping along at low level to stop German armour reaching the invasion beaches. Flying the 7-ton Typhoons at this altitude was incredibly dangerous and the casualty rates were enormous. Tom spotted the barrel of a tank under the fringes of a tree at the edge of a forest.

'I can see one,' he called on the radio/telephone.

'Skittle it,' replied Kelsic.

But Tom hadn't seen it quite early enough. He yanked the controls around too hard and started to lose control of the aircraft. It skewed sideways.

'I was skidding,' he told me. A strange notion for an aircraft, but I knew what he meant. He fired his rockets and missed. This gave the enemy the chance to retaliate and a machine gunner on the tank opened up.

Tom felt the thud of bullets hit his aircraft somewhere.

'I've missed him!' he called out.

The more experienced Kelsic did not, came in and set the tank on fire.

Back in England, the rigger looked over his aircraft in wonder.

'You've been lucky,' he said, and called Tom over to see the results of his day's work. Four bullets had struck the aileron, each missing one of the vital hinges by millimetres. If even one had hit, the aileron would have jammed, making the aircraft impossible to control, careering into the ground or upwards into a stall. And at the low level Tom was flying at, bailing out was not an option. That night, he quietly contemplated his situation for the first time.

'This game's for keeps,' he concluded. He would be needing a lot more of the luck that had saved him that day.

In late June, his squadron moved to France to its new permanent base, a rough airstrip bulldozed out of a Normandy wheat field and covered with steel matting known simply as B5. A line of tents, their new accommodation, awaited them.

Some mornings he would find himself waiting on a 'cabrank', one of four airborne Typhoons ready to be called in by the army to a pinprick on a map at a moment's notice. 'Red mortar smoke going down in one and a half minutes', would come over the air from an observation officer on the ground far below. And in they'd go. Sometimes the target would be a tank or a truck, sometimes lines of retreating German soldiers. In August at Falaise in Normandy, the Germans were corralled into a tiny pocket, with only one road left open to escape towards the east. It was carnage. As Tom says in his book:

> We rippled the rockets (fired them in pairs) then separately we did cannon attacks into the massed crowds of soldiers. We would commence firing, and then slowly pull the line of cannon fire through the crowd and then pull up and go around again and again until the ammunition ran out. After each run, which resulted in a large vacant path of chopped up soldiers, the space would be almost immediately filled with other escapees.

It was a long hot summer and clouds of dust blew up from the Typhoon's backwash, attracting German artillery. The pilots sweated like pigs inside the Typhoons' big perspex bubble canopy, encouraging them to dispense with the cumbersome Mae West life jacket. One afternoon in October, with Normandy long behind them, Tom watched as fellow pilot and Tom's long-suffering French teacher, Ross Clarke from Canada, bailed out over the B5 landing strip after having been hit by flak. All was well and a thumbs up given and returned. Then he could see Clarke panic as he realised he was heading for the middle of the River Meuse. He started swinging violently on his parachute to try and reach the bank, missed and went straight under. His body was later found downstream. Tom remembered Clarke's exasperated attempts to instil into Tom's Australian accent the subtleties of the French tongue.

After this fatality the order went out: everyone was to wear the Mae West at all times.

'Did you attack many trains?' I asked.

'Trains were our bread and butter,' he replied.

If they had steam up, he remembered, there'd be a tremendous explosion.

'How did you actually aim the aircraft? Was there a way of sighting it?'

'It was optical, a light that would appear as if 60 feet in front of the aircraft. We had to learn deflection shooting. Not easy.'

As the memories flood back like a tide, I could see that one particular incident still disturbed him greatly.

February 27 1945 was a miserable winter's day for the pilots of 175 in their forward base in Volkel, Holland. The weather was so bad there was to be no flying that morning. To pass the time many of them were playing bridge around a small table. Tom, one of the most senior pilots, was now often leading the squadron. The week before, he'd swooped down out of the sun to see a German V2 rocket about to take off to drop somewhere on London. The squadron fired and a massive explosion was witnessed. Then a call came through for four aircraft to take off and look for targets in the Lake Steinhuder area near Hanover. A ripple of unease went through the group as they glanced up at the heavy sky. The overcast cloud was down to 6,000 feet (1,800 metres). The commanding officer, Rollo Campbell, decided that his three wingmen would be chosen by the draw of a low card, but excused Tom due to the already high number of ops he'd completed, 120. Tom refused, and drew a three, along with Pilot Officer Ainsley and another experienced pilot and great friend, Warrant Officer Asher, an immensely likeable bloke from the West Indies.

The four took off, climbing through thick cloud and setting course for the target area, equipped with rockets and a single long-range fuel tank. Over the target, not one break in the cloud cover presented itself. It seemed a pointless exercise, but the four planes dived into it, line abreast. Diving down through cloud, Tom had a terrible, creeping feeling. As his airspeed built up, he counted off the seconds into the dive. There was, he knew, always a lag in the altimeter, and these instruments, bumped and thumped around daily in combat, were not ones he felt safe about relying on anyway. In front of him was nothing but white. The seconds ticked by, his airspeed increasing to over 500 miles an hour.

'You just couldn't see *anybody*!' Tom said, wringing his hands, his voice rising.

He wanted to open the radio and say to his commanding officer, 'We're too low, pull up!' But you never said that. Not ever. Not when someone else was in charge. But this time he had to. Tom pushed the button to transmit. As he did so, he heard his CO's voice.

'We're . . .' It was all he needed. The instincts of 120 operations kick in and he pulled the stick back hard, blacking out. The speed washed off as they broke through the cloud. Asher was missing. They circled and waited, then headed back to base in silence.

Tom remembered seeing the cards on the table, Asher's bridge tricks laid out from the game they'd played a couple of hours before.

Four weeks later the army advanced and found the remains of Asher and his Typhoon. For Tom, it was a terrible realisation. They had all been flying down into a valley, in cloud. Asher, on the far left, with 109 ops in his log book had hit one side and crashed. The others, similarly unaware, could not have been far away from catastrophe themselves.

Tom's face is dark with the memory of that fatal crash sixty years earlier. I looked at his book. The photographs of himself as a young pilot show the same troubled expression. Pictured in his flying gear mounting the wing of his mighty Typhoon, or against a hut, parachute pack slung over his shoulder, smiling weakly, the worry is evident behind the eyes.

Tom completed 122 ops on Typhoons – an astonishing tour and one he was very lucky to survive – and earned his DFC ten times over.

'I reckon I took other people's luck,' he said modestly. 'I saw boys on their first trip, dead as a doornail.'

As I left, Tom was calm and friendly. I didn't know who felt more drained after our conversation, me or him. I started to tell him what a privilege it has been to talk to him, but I sensed this would probably embarrass him. Instead I just said, 'It's been great to meet you.' And it was.

8

Bruce Clifton

Pilot

You just couldn't get your mind around the fact that you were going to get killed.

Bruce Clifton gave me one of the most extraordinary stories I had ever heard, on an afternoon I shall never forget. Not that I had any inkling of this on the long drive to his home in central Victoria. Every interview was like a lucky dip. Some were disappointing, while others turned up unexpected gems that made my head spin for days. By the sixth or seventh, I also started to feel that I was hitting my straps, and a pattern was starting to emerge as to how I would go about winning these peoples' confidence. First, I let them size me up. This usually took about twenty minutes while I made small talk over a mug of tea. Then I would casually drop something in to the conversation like, 'Ah, I see you have both the DFM [Distinguished Flying Medal] and DFC [Distinguished Flying Cross]. How long were you in the ranks?' Or, if my subject were a turret gunner, 'Did you ever use the Rose Brothers turret, or simply the Frazer-Nash?' These and other nerdy minutiae were designed to both impress and relax my subject. Sometimes it worked, sometimes it didn't.

All I knew of Bruce was that he had been a Lancaster pilot

at the very end of the war in Europe. He met me on the front lawn of his home, greeting me in front of a large, well-kept camellia. I immediately found him warm, intelligent and engaging, free of the residue of cynicism that people can sometimes pick up from a lifetime in the city.

He dashed about inside, making me tea, asking me about the drive up and introducing me to his wife, Marie. Sandwiches and biscuits of generous proportion emerged.

Bruce apologised for what he described as 'mess' on the kitchen table. It was in fact his mini museum, souvenirs from his few months flying heavy bombers. I noticed his badge of the 'Caterpillar Club', membership of which can only be awarded by bailing out of an aircraft with the aid of a parachute. As I cast my eye over the table, he handed me a leave pass from a Swedish internment camp and mumbled something about a funeral. I look at it, unsure of its relevance, feeling as if I'd lost track of a story I was supposed to have been following. I asked him to start at the beginning.

'Yes, let's not get ahead of ourselves,' he agreed.

One day at school, Bruce heard the news that his country was at war. He remembered the various reactions of the boys around him. Some cheered; others, especially those whose fathers had served in the First World War, were quieter. It was a Monday. Quite a way to begin the week. By the time his schooling had finished, the Battle of Britain and the legend of the sangfroid Spitfire pilot with a pipe and a cravat was already the stuff of schoolboy adoration.

Having qualified for pilot training, Bruce found himself at Nerrandra near Mildura, in the cockpit of a Tiger Moth with the instructor from hell. A screamer by the name of Dalby, any mistake from his pupils was met with a barrage of abuse: 'Fucking hell! Turn the bloody stick! Why am I wasting my friggin' time with you?!' Bruce's parody of his old instructor is amusing and comes out of nowhere, as if still smarting for torments afflicted sixty years ago and still hoping for a little revenge. Perhaps this is the very determination that got him through.

His first solo was one of the great moments in his life, akin he told me (out of his wife's earshot) to the birth of his children. He remembered it vividly. He had been practising landings all morning. On the runway in the dual control biplane Tiger Moth, his instructor (a different one of the non-screaming variety), who was seated in front of him, reached down and pulled out the split pin that secured his control column, removed it and threw it out of the aircraft. Bruce started hyperventilating. The other man climbed out, leant towards him and said, 'Right. All you have to do is exactly what we've been doing up till now.' Then he stepped back and sat down on the grassy verge. 'You're on your own, lad,' he called and Bruce was off. At 1,000 feet (300 metres), doing a circuit, he yelled a long, extended 'Yee-hah!'

Soon after, Bruce was posted to another school to progress onto flying the all-Australian built Wirraway, only to spend the next two months doing dishes. The sad story of the monster that was the Commonwealth Aircraft Corporation CA-1 Wirraway could fill a book on its own, but one of its more peculiar vices was that when being adapted from another aircraft, the North American Harvard trainer, the rudder axis was for some reason brought forward, making the pedals extremely hard to reach for any pilot under 6 feet tall. To compensate, the air force for a time resorted to installing wooden blocks on the rudder bars! Bruce was thankfully spared this ignominy but lost two months waiting for a place in another school. An entry in his log book summed it up: *Insufficient leg length for Wirraway aircraft.*

I could see that Bruce was enjoying himself immensely as we pored over the details of his log book and he explained the various codes of the training program. His memory was fabulous, recalling such details as the flavour of the ice-cream eaten onboard the American ship which took him to San Francisco, a trip he shared with several hundred American soldiers, who in the fighting in the Pacific had mentally and emotionally cracked and were being evacuated home. It was a sobering contrast to Bruce and his compliment of young air force graduates with their fresh faces and new dark-blue uniforms.

Upon arrival in England, he was sent to number 9 Squadron in Bardney, Lincolnshire, to re-start his training and to see just what went on at an operational heavy bomber base. Just eighteen, Bruce was younger than most pilots. As first, he would sit by the runway as the Lancasters were taking off at dusk, giving them a red or green light by hand-held lamp as they lined up to roar off into the night. Soon, he knew, the situation would be reversed and it would be him being signalled for take-off. Later the same evening, he would be on Flying Control, in the air as part of an airborne air traffic control system as the returning bombers came in, often with dead and wounded aboard. He would often hear the dramatic dialogue between radio operator and control tower. 'Hello Mayflower, this is A-Able. Request emergency landing. Two engines shot out. Mid-upper gunner dead,' and so on.

'My God,' thought Bruce. 'This is war.'

Bruce and I spoke amiably for a long time about training and flying. He loved the talk and the satisfaction he derived in answering my questions concisely and with as much relevant detail as possible was palpable.

His most serious incident was when training in the four-engined Stirling. While starting up for exercise, Bruce noticed one of the four rev counters not working properly and duly signalled the tower. A ground staff mechanic soon aboard began to remove the four screws which secured the recalcitrant instrument on the console. While doing this he fumbled and dropped the screws, managing to recover only two.

'I'll just put two back in and fix it up properly when you get back,' he said.

Bruce taxied to the end of the runway, then swung around onto the threshold for take-off. The throttles were open full bore, the tail was up, and they were tearing along at 85 miles (137 kilometres) per hour, his instructor next to him. The Stirling swung a little to the left with the torque as usual. This was nothing to worry about and needed just a touch of the rudder to correct it. Nothing happened. The rudder was rock hard, jammed solid with absolutely no give, and the aircraft was still wandering over to the side. The instructor had a go, but he too could not shift the rudder bar.

'Right,' he said, 'Cut throttles, cut switches, cut fuel!' One wheel was already off the runway, then another, and the big Stirling was at full power, heading straight for other aircraft dispersed around the perimeter track. At this speed, touching the brake was likely to lock one wheel, making the whole thing do a ground loop, digging the wingtip into the surface, wrecking the aircraft and endangering the crew. They decided to just hope for the best and let it run on. So 23 tons of aeroplane, completely out of control, bounced across the airfield until at last, it slowed quietly to a halt. A tender pulled up alongside and put the men immediately into another aircraft to complete the training exercise. Rather than let the nerves, or 'ring twitch' take a hold, the wartime rule was strictly 'get back on the horse'.

Later, enquiries would reveal that one of the two screws left on the floor of the aircraft by the mechanic had become jammed in a cogged wheel of the rudder control mechanism. Dangerous enough as this was, if it had become lodged in a slightly different part of the wheel, allowing them to become airborne but then preventing them from properly manoeuvring, it would have been catastrophic.

By December 1944, Bruce had trained up on Lancasters and was preparing to take his first operational flight, the mandatory 'second dickie' trip as an observer pilot with an experienced crew. He was so nervous he couldn't eat his pre-flight meal, then became so hungry he wolfed down his flight rations of barley sugar and chocolate, promptly making himself sick. Most of the flight was spent vomiting in the toilet at the back. The pilot advised he'd better come up the front and actually see something or he'd most likely have to do it again. Bruce staggered up to the cockpit, his head a blur of nausea and humiliation, icicles of vomit freezing around his face and oxygen mask in the sub-zero temperatures. The pilot had the perfect solution. 'Right, take over,' he said, and vacated his seat. Within five minutes, Bruce had forgotten he was sick, and even took the Lancaster back to base. It was a memorable first trip.

Bruce's tour was made up of attacks on oil refineries, railway yards and a few trips for the benefit of the army such as to the Ardennes Forest in Belgium when absolute precision bombing was needed to hit the German positions which were themselves close to the Americans, during the Battle of the Bulge. As far as he knew, he didn't make a mistake.

As one of the younger pilots, he felt the invincibility of youth that much more keenly.

'You just couldn't get your mind around the fact that you were going to get killed. We used to give it to the older crews. "You won't make it, your nerves won't stand it" – that sort of thing.'

Indeed, in twenty-eight trips, he was not once attacked by fighters, nor did he become trapped in searchlights, or have a close encounter with flak. Then came trip number twenty-nine.

On a big raid there was always a brief window between your slot in the complicated take-off schedule and being scrubbed altogether. Depending on the target, late starters were given a certain amount of time, after which you were deemed too far behind the others to make up the distance. On the night of 8 February 1945, it was set at thirty minutes. Bruce and his crew of seven were on the second last trip of their tour.

After their take-off meal, they sat in the briefing, listening with more intensity than they had ever listened to anything in their lives, to the information about the target, the weather and the expected defences. They had donned their flight equipment, parachute, life jacket, flying suit and boarded the crew bus out to their aircraft, Avro Lancaster PV382, with the identity code I-Item. They tested the equipment, the gunners working the turrets, the pilot and the flight engineer starting the engines and the flight systems. Then they shut everything down, climbed out and waited for their turn to start up and go. This was the waiting time, the time of the 'nervous pees' when you usually felt terrified but bored, sick with apprehension but nothing to do but think and a permanent urge to urinate. Usually, you couldn't, but the mere effort would alleviate some of the tension. Then at last the signal came. The Germans were already listening to the airwaves so it was always visual. The crew climbed back in and Bruce pushed the starter button. Number two, the inner starboard, was dead, not even a hint of turning over. A signal to the tower and in a few minutes ground staff put up portable scaffolding around the engine and the cowling was removed. All they could do was wait while the rest of the squadron took off in front of them.

Then a thumbs up, the cowling was replaced and the scaffolding removed. The inner starboard motor started immediately and they were cleared to go. It was the twenty-eight minute mark. Two more minutes and their mission would have been cancelled.

Their target was the synthetic oil plant at Politz, near Stettin, not far from Berlin on the Baltic coast. They were now flying alone over the North Sea with the rest of the bomber force of 485 Lancasters and seven Mosquitos 28 minutes ahead of them. Quickly, the navigator made a new course to cut two 14-minute blocks off the prescribed route, taking them over central Denmark, then down the Kattegat, the stretch of sea separating Sweden and Denmark, to re-join the stream. They would then ease back into the formation and swing south into northern Germany.

Near the rendezvous point the navigator, watching the second hand on his watch, gave the instruction to the pilot: 'Skipper, approaching change of course to 162.' It would be a turn to starboard so Bruce alerted the gunners to look out for other aircraft to avoid collision. 'All clear starboard, Skip,' came back from the gunners. Then from the navigator, 'Turn onto 162 . . . now.' They would be the last words Bruce heard him speak. He turned the Lancaster around to complete the delicate mid-air merge with the main force.

They had been over Sweden before. For them, it was an astonishing sight. As a neutral country it was at peace so instead of thc black-out, its cities were illuminated as in peacetime. But it also defended its neutrality. High above the city of Helsingborg, Bruce could clearly see the lights of the city 10,000 feet (3,050 metres) below. Slowly, eight of those lights began to move, gradually at first then speeding up rapidly and rushing towards them. Perhaps if he'd maintained a straight and level course they would have exploded behind him. But instead he made a fateful, shallow dive.

Sitting across from me, Bruce made four loud rapping noises on the table, *thump*, *thump*, *thump*, *thump*! The hairs on the back of my neck are standing on end. Four shells hit the belly of his Lancaster, I-Item. Pulling back from the dive, Bruce felt the control column go limp. In that instant, he knew the control cables were severed and the aircraft doomed.

'*Jump, jump, jump, jump*!' he yelled into the intercom but hears nothing back in his ears. It too is dead. Unable to communicate verbally, he gave his engineer a thump and pointed downwards. As pilot, Bruce was already sitting on his parachute pack, folded to fit into a scoop in his seat. The bomb-aimer was sitting behind him with the navigator, his chute on an adjacent shelf. Bruce distinctly remembered disconnecting his intercom, oxygen, seat harness and getting out of the seat, his priority in that instant to communicate to the rest of the crew to get out. Then, nothing.

Just a bright light, white and intense, and a clear, simple thought in his head, 'Hell, I'm dead! Mum's going to be upset'. There was no wind, no sound, no pain. 'It's funny how you remember these things,' he mused. Then, darkness.

I reached for the glass of water at my side but it was empty.

A shape appeared in front of him. The light faded slightly. It was moving. It was thin and dark and it seemed to be turning. At first he thought it was one of the crew, but watching it a little longer, he realised what it was. 'A cowling! It's only a bloody cowling!' Falling with a piece of his aircraft's engine cover seemed to restart some logical sequence in his brain: 'If that's a piece of the aircraft, it means it's probably disintegrated ergo I'm most likely in the air with it. Now, therefore, might be a good time to pull open the parachute.' He tugged on the rip cord, jolted upwards briefly and then descended through cloud.

He found himself standing in mud in a newly ploughed field. He stood up, half a mile away from the flaming wreckage of his aircraft. Ammunition was exploding and it was pitch dark, but Bruce began walking, ducking every time a bullet exploded from the wreckage. For some reason, he thought he was in Denmark. 'Bugger it,' he remembered thinking to himself. Soon he'd be picked up by the Germans.

He came to a rise in the ground, and an oil pipeline, suspended by concrete supports. He followed it and over the rise was greeted by the sight of the blazing lights of a city, Helsingborg, still very much in neutral Sweden.

I had been quiet for some time, mesmerised by this extraordinary tale. There was a pause. 'What time was it?' was all I could think to ask.

'Eight o'clock at night.'

'Were you in shock?'

'No,' Bruce answered calmly, 'just happy to be alive and grateful not to be in an occupied country.'

He couldn't know it at the time, but the Lancaster had ploughed into a local electrical substation, blacking out the entire area. He wandered towards the shape of a building some way up ahead. It looked like a farmhouse. A dog barked. A comical thought came into his head. Having survived being blown out of an aeroplane, was his fate now to be mauled by a dog? He found some steps, and went up to bang on the door. It opened, and Bruce could make out five or six startled people inside. He picked out a rather frightened-looking woman to address. 'Pilot. RAF,' he said, pointing emphatically to his uniform. No response. Then 'Australia'. This amazingly enough, seemed to spur them into action. They produced food – scones, bread and meat. Someone even removed and cleaned his muddied flying boots, and brought a basin with warm water to wash his face. No-one spoke English, but Bruce could tell questions were being asked. Ten minutes previously he had been blown out of a bomber at 10,000 feet. Now he was seated at a dinner table.

Soon a boy appeared in what looked to be a home guard uniform complete with a rather oversized, ridiculous-looking helmet. Unarmed except for a bayonet which remained firmly in his belt, he just stood there, agog, until the police arrived.

Bruce was arrested, put into prison with some local drunks, interrogated in the most gentle of fashions and marked for internment. At one o'clock that morning, he had the surreal experience of watching the formation returning home, roaring back overhead towards England at 4,000 feet (1,200 metres), their job at Politz done. The Helsingborg gunners again opened up and the shrapnel from the explosive shells rained metal splinters that tinkled on the roofs of the town.

Neutral Sweden had achieved what the Germans had failed to do in nearly thirty operations. The four flak shells had torn into the belly of I-Item, starting a fire in the bomb bay that set off several of the 500-pound bombs, tearing off the port wing, splitting open the cockpit and blowing the unstrapped Bruce Clifton into the night sky. In anyone's terms, it was a miracle of survival. Bruce's only injury was a tiny cut on the bridge of his nose. He lifted up his glasses to show me. I could just make out the tiniest of scars. The rest of his crew perished. Sixty years on, he gave a slight shake of the head in amazement.

The wing had landed about half a mile from the main wreckage. Not yet armed, the 4,000 pound Cookie failed to explode and rolled into a nearby orchard. The Swedish army asked if Bruce would consider disarming it. He politely declined.

A week after the crash, Bruce was given permission to leave his rather luxurious internment camp ('a bit like a holiday lodge in Daylesford') at Faloon, near Stockholm and return to Helsingborg to attend the funeral of his six crew members. His escort, a member of the British Legation, enquired if he was in possession of a hat. 'Can't go to a funeral without a hat,' he was told. In the town, they managed to borrow a Homburg hat for the afternoon from a fastidious shopkeeper who insisted on putting a sheet of paper inside it to keep it clean. Bruce showed me a photograph. There he is, a pale young man with a vacant look and a very odd, very new-looking Homburg, laying a wreath under a heavy sky on the fresh graves of six other young men without the benefit of Bruce's freakish good luck. In his pocket was the leave pass he had shown me earlier in the afternoon, still in remarkably good condition.

Bruce's wreath was not alone. The soldiers of the Swedish anti-aircraft battery that brought I-Item down, distressed at having caused the deaths of the six airmen, also sent one. Soon after, the Swedish parliament decided to desist firing at passing Allied aircraft altogether. His was the last aircraft brought down in Sweden for the entire war.

I think Bruce is still in awe of the good luck that has given him an extra sixty years of productive life. He told me at the beginning of our meeting that though he was not a cold-hearted man – and I could see that he lacked nothing in intelligence and sensitivity – when it came down to it, he really hasn't been too badly affected by it all. No guilt and remorse, no sleepless, screaming nights. Bruce was just one of those people with the ability to simply turn a corner and not look back. Lucky again.

A month later, he was repatriated to England, courtesy of a BOAC DC-3 from Stockholm airport. Back home, he was checked out and given a few weeks' 'survivor's leave' and then posted back to his squadron. There was talk of him going back on the battle order to complete his last trip, but the war ended a few days later.

Fifty years on, he returned to Helsingborg, sponsored by a Swedish bank and newspaper, now something of a local celebrity. He even met the woman who had given him a meal and bowl of water to wash his face that night.

On the drive back home, my football team was playing on the radio somewhere interstate, but I couldn't really concentrate. I thought about Bruce. He really was remarkably youthful for his age, as well as mentally and physically fit. Perhaps the drama of what happened that night had preserved in him an impervious joy at a long life happily lived on borrowed time.

9

John Trist

Bomb-aimer

I wasn't very good to start with. If I wanted to hit Essen, I'd aim for Cologne.

Originally a Queenslander, John began his war marching all over the Blue Mountains (or, as he called them, the 'Black and Blue Mountains'), wearing not an air force uniform, but the scratchy, ill-fitting khaki of an army recruit, and he hated it. 'I don't want to walk. I'd rather be carried somewhere,' he decided, so a career in the air force beckoned. The army however, were anything but happy when his transfer came through. 'You're running away!' they said to him, attempting to apply some guilt-assisted leverage. It was never going to work. Sitting with him in his living room, surrounded by the library of an obviously erudite man, listening to recordings of great operas and sipping some excellent wine to accompany the three-course lunch that John had prepared, I can see why the army was never for him. Nothing to do with his education at Brisbane Grammar, then Latin at Queensland University. He simply prefers the good life.

The first time I met John was at the tail end of a long lunch in a suburban Melbourne pub, put on by the association of former members of 'EATS', the Empire Air Training Scheme.

This remarkable, as well as remarkably efficient system of aircrew training was instigated at the beginning of the war and stretched over several continents in places such as Canada, South Africa, Rhodesia and, of course, Australia, and just about every aircrew who served in Europe went through it.

From what I remember, it was a wonderful afternoon, despite being the youngest there by a measure of my own lifetime, a fact that in itself gave me some kind of odd celebrity, like the solitary young child that is fussed over at a grown-ups party. After drinks and lunch, speeches and a great many toasts (including of course the Queen), the volume level gradually rose to a cacophony as groups of men formed and reformed as acquaintances were renewed and memories re-visited. Someone introduced me to John and mentioned my project. He immediately laughed loudly and put his number down in the notebook I was holding hopefully in my hand.

I drove up to John's place and immediately noticed his front garden dominated by two massive full-grown white gum trees. Such an odd sight in a small, suburban garden, I thought as I looked up at them towering over house and street. I liked the fact they were there, and that its owner had remained resistant to the warnings of falling boughs and damaged drains. The afternoon was cold and gloomy and it felt good to be inside John's cosy living room. He shook my hand wearing an apron. A strong smell of cooking was in the air and a table was set, complete with an already decantered bottle of red. 'Lunch won't be long,' he stated in an easy assumption of hospitality.

An eyesight problem meant that John didn't even get a chance at being a pilot so after Initial Training School at Bradfield Park in Sydney, he was marked down as 'observer' and put on a ship to Canada to undertake training in whatever occupation the air force saw fit.

'Actually,' he told me, 'it was all done alphabetically. If your name started with "t", you were a bomb-aimer.' And so a bomb-aimer he became. I must have seemed sceptical at this arbitrary method of selection but he assured me it was true, even though, initially at least, he wasn't very good at it.

'If I wanted to hit Essen, I'd aim for Cologne,' he joked.

The bomb-aimers were promised training in the warmth of Florida, but instead were put on a train north to icy Canada. First came a stint at Bombing and Gunnery School at Lethbridge in Alberta, flying very old Blenheims and shooting out the back of the aircraft at ground and air targets. In the tight turns, John found out just how strong a stomach he'd been blessed with as he watched his fellow students succumb to nausea.

'Once there were three of us in the back of the plane, and I had to complete the firing practice for all of us,' he said.

Australians had a reputation for harbouring a healthy disrespect for authority, so John was duly nominated as complaints spokesman for the course, a role he didn't relish and which, he reckons, probably cost him an on-course officer's commission.

In canvass-skinned Ansons, John began flying over the snowy Canadian wilderness on training exercises, where raw crews were expected to fly to a pinpoint position, a near impossible task in the endless expanse of white.

'The only way we could work out where we were was to fly down very low and read the names on the silos. It was amazing how much our navigation improved after that.'

Amazing or not, it got them through, and John was sent to England. After a spell in Brighton's Metropol Hotel, looking out over the uninviting beach cut off by mines and coils of barbed wire, followed by a train trip north, John arrived at a bitterly cold and dreary Advanced Flying Unit in West Freugh, Scotland.

Gradually, he got the sense that things were starting to progress. A little later, he found himself at an Operational Training Unit in Lichfield crewing up, or as John puts it, 'wandering around a big room, trying to find your soulmate by the look in his eye'. Someone tapped him on the shoulder. 'I like you,' he said and John had met his pilot, Allan Baskerville, a fellow Queenslander. The rear-gunner, Jack McQueen, made three 'banana benders', and John already felt he was lucky.

It was spring. A time, John says, of 'lambs gambolling in the fields, airmen gambling in the huts' and flying Wellingtons on cross-country exercises over the fair face of England. John's skills began to improve. Then came his first flight over enemy territory, a 'stooge' raid just before D-Day, dropping propaganda leaflets on the French, informing them their day of liberation was fast approaching. They were also intended to convince the Germans to get going while the going was good. They didn't, and all John's crew gained from it was a false sense of security. Soon they were to be posted to the squadron which suffered the highest casualties not only of any other Australian squadron, but of the entire Australian armed forces for the Second World War, number 460 Squadron, RAAF.

'I can still hear the note of the Lancaster's four synchronised engines,' John remembered wistfully, as have many others who flew in them. Initially, however, he was unimpressed with the prospect of flying with four engines instead of two, training on a very rickety early mark Halifax. But the Lancaster was a different story.

'It really was a wonderful aircraft,' he said. 'The sound of those engines . . . it was a very comforting feeling.'

Actually, I knew just what he meant. I've heard a Merlin engine and it really does have a special quality – smooth and rich, but somehow understating its immense power, and quite hypnotic.

Number 460 was an established Australian squadron with an enormous reputation. As the history book says, 460 'carried out the most bombing raids, flew the most sorties and suffered the most losses in Australian squadrons'. It also holds the record for most bombs dropped by any squadron throughout the whole of Bomber Command – a whopping 25,000 tons. In doing so it achieved another grisly record, over a thousand men killed in action, the highest for any World War Two Australian military unit. Into this formidable establishment came John and his crew of new boys.

'It was just like being back at school,' he said. In briefings he would sit at the back of the room, awed by the 'easy nonchalance' of the experienced crews.

John's tour began quietly enough, at a time when, during the latter months of 1944, much of Bomber Command's strength was taken off attacking the big German cities in favour of tactical raids in support of the armies in France. His first proper trip was again almost anti-climactic, a three and a half hour flight over to Le Havre. No fighters, hardly any flak and a quiet trip all round.

This easy introduction, however, was deceptive. The first few operations of a tour in Bomber Command were by far the most lethal. Hank Nelson's superb book on Australians in Bomber Command, *Chased by the Sun*, details a survey of men killed in action in 460 Squadron, finding that 'over 11 per cent died on their first operation' and nearly half of all deaths occurred on the first six! After this, the 'chop rate' began to fall dramatically as men accrued the experience that would help keep them alive. Even so, John reckoned his was an outstanding crew.

'Without doubt, I owe them my life and my undying gratitude.'

One of the bomb-aimer's tasks would be to take over from the pilot in case of death or incapacitation. In preparation for this dreaded, though not unanticipated event, John practised in the Link trainer, an early form of flight simulator, as well as the odd stint flying straight and level on the way home.

'If anything happens to Allan,' John assured his crew, 'don't worry, I'll get you home.'

They remained sceptical.

'What you'll actually do,' they said pointedly, 'is take us over the airfield at 10,000 feet and we'll bale out. After that, you can do what you like.'

As the war progressed satisfactorily on the ground, the bombers were put back on attacking the big industrial and population centres of Germany. On one occasion, over the fires of a burning city, John lined up the target below, his finger poised on the release button.

'It was night, but in the fires below it was like a scene out of Dante's *Inferno*.'

Then the great shape of another Lancaster below began to drift sideways, cutting across the view through the bombsight. He couldn't risk it, and told the pilot to go around again.

'I wasn't popular, but I wouldn't have had that on my conscience for the world.'

It's an astonishing image, turning around, at night, with no lights, flying directly into a stream of hundreds or more aircraft.

'How did you manage it without collision?' I asked.

'Put your hands over your eyes,' he told me, and did so, chortling darkly.

In the perspex nose of the Lancaster, John saw everything, and it was colourful. There were the target indicators dropped by the Pathfinder aircraft above, often a different colour each trip, the orange *crump* of exploding flak, the fires themselves and the coloured tracer winding its way up towards you, slowly at first, then passing by in a rush. He also witnessed the full effect of being 'coned' in a web of searchlights. On one occasion, they encountered the feared 'master' light, an enormously powerful beam with a distinctive cold and evil-looking blue hue. This monster would latch onto you, alerting both fighters and anti-aircraft gunners to your presence with naked illumination, and was hard to shake off. Once caught, and blinded by literally millions of watts of candlepower, it seemed the seconds to your imminent demise were counting down. But John was lucky enough to have an excellent pilot in Allan Baskerville. His quick and violent evasive 'corkscrewing' managed to shake the lights, and also keep the aeroplane in one piece.

On returning from Essen one night, the aircraft was again illuminated but this time by the hand of Nature. John feared the worst from a sudden flash, but the Lancaster had in fact been hit by lightning, and for a while the electric current made the aircraft glow with a strange, dancing blue iridescence.

Stuttgart – mid-upper turret holed I read aloud from the log book entry written in John's neat hand. A big chunk of flak had missed the lucky gunner's skull by about 3 inches (8 centimetres).

'I was a bit lucky like that myself,' he told me.

Over one target on the run-in, he had just vacated the nose position to briefly check the camera that would soon record the success (or otherwise) of his bomb aiming. Then *bang*! Normally, you could never hear the flak bursting above the throb of the engines. But when it was really close you not only heard it, you smelt it. A red hot chunk of iron tore through the thin perspex bubble right where John's head had been seconds before. A lucky escape certainly, but something had hit him in the face nonetheless, and liquid was oozing from his mask.

'Are you alright, Oliver?' asked the pilot (they called him Oliver. Trist – Twist – Oliver Twist).

'I – I think so,' answered John feebly. After a moment of

watching his life flash before him, he realised that he wasn't that damaged after all. A piece of the perspex had flown off and whacked him on the nose. The liquid was simply water from the condensation in his mask, and he was basically unharmed. He laughs now, but I don't suppose he was then.

Immediately above the bomb-aimer's position sat the rarely used front gun turret. A large part of John's training had been as a gunner, so it seemed a shame to go through the entire tour without at least giving them a go in anger. One day, in late 1944, he got his chance when he spotted a small, unusual looking aircraft heading straight towards him. Unusual, in that it lacked propellers. In fact, it was the first jet John had ever encountered, the famous Messerschmitt 262 jet fighter. The closing speed of both aircraft would have been astronomical and it just wooshed past in a flash, but John at least had time to clamber up and get off a few satisfying, if ineffectual rounds.

Despite this, John was becoming comfortable in his 'office' and more confident with his skill as a bomb-aimer. He had learned a lot in a very short time: distinguishing the real from the dummy targets the Germans set fire to on the ground, learning to bomb on the right coloured target indicator markers and avoiding the tendency to 'creepback'. This unfortunate but understandable phenomenon occurred when, directly over the cauldron of the target, the bomb-aimer would be in such a hurry to 'just drop the bloody things' and get out of there, that he would do so slightly short of the target. Thus, the target area would expand, or creep, often several kilometres back towards the direction of the oncoming aircraft, the fire engulfing whatever stood in its way, military or civilian.

John would make himself count a full second when directly on target, a decision often vindicated by his camera shots the next day. A set of five photographs were taken automatically after the bombs' release and ideally, the target itself should be visible in frame number three. Otherwise, you had released too early.

Overall, John reckoned he preferred the daylight trips, and the satisfaction of seeing the results of the work he was doing. One such was Wanne-Eickel in the Ruhr Valley for which John's log book reads *Lots of explosions*.

It was the site of a large synthetic oil and benzol plant and was hit hard by the RAF in mid-November 1944. It was one of the rare occasions John could actually see the damage his bombs were doing to an unequivocally industrial target, with large explosions ripping apart whole sections of the plant, ensuring the fuel it produced for the tanks and trucks and planes would never arrive. Daylight missions had their disadvantages, however. Once or twice he saw another Lancaster go down and was aghast at the black carpet of flak he was expected to fly through. 'How the hell are we going to get through this?' he thought. At night, the danger was still there, of course, only less visible.

Another satisfying trip was St Vith, in the Ardennes forest on Boxing Day 1944, when the weather at last cleared enough to allow the RAF to intervene in the Battle of the Bulge. They attacked at low level, destroying an important rail head crammed with German tanks on flat cars waiting to be unloaded, on their way to join the battle.

'Gee, it must have been frightening for them, though,' John reflected.

Ten thousand feet is low enough to easily make out people on the ground, so their terror would have been clearly visible.

Then, quietly he said, 'The one I regret is Ulm.'

Ulm sits on the left bank of the Danube in the south German state of Baden-Württemberg looking across at Neu (new) Ulm, its reflection on the other side of the river in Bavaria. Ulm itself goes back to the twelfth century, when it was a prosperous centre for the manufacture of linen. It was swept up in Martin Luther's Reformation, becoming Protestant in 1530, and is dominated by a magnificent Gothic cathedral, founded in 1377, with one of the highest spires in the world.

By late 1944, Ulm had managed to come through the war completely unscathed until, on the night of 17 December 1944, Bomber Command made its one and only visit to the town, sending 523 bombers to attack it. In the nose of one of those aircraft was John Trist. Among Ulm's industries at the time were two large lorry factories, a barracks and a depot, but John can't now recall just what it was that he was supposed to be aiming at. He remembered approaching Ulm in moonlight and seeing a pretty medieval city on the banks of a big river.

'It was just sitting there in the moonlight, and we plastered it. It looked so beautiful and . . . *bang*.'

Nearly 1,450 tons of high explosive were dropped on Ulm that night in a raid that lasted just 25 minutes. A large fire started in the centre of the town and crept back into open country, gutting an entire square kilometre, killing over 700 people, wounding 600 more and leaving 20,000 others bombed out of their homes. Eight bombers were lost.

In that part of his log book where details of the target are often recorded, he has simply written *Ulm – city itself*.

'I've never been very proud of that,' said John.

The attack on Ulm never engendered any controversy. It wasn't a Caen, or a Dresden or a Hamburg. There was no talk of war crimes and history has largely forgotten it. When the war ended sixteen weeks later, it became just one of the hundreds of maimed European cities, the reasons for its destruction quickly forgotten.

John, however, has never forgotten, and the brief clouding of his sharp, lively eyes told me he is haunted by it still today.

He finished his tour, plus one extra trip. His wireless operator had been sick for one mission and was required to make it up after the rest of the crew had finished. Rather than make him go with a strange crew, they all of them volunteered to do one extra to finish together.

The wireless operator, however, received a word of warning.

'Listen, Harry,' said John before take-off, 'if anything happens to us on this last trip, I'll grab the aircraft axe and get you on the way down.'

All of them made it back to experience that wonderful feeling of completion and life suspended no longer.

'I still can't stand fireworks, though,' said John. 'Kids reckon they're wonderful, but I hate them. Been there, done that.'

He had seen enough bright colours in the sky for a lifetime.

It was time to go, and as we went outside, I admired his enormous gum trees once again.

'I planted them,' he told me, proudly looking up at the crowns high above our heads, 'just after the war. You might one day read about someone being crushed by a falling bough.'

I laughed, and he too was smiling.

'But there you go,' he said. 'History is told by the survivors.'

10
George Gilbert
Spitfire pilot

The most dangerous part was flying those aeroplanes.

George, from Tasmania, began his training in the winter of 1942, and in the open cockpit of a Tiger Moth, it was bloody cold. He joined up in Hobart then did three stints of four months each at Somers in Victoria, back to Tassie at Western Junction, then Deniliquin in New South Wales, seeing a great deal of Australia in a very short time. Starting from scratch and learning to fly full-time was extremely stimulating, but extremely intense. It was too much for one fellow student, he remembered, who attempted to bail out of the dormitory window in the middle of the night. However, the feeling of collecting his flying gear and walking towards the aeroplane for his first solo was one he'll never forget.

George was something of a natural pilot, quickly learning to command the aircraft while gaining experience from its individual foibles, much like learning to ride a horse. The Tiger Moth was a quaint-looking little biplane, but not actually easy to fly. Once, in a mock dog-fight, he attempted to pull the stick in one direction, but the aircraft insisted on going another. Looking around, he suddenly realised he was in a stall. Instinctively, he took his hands off the controls and let the aircraft do what it wanted. It recovered, and as he puts it, 'flew off, sweet as a nut. They have a mind of their own, you see.' His instructors spotted his talent and so marked him down to complete the final leg of training at number 2 Operational Training Unit in Mildura, then Australia's premier school for fighter pilots.

Sitting in the cockpit of a 700 horsepower Wirraway was a step up from the 100 horsepower Tiger Moth but that's where the glamour ended.

'The Wirraway was an aircraft that had every vice in the world,' he said flatly.

The Commonwealth Aircraft Corporation built no less than 755 Wirraways between 1939 to 1946, and all of them were rubbish. *Wirraway* is apparently an Aboriginal word meaning 'challenge' and indeed, what a challenge this great lump was to all who flew in it. Much to the disgust of the British, the design was adapted from an American training aircraft, the Harvard. In 1936 it became the first project undertaken by the newly formed Commonwealth Aircraft Corporation (CAC), being duly given the designation CA-1 and built at Fishermans Bend in Melbourne.

Because the Wirraway was not particularly good at anything, it was given the classification 'general purpose aircraft' and forced into a variety of ill-fitting roles including fighter, bomber, reconnaissance aircraft, army-co-operation and trainer. There was even a madcap plan to turn it into a dive bomber but common sense prevailed and this particular fantasy was abandoned. A moment's lack of concentration by the pilot could result in a stall at just about any speed, then a series of virtually uncontrollable flicks onto its side and back. Landing could also be a problem as it tended to suddenly drop a wing if the angle of attack was marginally too high.

They were inadequately armed with two .303 Vickers machine guns mounted in the cockpit right in front of the pilot, firing through the propeller with the aid of a synchronising device. Even so, said George, there were few Wirraways without a couple of holes in the prop where the synchroniser had failed, and he himself would hear the occasional *ping* as a bullet struck.

The Wirraway's most infamous hour occurred in 1942 when it was sent into combat against Japanese aircraft in New Guinea, and a more David and Goliath encounter never there was. They were massacred by the nimble Japanese fighters and suffered terrible losses. Once, and only once did a Wirraway manage to shoot down a Japanese plane when, on Boxing Day 1942 Pilot Officer J. Archer surprised a very unlucky Zero pilot near Buna on the northern coast of New Guinea, diving hard and sending him crashing into the sea. Archer's award for his astonishing feat? Six bottles of beer.

'They weren't even well made,' George recalled. One day at 8,000 feet after finishing some formation training, he was flying on his own when his engine blew a bearing, pouring choking smoke into the cockpit. This was it, he thought. He trimmed the aircraft and climbed out onto the wing, ready to jump. Then he noticed the smoke had cleared so, happy to save the government several thousand pounds, climbed back in and looked for the nearest open paddock. Being near Mildura, he didn't have to look very far, and was even able to manually lower the undercarriage. The prop windmilled away and the Wirraway, its engine well and truly dead, glided down in one piece. But any thought that his thrift would endear him to the authorities was sadly mistaken. They were furious, preferring him to have written the plane off, rather than going to the expense of recovering and transporting it back to the airfield, with all the associated paperwork. (Public service attitudes, it seems, go back a long way.) They didn't even send another plane to pick him up so, somewhat comically, George had to sit in the cockpit of his lame duck as it was towed the 30 miles back to Mildura down the highway behind a lorry.

'A vicious, vicious thing,' said George of the Wirraway shaking his head, and was glad to be rid of it. He then graduated onto the P-40 Kittyhawk, another aircraft which left much to be desired but a definite improvement nonetheless.

As a single seater with no dual controls, the only way to fly a Kittyhawk was to do it yourself. So for a couple of days, George was made to sit in the cockpit familiarising himself with the instruments. Then one day, he taxied out to the edge of the runway and was signalled to take off.

'It was one of the most frightening experiences I've ever had,' he said.

In the air the noise from the Kittyhawk's Allison engine was deafening and with the cockpit open, the wind came in from the side and forced your head forwards. But he managed to pull his wheels up, then turn around and land. That was it for his first flight, but he'd got the feel of it.

It was a modest debut, but being cocky didn't do you much good either. A fellow Tasmanian who joined up with George had the temerity on his maiden flight to execute a slow roll over the airfield. The CO was not happy, and the entire unit was made to form a line behind the unfortunate young man and administer a kick in the pants next morning on parade.

George's training was nothing if not thorough. By the time he passed out, rated as 'average' (everyone was rated 'average' – the CO looked better that way) he had already clocked up 226 hours in the air on Wirraways and Kittyhawks. He had learned about strafing, formation flying, air combat tactics and had even learned to skip a bomb along the water to hit a ship. As fond as he had become of the Kittyhawk, it was time to say goodbye to it too, because George was off to join a brand new RAAF squadron, number 79, flying Spitfires.

I'd noticed when discussing the Spitfire, that almost anyone with even the slightest interest in aeroplanes went into a kind of love-struck, reverential trance, spouting absurd anthropomorphising platitudes about this aeroplane's 'beauty', 'grace', and even 'mystery'. George, who actually flew them, didn't much like them at all, and in the context of the enduring legend, it was one of the most refreshing, amusing – not to mention authoritative – views I'd ever heard.

'Austere,' is how he rated the Spitfire. 'No creature comforts at all.'

Compared to the roomy Kittyhawk, the Spitfire was cramped and uncomfortable. Your head hit the top of the canopy, your shoulders touched the sides and your feet had to be hung in straps on the rudder pedals to prevent the blood rushing down into your legs and blacking you out. In the cloying heat of the tropics, it would have been less than pleasant. To be sure, the British wartime economy was bare-boned and the government was churning out Spitfires as fast as it could but compared to the relatively luxurious American aircraft the Spitfire must have seemed miserly indeed.

After picking up his Spitfire at Laverton in Victoria, George's log book tells the story of 79's long journey north to take part in the Pacific War. From Laverton to Richmond in New South Wales, Richmond to Amberley in Queensland, then onto Townsville, where the aircraft were tested and adjusted for the tropics before leaving Australia. Then to Horn Island off the tip of Cape York, Port Moresby (where the squadron became operational), Seven Mile Airstrip in New Guinea, Milne Bay, and then to tiny Goodenough Island, off the eastern tip of Papua, part of the small archipelago known as the Entrecasteauxs.

As a Tasmanian, George found adjusting to life in the tropics challenging. Snakes, bugs, spiders the size of your hand, and rudimentary accommodation in tents with no relief from the unbearable humidity. To pass the time, the men would collect white coloured ants, put them in among black-coloured ones and, as George says, 'watch the massacre. Terrible. The white ants would cop it the worst'.

The isolation had its own dangers. Once when over the big Japanese base at Rabaul, on New Britain, a fellow pilot suffered engine failure at high altitude, so George decided to stick with him. Flying alongside, George watched as the pilot prepared to abandon the stricken Spitfire.

'I expected him to do the normal thing: roll the aircraft onto its back and fall out.'

Instead, he watched as the pilot trimmed the aircraft and pulled the stick back to fly straight and level, then suddenly let it go, causing the Spitfire to 'bunt', ejecting the man like a bucking brumby at a rodeo. The Spitfire proceeded to the bottom of the sea, and a Catalina flying boat was sent to rescue the pilot in the water. But his ordeal was not yet over. Rough seas swamped the Catalina's motors, so it too had to be rescued and towed back to base the next day.

The prospects of bailing out over Japanese-held territory was a sobering one, as the stories of abuse of POWs were already well-known.

'We all wore officers' ranks, even those of us that weren't,' George remembered. 'We knew they treated the officers slightly better than the men. We thought it might give you a little more time before they chopped your head off.' And the Japanese were not the only danger to a downed airman.

'To the north of New Britain were cannibals, and yes, we were told they would eat us.'

In the tropical extremes, the Spitfire proved less suited than to its original task of short-range defensive fighter in the cool skies of northern Europe, and mechanical failures accounted for a disproportionately high number of casualties. Often, said George, airmen would simply vanish into the sea.

'One disappeared north of Horn Island. Never saw him again.'

A particular danger was the Spitfire's oxygen system which, amazingly, had no indicators. The only way you knew you were running out of air was to keep looking at your fingernails.

'If they were pink, you were getting oxygen. If they were white, you knew you were in trouble.'

At 40,000 feet (12,000 metres), George reckoned, you had about 8 seconds before your oxygen-starved brain lapsed into unconsciousness. One pilot, on his very first high altitude flight, suffered such a fate, slumping forward onto the stick and sending the aircraft straight into the ground at over 400 miles an hour.

'He just left a little hole.'

Another drawback was the Spitfire's restricted range, limited by its relatively small 80-gallons in the main fuel tank, supplemented by another 80 in the drop-tank slung under the belly. Even with the engine operating nowhere near full power it only had a flying time of about 5 hours. The trouble with the drop tank, however, was that occasionally, you had to drop it.

'If we needed height in a hurry, we'd let it go, and then we were very restricted,' George explained. 'Usually, we'd come home with only 2 or 3 gallons left in the tank.'

For all its faults, the Kittyhawk's range was superior, and later the Mustang could be in the air for as long as 8 hours at a stretch.

Maintenance of these complicated machines in such climes was a truly Herculean task, carried out by dedicated groundcrews. George had a theory, though, that sometimes it was not just the elements and the Japanese working against them.

'Some of the motors were sabotaged,' he claimed.

This was certainly a new one for me, and I pressed him on it. After every 80 hours of flying, a Spitfire required an engine change, and the changeover Rolls-Royce Merlin engines would arrive in big crates from England. Occasionally one would be missing a vital circlip off the little end, causing the pistons to slowly wear a hole in the cylinder sleeve. Whether it was sabotage or carelessness of the part of the weary English factory workers, once this occurred, white smoke would spew from the exhaust and the pilot would need to quickly cut the engine electrical switches to avoid a fire, and either bale out, or use the Spitfire's excellent aerodynamics to glide its way in.

Once, a fellow pilot radioed in saying he was in just this kind of trouble at 25,000 feet (7,600 metres). On the ground, George could see the tell-tale white vapour and watched him come all the way in on a long glide. Obviously thinking that he might be a little short of the end of the runway, he suffered a momentary mental lapse and switched on the engine electrics, hoping for a brief boost that would bring him safely down.

'He just blew up. Right in front of us,' remembered George. 'Just like that. *Boom*, in a big flash. We lost a lot like that.'

George's nine month Pacific tour included shipping patrols, base patrols, weather patrols, reconnaissance patrols, night flying, searches for downed pilots in dinghys, ground strafing, and a great deal of other flying besides. Later, 79 moved a little further north to Kiriwina, the largest of the Trobriand Islands, and would scramble to have a go at intercepting the Japanese bombers as they flew over to raid Port Morseby.

At dawn every morning, a marauding 'Tony' – Japanese aircraft were all issued with anglicised names by the Allies to aid recognition – fighter bomber would drop one on 79's airfield and speed off, until on 31 October 1943, Flight

Sergeant I.H. 'Kid' Callister brought it down with a lucky piece of interception and cannon-fire. A week later, Callister was dead, killed in a take-off collision with another aircraft.

'The other bloke ended up in hospital, completely burned, with just his eyes showing,' remembered George.

Then one night it was George's turn to chase down a high-flying Japanese bomber. High above the island in darkness, the only way he could spot it was by looking for the glows of the engine exhaust stubs, but try as he might, the bomber remained elusive. Then, looking down, George spotted lights of a different nature. It was anti-aircraft fire being aimed in his direction.

'The Yanks are having a go at me!' he thought indignantly.

Then a searchlight opened up. Thinking this was getting 'bloody ridiculous', he turned away in a wide arc out to sea, then came back to sneak onto the strip, aided only by the dim light of kerosene lamps.

'They would just shoot at anything,' he said.

Having said that, he was grateful for the Americans' generous supplies of cigarettes, chewing gum and toothpaste. The chewing tobacco was, however, politely declined.

The mid-to-latter stages of the Pacific War were an odd time for the Australians, the bulk of the fighting having been taken over by the Americans. They were now travelling north, pushing the Japanese back towards their homeland. The Australians were restricted to the secondary, some have argued superfluous tasks of mopping up the remnants of the Japanese who, cut off and unsupplied, were going nowhere fast and possessed little or no offensive potential.

Later, Kiriwina would play host to the Americans, who not only provided the ground defence but used 79's airstrip as a base to attack Rabaul, and continue on to places further north. George would watch them fly in, their factory-fresh

P-38 Lightning, twin-engined fighters finished all over in gleaming silver aluminium, and looking magnificent beside the drab camouflage of their well-worn Spitfires. 'Why shouldn't we have nice shiny aeroplanes too?' thought George along with a couple of the pilots, and proceeded to strip the paint off some of their mounts. However, instead of shiny silver, all this revealed was an ugly patchwork of low-grade metal panels, each a slightly different, slightly dirty shade of grey. All the stories of Spitfires being made out of the donated pots and pans of patriotic British housewives seemed a little less apocryphal. The bare patches were painted over again. 'At least we were better trained than they were,' said George as consolation.

He also did his fair share of ground strafing, although remains doubtful as to its efficacy.

'We were told there were Japs in a plantation on an outlying island, so we flattened it but didn't see anyone. Whether they were there or not, we didn't really know.

The tiny New Guinea island of Pitilu was clobbered by just about everyone.

'The navy shelled it, we strafed it, the bombers bombed it and then the Yanks came to take it over. But thc Japanese fired a mortar round into one of their landing craft, so we all had to do it all over again.'

Later, George heard that there had been fourteen Japanese there at the beginning of this quick mini-campaign, and fourteen at the end, all secure in underground shelters.

But strafing could be dangerous as well, and the Japanese had a particular fondness for laying traps. George was leading a flight of four Spitfires investigating a lone barge tied up on a beach on a remote island. Unable to detach his drop-tank, he remained at about 1,000 feet (300 metres) while the other three went in at tree-top level. Then all hell broke loose and big black puffs of smoke erupted right beside him and bullets streamed up in all directions from the jungle.

'Let's get out of here!' George yelled and swooped down to join the others, hightailing out of the trap. 'None of us were hit, but we were very lucky.'

On the Japanese airstrip on Gasmata on the south-west coast of New Britain, the Japanese planted dummy aircraft to lure the Australians into strafing attacks. This time it was not anti-aircraft fire that was waiting for them, but as George found out when screaming in at zero feet, land mines buried in the runway and set off remotely. Luckily, the Japs' timing was out and they exploded harmlessly behind the Spitfires as they whooshed past.

After his tour, he came home to a job at his old alma mater, number 2 Operational Training Unit in Mildura, where he was reintroduced to his old friend the Wirraway. This time, however, he was flying in the back seat as an instructor, continuing to do so until after the war.

'What's the most dramatic thing that happened to you?' I asked as the meeting came to an end. I expected him to nominate the strafing or anti-aircraft episode and send me on my way, but instead he surprised me.

One day the whole squadron of twelve Spitfires was in formation over the sea, on their way to intercept a formation of Japanese, when the CO's voice announced, 'Righto, we've got to get some height, drop your belly tanks,' and away they fell into the sea. Then George's engine started to lose power. The revs were there, but no boost, and he started to fall back. 'Come on, George, pick up,' said the CO, but his engine just wouldn't respond. Eventually he was instructed, 'George, go home,' and peeled off, heading away from the formation.

'And there I was, all by my little self,' he said, in a tone making fun of himself slightly, but I could see he also meant it. It was a poignant image to end the interview – this young man way out over the endless sea all on his own in a small aeroplane, feeling extremely vulnerable.

'All the boys had gone and left me on my own and were out of sight. That was my most worrying time.'

11

Les Gordon

Air-gunner

Ours was called the Chop Squadron.

Les described himself as 'a baby boomer of the First World War', but could almost pass for one from the Second. What is it about the English? How is it possible that, even into their eighties, they can manage to look so uncannily young? Perhaps a lifetime not spent baking under the Australian sun might have something to do with it, but I reckon a lot of it simply comes down to attitude.

Les, originally from Bristol, now lived very much under the baking Australian sun at the Bull Creek Estate in Perth, where the streets and buildings bear the names of the aircraft once flown by many of the residents of this air force retirees' village – Anson Court, Spitfire Street, Sunderland Road, Beaufort Crescent and so on. The poor buggers must feel they can never get away from the war, especially when someone like me shows up with a tape recorder, hell-bent on wrenching them right back into the middle of it.

Les was the head of the Bomber Command Union of former members, looked after the estate's chapel, and seemed to know just about everyone.

Les joined the RAF at Lord's cricket ground at the minimum acceptable age of seventeen and a half. 'I was so *keen* to go to war,' he said, shaking his head with disbelief at the enthusiasm of his youth. This, despite having already lost a brother – killed by a Japanese sniper while rescuing a fellow soldier in Burma – as well as a cousin shot down over Calais on his first trip. Even still, he never thought it would happen to him.

While pilot training on Tiger Moths in Carlisle, the numbers men looked down at their list of recruits and realised they had a glut. So, a line on the page was drawn, and an announcement made: 'Those above the line will be pilots, those below, flight engineers or gunners'. His piloting days were over.

At the crewing-up stage, Les found himself in among a strange and unfamiliar tribe – New Zealanders – and was duly assigned to be a rear-gunner with 75 Squadron, Royal New Zealand Air Force at Mepal in Cambridgeshire. Being forced to fly with a bunch of antipodean colonials might have dampened the fervour of some Englishmen but, as Les soon realised, he'd joined the 'A' team.

Number 75 Squadron was the only dedicated New Zealand unit in Bomber Command, and a more impressive flying unit was there none. We Australians are never happier than when banging on about our proud-albeit-rugged military heritage, but when it comes to the warrior stakes, New Zealanders are second to nobody. It's just that they go about it a little more quietly. (The bravery of the Second NZ Division at the Battle of Monte Cassino in Italy is but one of many barely known feats of Kiwi valour.)

The medal tally for 75 Squadron – which took for its emblem a tiki, and a Maori inscription meaning 'for ever and ever be strong' – speaks for itself: one Victoria Cross, *six* Distinguished Service Orders, an astonishing *eighty-eight*

Distinguished Flying Crosses, and over twenty bars and other decorations besides. A more sobering statistic is that 75 suffered the second highest loss rate of any Bomber Command squadron – 196 aircraft lost on operations – exceeded only by 115 Squadron with over 200 aircraft lost and which was, oddly enough, 75's next door neighbour, at nearby Witchford. Les later found out that 75 was known as 'the chop squadron'.

The four New Zealanders in Les's crew had all topped their individual courses. The gunners had also proved themselves in battle. Later on operations, this was borne out by the decision to paint yellow stripes on the tail fin of their Lancaster, identifying their aircraft 'G-H leader', a vital role that involved leading the bombing in daylight for the entire formation. The moment they dropped – so would everyone else.

Les's tour would see him operating largely in daylight in late 1944-45, often adopting the tight 'box' formation of the Flying Fortresses of the United States Eighth Army Air Force, instead of the much looser arrangement of Bomber Command which simply told an individual aircraft to be over a certain target at a certain height and time, and to try not to get in anyone's way.

This particular strand of conversation leads us onto one of the great talking points among plane geeks like me: the respective merits of the two main Allied aerial weapons of the European bombing campaign, the B-17 Flying Fortress versus the Avro Lancaster, a contentious argument still, which I will attempt to summarise here.

Regrettably, I have never had the chance to meet a Fortress crew member, but those who flew the Lancaster are universal in their dismissal of their American counterpart for one particular reason: the B-17 could barely lift a cooked sausage. That's untrue, of course, but such is the implication in their tone.

The lifting power of the Lancaster was, admittedly, extraordinary. Its four Merlin engines (the same ones that powered the Spitfire) allowed it to pull a whopping 14,000 pounds of bombs into the air, more than a third of the aircraft's actual weight. The Fortress, on the other hand, jammed-packed as it was with extra crew (the 'G' version having five dedicated gunners to the Lancaster's two), thirteen .5 Browning machine-guns (the Lanc had eight smaller .303s), extra turrets and all that heavy ammunition, could manage just 6,000 pounds, less than half the Lancaster's payload, or the equivalent of just one RAF 'Cookie' plus two ordinary general purpose 1,000-pounders.

'When we were both bombing oil refineries and the like, our bombs did much more damage than theirs,' Les asserted, as if discussing rival football teams. Of course, the Americans would argue that the Fortress didn't *need* to carry so much because in daylight they could actually *hit* the target, unlike the British 'area' bombing policy (which hit everything and hopefully, the target as well), about which the Americans remained highly dubious until the end of the war.

Les began his tour late in November 1944, when the threat from fighters had moderated, but thc flak, as well as the other hazards of flying in wartime, was still real and deadly.

First up was a daylight trip to the benzol plant at Osterfeld near Stuttgart in south-western Germany, and he had no idea what to expect. Another Lancaster was hit and he watched it fall out of the formation, slowly head towards the ground and explode. This was appalling, he thought. Was it usually like this? With nothing to measure the experience by, he nonchalantly asked some of the more battle-hardened crews upon returning, 'So, er, what was that one like?' Ashen-faced, they told him that it had indeed been extremely heavy. His had literally been a baptism of fire.

'We used to like it when it was nice and cloudy – they

couldn't see you then. Once we got hit over Cologne and got two engines knocked out,' he said, with a tinge of excitement. '*Boom*! First the port outer' – this also hit the motor powering Les's turret, rendering it useless – 'Then, *boom*! the starboard outer went!' Les became more animated, as if telling an adventure story.

Peppered with holes and with two out of four engines gone, they zoomed down low to escape the flak, but still had a full bomb load onboard. The bomb-aimer looked for a suitable target and announced casually over the intercom, 'I'll think I'll get that farmhouse over there.' The chorus of disapproval from the rest of the crew was, to say the least, overwhelming. As Les said, 'If that farmer only knew how lucky he was. Public opinion saved his bacon that day!' The bombs hit a field, ploughing it up from one end to the other. After the war, Les and his crew travelled back to inspect the damage first hand.

It is testament to the Lancaster's strength that they made it home at all. They arrived two hours late on their two good engines at Mepal, where the rest of the squadron had turned out to greet them, including the CO. Relieved but unharmed, Les emerged to the welcoming entourage, then tripped head over heels on the ladder getting out of the aircraft, landing in a heap on the tarmac.

'It was a brand new aeroplane on its first trip, and we brought it back full of holes.' I asked whether his pilot received a decoration for his efforts and Les laughed. 'They probably just gave him the repair bill!'

Sometimes the dangers were not from the enemy. On a daylight trip to Munster in March 1945, the senior navigational officer for the squadron was out with his timings by 4 minutes, resulting in a late arrival over the target. Les's crew were supposed to be part of the lead formation that day, but instead found themselves right underneath another squadron

B-24 Liberators of 23 Squadron head out from their Northern Territory base in the latter part of the Pacific War. (Arch Dunne)

Lancaster LL848 X X-ray of 463 Squadron flies high above the patchwork fields of England. Note the exhaust stains from the leaded petrol streaking the wing upper surfaces behind the engines.

The slow but sturdy Avro Anson, the training mainstay of almost every Australian multi-engined crewmember.

An RAAF 455 Squadron Handley-Page Hampden. Fast, but underarmed and impractical, deserving of its nickname, 'flying tadpole'. (Australian War Memorial UK0166)

The infamous Fairey Battle at an Australian flying training school. Almost useless in combat, they were relegated to trainers. Air-gunners remember them reeking of a mixture of glycol and vomit. (Tom Saker)

A fine line-up of 3 Squadron Tomahawks somewhere in the Western Desert. (Tom Trimble)

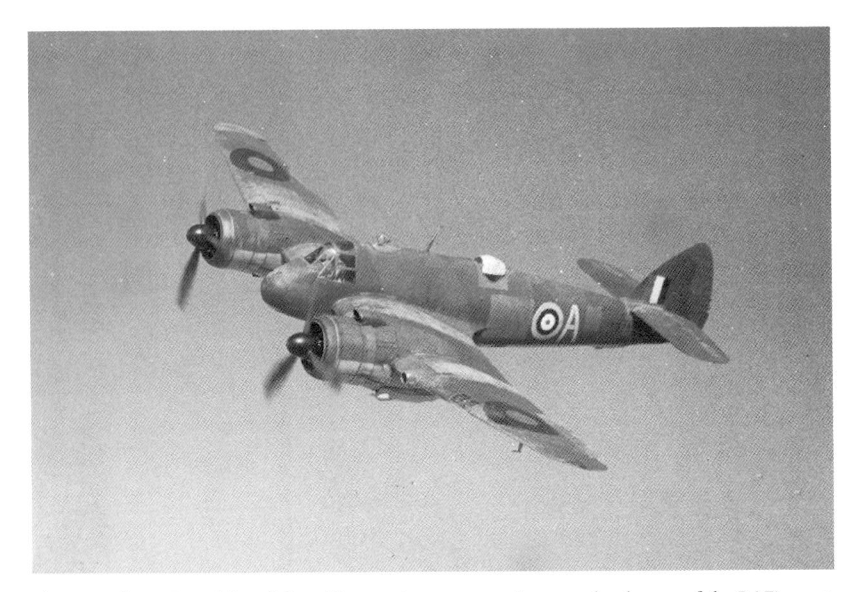

The magnificent Bristol Beaufighter. This wartime compromise proved to be one of the RAF's most successful and adaptable heavy fighters. (Tom Trimble)

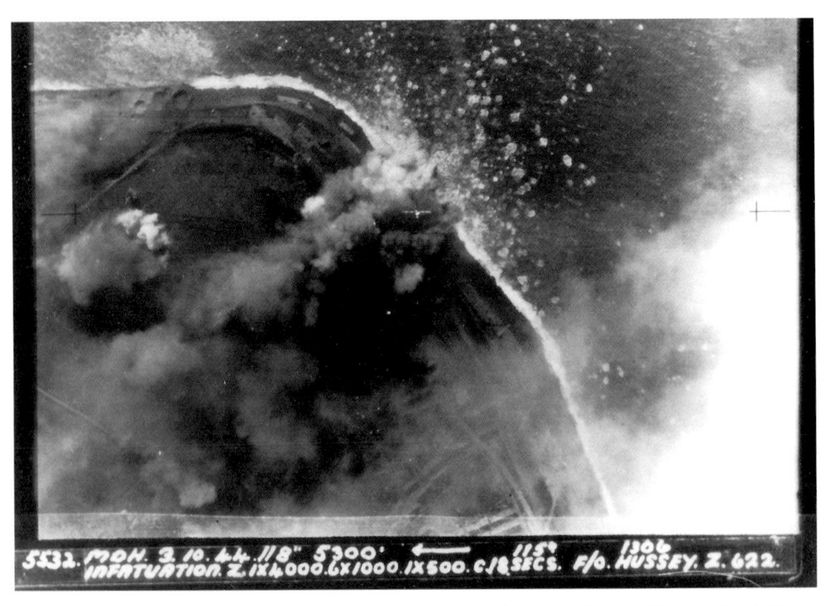

Gordon Dalton's aiming point photograph of the breach in the sea wall on Walcheren Island. Note the splashes of debris in the water. (Gordon Dalton)

RAF B-25 Mitchells of 180 Squadron, Second Tactical Air Force, in early 1945. Dick Levy's aircraft is closest to the camera. (Dick Levy)

One of 11 Squadron's Consolidated Catalinas in Port Moresby shortly before Pearl Harbor. The popular and reliable 'Cats' had an extraordinary range, being able to stay in the air for twenty hours at a stretch. (Australian War Memorial 009102)

No. 1 Squadron's Lockheed Hudsons line up on a training flight over Singapore before the start of the Pacific War. Few of these aircraft would survive the onset of hostilities. (Australian War Memorial 006647)

A 4,000-pound 'Cookie' is loaded into the bomb bay of an Australian Lancaster. These bombs were so sensitive it was forbidden to land with one still on board.

The view from the bomb-aimer's position inside a 12 Squadron RAF Lancaster. The navigator, pictured left, seems none too happy at having emerged from his windowless 'office' behind the pilot. (Australian War Memorial P01573.011)

This young mid-upper Lancaster gunner seems dwarfed inside his lonely turret high up on the back of the aircraft. (Alec Hurse)

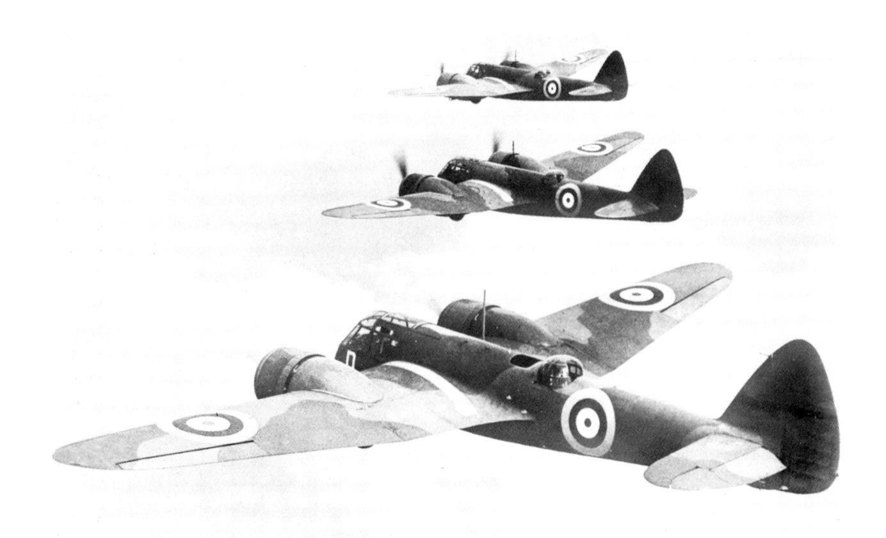

The Bristol Blenheim was used as both a light bomber and fighter, with little success in either role. Few crews mourned their withdrawal from service in 1941. (Australian War Memorial 072930)

The Boulton-Paul Defiant's rear-facing turret armament momentarily surprised the Germans over France, but its lack of speed and power saw it subsequently decimated and relegated to night fighting. (Australian War Memorial 001208)

Long .5-inch ammunition belts go into the wing magazines of this 3 Squadron Tomahawk in the early Mediterranean light. (Tom Trimble)

A Hawker Typhoon of 137 Squadron RAF, laden with rockets, taxies to take-off in Holland in late 1944. Rushed into production, the Typhoon became one of the war's superlative ground attack aircraft, despite disastrous teething troubles. (Australian War Memorial UK2037)

With characteristic insouciance, Australian 3 Squadron pilots pose around the open cockpit of a Tomahawk. (Tom Trimble)

RAAF Spitfires from Number 2 Operational Training Unit in Mildura formate over the outback. While brilliant in Europe, the Spitfire proved problematic in the tropics. (Australian War Memorial AC0123)

RAAF Lancaster crew from 460 Squadron at Binbrook, taken on 8 April 1944. All but one of this crew, Pilot Officer T.J. Lynch of Toowoomba, pictured rear left, would be killed less than three weeks later in a raid over Friedrichshafen. Some of the men seem to sense their fate. (Australian War Memorial UK1175)

Lancaster rear-gunner in his power-operated turret. Inside it was so cramped, there was no room even for the gunner's parachute. (La Trobe Picture Collection, State Library of Victoria H98.100/4257)

Lancasters line up for take-off on a base somewhere in England. Note the wartime censor has scratched the closest aircraft's airborne radar aerials from the negative.

The 'Wooden Wonder', the De Havilland 98 Mosquito. An aircraft virtually without a vice, it was tremendously popular with the crews who flew it. This example is painted in the black and white 'invasion stripes' applied prior to D-Day. (Australian War Memorial AC0092)

The RAF's first four-engined bomber was the Stirling built by Short Brothers. It was beautifully engineered but crippled by a lack of ceiling due to its narrow wingspan shortened to fit through the door of the standard RAF hanger. (Australian War Memorial 069307)

The ubiquitous Douglas 'Dakota', built in enormous numbers and in service throughout the war in every clime and theatre. (La Trobe Picture Collection, State Library of Victoria H98.100/624)

This 460 Squadron Lancaster crew seem pleased to be home after a raid on Peenemunde in 1943, where flak tore a gaping hole in the starboard elevator. (Australian War Memorial UK0393)

The business end of a Lancaster bomber, the bomb-aimer's position. Here, for the cameras, the bomb-aimer peers over his Mark V11 bombsight. (La Trobe Picture Collection, State Library of Victoria H98.100/4254)

Australian-built Beauforts of No. 1 Operational Training Unit at Bairnsdale, Victoria. At a time when Australia produced not so much as a motorbike, these modern bombers were built under licence and quickly rolled off the production lines at Fishermans Bend. (Australian War Memorial AC0216)

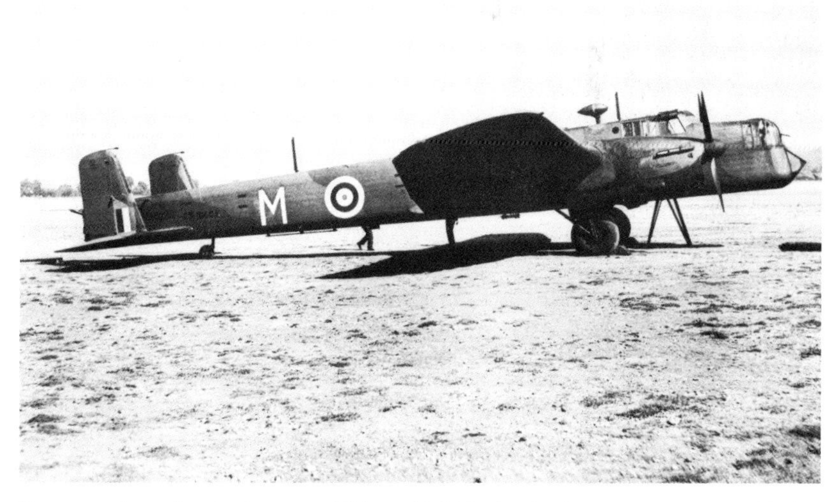

The very under-performing Armstrong-Whitworth Whitley bomber. It was so un-manoeuvrable that according to pilot Brian Walley, to turn left, you would 'turn the wheel, slowly count one-two-three-four-five, then gradually the wing would start to drop'. (Australian War Memorial 072929)

The Messerschmitt Bf 109, Nazi Germany's most famous fighter. Ironically, in 1935 the prototypes were powered by Rolls-Royce Kestrel engines. (Australian War Memorial P02994.010)

Relief on the faces of this Australian crew at the completion of their first tour of thirty operations. Behind them is their reliable, fabric-covered Vickers Wellington bomber. (La Trobe Picture Collection, State Library of Victoria H98.100/4261)

of Lancasters, watching its bombs falling just a few yards from their tail fin. Added to this, the pilot was forced to dodge burning aircraft which had been hit and started drifting towards them.

'Yes, it was all quite scary,' he said in masterful understatement. It was indeed another bad day for 75, whose three Lancasters lost comprised all the losses for the entire raid. On one occasion, the Pathfinders were late (Les has forgotten the target) and the whole formation, at night, had to circle the heavily defended aiming point while waiting for the coloured indicator flares to be dropped.

Les's earlier enthusiasm soon transformed into a more practical philosophy based on doing the job as unobtrusively as possible, and surviving at the same time.

'The bomber is not a fighter. You learn to leave well enough alone. You were very grateful not to have been seen.'

Although diminished, the German fighters were still out there, and Les had the odd encounter. Over Dessau Les's Lancaster nearly collided with a Focke-Wulf 190 whose pilot happened to be looking the wrong way.

'I just heard the mid-upper gunner say "*ah* . . .", and the German fighter cleared the top of the turret by 3 feet.'

Les, for some reason, finds this brush with death terribly amusing, and his voice almost breaks up with laughing at it all.

'He just zoomed over the top of us!'

Over Mersberg, on one of Les's few night trips, he had another close call, this time with a twin-engined Junkers 88. Immediately after the Lancaster had dropped its bombs, he spotted it, like a cat in the night waiting to pounce, except that in moving into position, it was startlingly revealed in silhouette between Les's guns and the fires of the burning city below. It turned and flicked away.

Les was lucky but several times witnessed others who were not. When a Lancaster exploded as a result of flak hitting the bomb load or the fuel, the residue of the petrol from the self-sealing tanks burned, leaving an eerie red orb hanging ghost-like in the air.

'You just hoped the crews got out. Then you'd come back and lie down on your bed and think about it.'

By this stage in the war the rear-gunner's chances of survival had been increased by the introduction of parachutes that could, pilot-style, be worn inside the turret, as part of the gunner's seat. Previously, the rear-gunner needed to exit the turret, retrieve his 'chute from inside the fuselage and then clip it on before escaping the aircraft. Now, he had simply to swing the turret 90 degrees, then push back and fall out through the doors behind him. Flying in daylight revealed many gunners had survival on their minds. On difficult targets, Les would often look around and see the rear turrets of other Lancs already swung fully around just in case.

Then there was the trip to Potsdam, in April 1945, barely a month before the end of the war. Potsdam – the old seat of Prussian power, untouched and just a few miles from Berlin – had so far escaped the bombing, and when the sirens sounded, many of its residents assumed the target to be once again Berlin and failed to take cover, even emerging from their homes to watch the planes go over. The death toll for the Potsdam raid is still not known but it was high – somewhere in the thousands – and at the post-war conference held there in July, the place still reeked with the dead.

On Hitler's birthday, 20 April 1945, Les made a seven and a half hour trip to Regensburg to attack oil facilities. It was an easy target, with only one aircraft lost out of the formation of 100. Afterwards, however, Les learned that they had hit a bridge over the Danube at the precise moment that a large group of Allied prisoners of war were crossing and that many had been killed. 'I hope they weren't our bombs. It was very impersonal up there.'

Les's last trip was flown in perfect conditions, and the trouble came on the way home. Attacking the railway yards at Bad Oldesloe in Northern Germany on 24 April 1945, there was not a puff of flak over the target and after bombing, the individual aircraft raced each other home to base, even cutting a corner off the route to expedite the journey and be first to get to the de-briefing. This, however, took Les's crew over one of the Dutch islands still being held by the Germans who duly opened up with their anti-aircraft guns. Big black puffs of smoke burst all around the aeroplane. The crew was caught off-guard. Things had been so relaxed that the pilot was not even at the controls, allowing the flight engineer to have a go. It was a reminder, said Les, that you could never be too careful.

The war was winding up, but Les's flying career was not over. His last few trips, however, were missions of mercy. Holland, already denuded of food by the Germans endured one of the harshest winters on record in 1944. 'Manna' was the code word for a series of nearly a hundred emergency food and supply drops to the starving populace, delivered by the same aircraft that a few weeks earlier had been dropping TNT, Amatol and RDX. The Germans in Holland, no doubt hoping to curry favour after the war, agreed to hold their fire. The method of delivery was crude but effective. Sacks of food were simply stuffed into the bomb bays of the aircraft and away they went to their pre-designated drop zones. Les and his crew set a course for the racecourse at The Hague.

'We didn't know if the Germans were going to fire at us. Arrangements had been made but you never knew.'

Coming in low over the Channel, Les could see the water being disturbed by the aircraft's slipstream.

'We could see the civilians waving Dutch flags out of sight of the Germans, who were just leaning on their guns.'

Over the 'target' the bomb doors were opened and the 'manna' rained down.

'We watched the people run from everywhere onto the racecourse to pick it all up.'

A little later, at war's end, Les was over the Continent again, this time to pick up ex-prisoners of war. Never made to take passengers, every inch of the Lancaster's interior was nevertheless crammed with relieved and disbelieving soldiers, sailors and airmen, on their way home after, in some cases, nearly five years in captivity. Les let them clamber into the turret and observe the Europe of their incarceration disappearing below them.

Then it was time for some grandstanding. To see at first hand the devastation they had wrought, many crews made tourist or 'Baedeker' flights (called after the famous European guidebooks) over the cities they had attacked. Many were shocked by the extent of the ruin: sometimes a seemingly endless sea of roofless houses and the charred, twisted beams of wrecked factories, docks and train lines. Les returned to the scene of his closest brush with oblivion, Cologne, sweeping in low and lifting a wing over the famous twin steeples of the Gothic cathedral. Unlike his earlier visit, this time no-one was shooting at him.

His wife, Molly, was, I discovered, worth an interview all on her own. As a kid, she had watched the Battle of Britain rage overhead and her family's house was bombed out in Portsmouth. Later, she worked as a radio operator at RAF Mildenhall in Suffolk, providing pilots and navigators with the radar and electronic beams, that guided aircraft onto the target.

It was a bright blazing day in Perth, with the intense Western Australian sun obliterating my vision for a moment as I walk out into it with Les. It's a far cry from the damp climate of his birthplace, or the freezing skies over Europe which made his tears turn to ice. Five pairs of gloves and an electrically heated suit only barely kept out the cold, he remembered.

The last story Les told me stayed with me for a long time. Les was just a boy of nineteen when he began operations. Taking off on his first ever night trip to Germany, he happened to pass right over his home, the little village of Aldbury in Hertfordshire. Down below in the gathering dusk, he could clearly make out the route of a walk he had often taken. There was the familiar landmark of the Bridgewater Memorial, as well as the grand estate of Ashridge itself, where his father, who himself had been badly wounded in the First World War, worked in the large stately home – transformed into an emergency hospital. Looking down, it must have seemed so familiar, but inside his small rear turret, flying away into the night and the furnace in the skies over Germany, very lonely indeed.

12

Charles 'Bud' Tingwell

Photo-reconnaissance pilot

On most ops, I expected to be shot down.

Charles 'Bud' Tingwell is a much-loved icon of Australian stage and screen having spent over half a century acting in films, plays and television shows. His break came just after the war, when his mother told him someone was making a film about Charles Kingsford-Smith down the road, and that if he turned up in his air force uniform, he'd get a part. So, he was cast as a control tower operator speaking about two lines, and wearing his own uniform.

Late, panting and slightly panicky, I rolled up to his modest Melbourne house, apologising for my lack of punctuality. Bud not only makes no fuss but welcomes me in, past a small front garden at the end of a suburban court, and a dead white Triumph slowly decomposing on the front lawn.

Bud has played many parts: a doctor in a medical series, a policeman in the series *Homicide*, films with Chips Rafferty, and (this really impressed me) one of the voices on *Thunderbirds*. But, impressed by his long acting career, it's what he did before it started that interested me. Because in 1944, Bud had one of the most specialised, unique and dangerous jobs in the air – flying photo-reconnaissance operations over enemy territory.

He's done some digging about for my visit and has rediscovered his log book, dragged out a sheaf of yellowing documents and has even found some of the photos he took from his Spitfire. They're in amazing condition.

'These are some of the obliques from the Greek islands,' he told me, and in crystal-clear monochrome I could almost make out the name of a ship in a harbour, and a rocky, Mediterranean hillside rising behind. Not bad for snaps taken from a passing aeroplane at 400 miles an hour more than sixty years ago.

'What's this one? Greece?' I asked.

'No. Sydney,' he answered. Perhaps we'd better start at the beginning.

Oddly enough, Bud didn't even want to join the air force, preferring to be with his mates who had signed up for the infantry. His father, however, having been through the carnage of the First World War, wouldn't have a bar of it. 'Too bloody dangerous,' he said. As it turned out, Bud's dad was wrong. In the Second World War, it was the air force which, statistically, gave you the smallest chance of coming home. It was, however, a good ploy to keep his boy safely in training for as long as possible, and it was not until September 1941 that he began in earnest, at number 2 Initial Training School at Bradfield Park in New South Wales.

Marching, drill and classes were all rather tedious. Then, in December, Bud was digging a slit trench when someone told him that the Japanese had attacked Pearl Harbor. 'Then it was on for young and old.' But all it meant for him was more delay as the government absorbed the shock. It was not until April 1942 that he finally had his first flight in a Tiger Moth at Narromine in central New South Wales.

Having delayed Bud's training by months, the air force then rushed him through it, and after just twelve days, he was going solo. He read from his log book as if it were a scene from a play in which he is a character: 'Taxying – S and L' he announced in a stentorian voice, though he'd forgotten exactly what S and L stood for.

I asked him if he felt a natural aptitude for flying.

'Never,' he said, somewhat to my surprise. 'It was just hard work'.

In fact, he never really felt comfortable flying until much later when he was instructing on twin-engined Mosquitos. He could still hear the voice of his long-suffering instructor, a Sergeant Castle, and mimicked for me the weary, rising inflection of his endlessly repeated instructions. 'Climb at sixty-six . . .' followed by a pleading, exasperated sigh.

Exasperated instructors notwithstanding, Bud, at the completion of his course, was selected for further training on single-engined aircraft in Canada. That is, if he survived the journey over.

'We were sent on a condemned ship,' he remembered. Up until Pearl Harbor, Australians travelling to Canada went in virtual luxury as passengers on liners, and would compare notes at the other end about the standards of service experienced. Not so after the Japanese attack when everything that floated became requisitioned to the war in the Pacific. So all that was left was the bottom of the barrel.

One particular American bucket, the curiously named *Tasker H. Bliss* (after a senior US staff officer at the beginning of the twentieth century), was inspected, then duly rejected by the RAAF as below the required standard for the transportation of their precious volunteers. 'Take it or leave it', replied the Americans, and the RAAF backed down. So, like a US conscript, Bud travelled in the hold.

It was an awful journey, not helped by the fact that it lasted not the scheduled three weeks, but seven, and the food ran out after three and a half.

'We survived on tea, bread and jam,' said Bud.

There was even a minor mutiny on board during the 'crossing the line' equator ceremony when the American in charge ('a genuine Captain Queeg', said Bud) was locked in the brig and had the fire hoses turned on him.

'The only reason we got away with it is because we kept laughing while we did it – it was a very Australian mutiny!'

There is still an association for those who survived their journey on the *Tasker H. Bliss*. Possibly it's a support group.

Bud found the Canadians far more convivial, and never more so than when he almost wrote off a Harvard trainer. A strange characteristic of this aircraft was its tail wheel, which free-wheeled like a caster if the pilot applied more than 70 degrees rudder, a feature which improved manoeuvrability when taxying, but could make for a very nasty landing if an inexperienced pilot like Bud was too heavy on the rudder bar. On his very first flight in a Harvard, he touched down, over-corrected and the whole aircraft spun like a top, breaking the undercarriage and ploughing the propeller into the ground.

The Canadian chief flying instructor raced over, asked what happened, then casually leaned over Bud and turned off the aircraft switches to prevent it blowing up.

After his ground loop, Bud thought he would be scrubbed, but they were kind and kept him flying until December 1942, when he received his wings with the distinction, 'high average'.

After training he was sent to England, this time on a neat 5,000 ton banana boat, complete with cabins, dining room and an attractive contingent of Canadian WAAFs who were also on their way to their new jobs. It all seemed too good to be true, and it was. A day out, the Atlantic weather turned the sea into a mountain range, threats of U-boats were the talk of the ship, and a gigantic wave broke over the bridge, damaging the vessel and sending water cascading down below, leading to a panic that they had been torpedoed. The sight of dreary, wartime Liverpool was, for Bud, a welcome one.

Taking an extra navigation course in Canada (in fact, a fruitless attempt to be posted back to Australia) Bud had put himself in that category of pilots eminently suited to flying photo reconnaissance. This idea was much to his liking, for the simple reason that the Operational Training Unit was at Dyce in Scotland, near his fiancée's home town in Aberdeen. Also, two mates had recently been selected for Dyce and he was keen to join them. In the weeks spent in Bournemouth waiting to be transferred, he had been able to visit Aberdeen regularly and no-one seemed to mind too much if you were a day or two late. That is of course, provided you weren't posted in your absence.

Upon returning to Bournemouth, having overstayed his leave pass by a couple of days to attend a dance, Bud was told, 'Don't unpack, get up to the embarkation depot in Blackpool quick smart, you've been posted to the Middle East.' He just made it.

On to another ship, this time heading to South Africa to pick up another vessel going north in a roundabout but safer route to RAF Middle East Cairo, and then on to number 74 Operational Training Unit, Pethah Tiqva a few miles from Tel Aviv, in what was then the British mandate of Palestine.

The war for Bud was slowly getting closer. But after being absent from the cockpit for so many months, he felt rusty. However, here he was, on an airfield in one of the Empire's far-flung corners with some superseded mark V Spitfires in which he was expected to learn the fine art of aerial photography.

I asked Bud what it was like flying a Spitfire for the first time. 'Dangerous', he said. The Spitfire, for all its wonderful handling characteristics, had some nasty features, one of which was the length of its engine. This extended way ahead of the cockpit, effectively obscuring much of the pilot's view, not only when taxying on the ground but also in the air.

'For us it was a real problem. If you came straight in to land, the nose obscured the runway.'

The first thing Bud had to learn was a difficult curved landing approach in which the pilot had to turn onto the runway, then straighten up just before he touched down.

'It was completely outside our range of experience. Every other time I'd landed was straight on, like an airline pilot.'

Aerial photography was, in 1943, a very recent art, having been developed only in the late 1930s and in the face of much scepticism from the RAF establishment. But in 1939, the head of Fighter Command, Hugh Dowding, reluctantly allowed a couple of Spits to be earmarked for the purpose, and the early results spoke for themselves: clear pictures of the German defences around Aachen, and later, in May 1940, daily flights over the advancing German army revealed to an awestruck world the lightning-fast dismemberment of France. PRUs – Photo Reconnaissance Units – had come into their own, and in the Spitfire, had found the method to transform their art into a science.

And not just any old Spitfires. These beauties were specially modified numbers, stripped of every ounce of excess weight – guns, armour-plate, radio – and fitted with a souped-up engine, retractable tail wheel and pointed fins for greater streamlining. They were then finished all over in a sleek, polished, powder blue to blend in with the high altitudes in which they would operate. They were quite a sight.

But as Bud recounted, the early techniques of photo-rec were far from exact, and the only real training for a new pilot was trial and error.

The pilot of a bomber was completely dependent on his crew, and even a conventional fighter pilot was rarely all alone, flying in formation and relying on his squadron for support and protection. The pilot of a photo-rec aircraft was, however, a true loner, operating entirely by himself, flying fighter aircraft but never required to fight. Bud, even now, is uncertain as to what made a good photo-rec pilot.

'It would have been interesting to see how they selected our lot,' he said. You'd need to be a good pilot, certainly. One who was an excellent navigator, definitely, but also a person who could be relied upon to carry out extremely dangerous tasks all on their own. The way Bud speaks about it, it seems he finds it hard to understand why he himself was chosen for the job.

At one stage, the doorbell rang with a courier delivering the instructions for Bud's upcoming appearance at the AFI awards. 'Your sealed orders', I remarked. 'Yes', he laughed, 'to be opened only in times of emergency'.

After months of delays and training, being posted to operations was indeed a good feeling. Bud found himself in Matariya on the outskirts of Cairo as part of 680 Squadron, which at that time was operating over the German-occupied islands of Greece as well as targets further north in the Aegean Sea and mainland Greece itself, including the particularly 'hot' target of Athens itself.

Bud's first op, however, was less than successful. His brief was to photograph various installations at specific points along the coast and harbour of Rhodes, but all he could now remember was 'seeing an enormous ocean of cloud and thinking, Turkey should be on my right'. He failed to find the target, so turned back empty-handed.

The success or otherwise of photo-reconnaissance missions was fairly easy to quantify: either you got the pictures or you didn't. And if you didn't, either you or someone else would have to go back and try again. Failure left a sour taste in the mouth, particularly when another pilot had to go and take the shots you missed.

PRU Spitfires carried two sets of cameras positioned behind the pilot, one to shoot vertically, the other on the oblique, aimed sideways but a few degrees below the horizontal for low-level passes. However, no effective aiming device had yet been developed, leaving the pilots effectively blind and needing to develop their own 'sixth sense'. The technique was to drop a wing on approach to the target, then flatten out and 'feel' the precise moment to hit the camera button, trusting that what you were photographing was directly underneath you. Bud's early trips sometimes caught only a chunk of the target, or else missed altogether. But he learned quickly.

He also learned about the rosters, both high and low. It was a fair system, with every pilot getting his fair share of both the dangerous low-level trips and the safer (but by no means safe) high altitude ones. But it was the low altitude roster, the dicey jobs, that mattered most.

He also had to deal with the new phenomenon of people shooting at him.

'Were you fired at much?' I asked.

He guffawed loudly. 'All the time, all the time!'

Foolish question, really. Everyone, including the enemy, appreciated the importance of photo reconnaissance, knowing that the appearance of one lone blue-painted Spitfire high above, could mean the arrival of a squadron of bombers in the not-too-distant future. That was another hazard of photo-rec. 'We would cop everything that was meant for an entire squadron.' Bud was one of the few pilots I'd met who was aware of the different types of anti-aircraft fire directed against him, rattling off the difference between the famous 88-millimetre guns, which could fire a 10 kilogram shell up to 30,000 feet into the sky at the rate of 10 per minute, but also the nastier 105 mm high altitude and the low-level 'light' stuff.

I can well picture Bud coming in at high speed in his bright blue Spitfire over the harbour at Rhodes, because I have been there. It's a busy place, crammed with tourists and rather hideous hotel blocks, and is also a large fishing port and ferry terminal servicing the many islands of the Dodecanese Archipelago. According to legend, the gigantic Colossus of Rhodes, an enormous statue and one of the Seven Wonders of the Ancient World, straddled the harbour entrance.

Many years ago, I took a ferry from Rhodes out to a smaller island called Simi – a speck of a place which apart from two very ordinary restaurants and several pushy vendors flogging off the area's few remaining natural sea sponges had very little to say for itself. When walking along a rocky shore at the back of the island however, I came across the barrel of a half submerged and very rusty German 105-millimetre anti-aircraft gun, the 'Krupp' stamp and year, 1942, still visible on the breech block.

In the more than ten years since visiting Simi, I have neither read nor heard a single word about the place, but there it was in Bud's log book, listed as one of his early trips, making it a reasonably high possibility that he photographed the very same gun that fifty years later, I stumbled across on a quiet, rocky beach. I begin to tell him about this remarkable co-incidence (well, *I* thought it so), but the phone rings once again, and Bud is obliged to have a brief, genial phone conversation with an old mate who just happens to be a former CEO of the Royal Flying Doctor Service.

On another trip, Bud was on a low-level, looking for a suspected German radar station on the north coast of Crete. He found a building that looked like a contender so made a run using his oblique cameras at about 300 feet (90 metres). He knew there were a few troops in the area, but could see no-one about save for a sole figure in a grey suit, looking skyward and doing something that looked very much like waving. With no-one shooting at him, Bud made another series of runs – five in all – the figure in grey remaining on the spot, waving all the while.

'I nearly waved back at him,' he said.

Job done, pictures taken, Bud headed back to base in North Africa. Coming into land at the desert strip, he put the flaps down and . . . nothing. On a Spitfire, flaps and brakes were both activated by air pressure, so if your flaps weren't working, you knew your brakes would be out of action too, and a Spitfire without brakes or flaps is in no hurry to slow down once it hits the ground. Checking out the end of the runway, Bud noticed the tents of the Arab laundry, used by the base to wash the men's shirts, and decided that all in all, he would prefer not to hit it.

'What I was trying to do was a nose-up landing with a lot of power, coming in as slow as possible just above stalling speed,' but he was tired after his second trip of the day and his skills deserted him. The tyres hit the ground, but without brakes or flaps to arrest the speed, the aircraft just kept on going. He slid the throttle forward, powered up, took off and came around again.

On his second go the Spitfire once again refused to slow down and the tents of the laundry loomed up fast at the end of the runway. Once more, he took off. By this time the rest of the squadron, knowing Bud had come back from a low-level, had come out to watch, pray and cross their fingers.

'I could see myself running over the tents at the end, so I had to do something dramatic,' he said and so he did.

On his fourth attempt to land, he touched down and kicked the rudder bar over hard to force the aircraft off the runway onto the sandy ground on either side, a terrible risk both to himself and the machine and one he was worried would not pay off.

The Spitfire bounced roughly along the sandy, uneven

ground. Even on strips that were as smooth as billiard tables, the chances of tipping were high as the Spitfire's extended under-carriage was notoriously narrow.

'I thought it would go up on its nose, sure as eggs.'

It began to tip up, but then bounced back down again safely and came to a stop.

'It was pretty bad flying and I was lucky. *Really* lucky,' Bud remembered.

The ground staff chief, a big Cockney, came up to Bud, who was still in his aircraft, and gently enquired, 'Did you cop any shit, sir?'

Unaware of having been hit by anything, Bud replied innocently, 'Er, no', which prompted the flight sergeant to let loose, as only Cockney sergeants can, even to a superior officer.

'You stupid bastard, Bud! You nearly wrecked the best aircraft we have!'

Bud even remembered the serial number of the machine he nearly sent to an early grave, EN 845, the squadron's prize Spitfire and in perfect nick.

Upon examining the aircraft, Bud to his amazement found a bullet hole in the tailplane, and then put the puzzle together. The figure he had seen in grey (a grey uniform, he later realised) had indeed been doing something very like waving. He had been firing a pistol. Bud never discovered whether the bullet had ruptured the air pressure mechanism because, feeling foolish at having been nearly brought down by a single individual with a Luger, he never reported it, excusing the hole as a stone thrown up by the rough landing. He told me it was an incident he's re-lived many times.

The Spitfire was fine for medium range photography, but for targets further afield, Bud soon began to convert to the 'wooden wonder' itself, the De Havilland Mosquito. Apart from being a marvellous aeroplane to fly, the Mosquito made

Bud's job that much easier, as it allowed a navigator to sit in the nose and take the guesswork out of the exercise by taking the pictures himself.

No-one has ever had a bad word to say about this remarkable machine, least of all the people that flew it. It started life simply as the De Havilland 98 and was a superstar from the very beginning, surpassing its manufacturer's expectations on its first test flight in January 1941. Built as a medium bomber, they soon realised it could do just about anything and ended up performing almost every combat role in every theatre from photo reconnaissance to fighter-bomber and everything in between. It remains even today one of the most attractive aircraft ever built. Even, understated lines, an almost feminine sleekness with a long tapered fuselage, high noble tail fin and two prop hubs protruding slightly past the tip of the nose, a pillar of aviation aesthetic.

However, its most remarkable feature is not what it looked like but what it was made from. Early in the war, as Britain's industries geared up to war manufacture, it was realised that the skills and materials of certain trades had not been sufficiently utilised. And so it was decided the furniture industry would contribute its very own aircraft. Hence, the Mosquito was made entirely of plywood and glue. This helped account for it's remarkable speed, manoeuvrability and smooth, rivet-free surface but also gave an army of carpenters and joiners a sense that they were contributing in a serious way to the war effort.

Once, over Athens, Bud got a touch of stage fright. The usual method of approaching such a heavily defended target was to fly downwind, thereby adding anything up to 100 extra miles to the speed, but this afternoon he must have been a little lazy, and found himself flying against a powerful headwind to photograph the Greek capital at 28,000 feet. This was also the day the cockpit heater decided to pack it in, icing up the inside of the windshield 'a bit like a misty car'. He scraped out a patch in the ice with his glove that was just big enough to see through, and was happy to leave it at that. Bill, the Scottish navigator, was down in the Mosquito's nose guiding Bud onto the target, with the same 'left, left, right a bit' manner used by bomb aimers. Suddenly, Bud saw an enormous and extremely close burst of flak explode right in middle of the little viewing hole he'd just made for himself, but when he tried to say, 'Gosh Bill, flak,' all he could make was a low gurgling sound and a hollow 'err . . . er', as his vocal chords became immobilised by a rush of panic.

'What? What are you saying?' asked Bill, busily lining up in the nose.

Eventually Bud managed to blurt out an astonished, 'Gosh, flak!'

'Well, do something about it!' was Bill's short reply.

Obligingly, Bud made a sharp turn and was confronted with, as he puts it, 'a bloody ocean of black puffs'. Unbeknownst to them both, they had been flying through a box barrage – multiple, closely-positioned guns ranged and firing simultaneously into the same coordinates. Lucky for both, they were falling slightly to the rear, out of sight and out of mind. When the photographs were later developed, big bursts could be clearly seen, mid frame.

'No, they were never very pleased with us being over the harbour area of Athens,' Bud said.

A tour for a photo-rec pilot was measured not by individual trips, but 300 hours of operational flying time. According to his log book, Bud would sometimes be up more than once in a single day, ranging over the Greek islands to places such as Cos, Leros and Samos, making his war sound strangely like a modern European holiday destination. Towards the end of his tour, however, Bud's squadron received a request from the army that made his blood run cold.

What they wanted was a full photographic survey of the potential invasion beaches on Salonika, a large peninsula of the Greek mainland in the northern Aegean. It would be a long trip, taking the Mosquito to the edge of its range, and the run would have to be at low-level. Bud and Bill pored over the map, but the more they thought about it, the more their chances of surviving seemed to diminish. As photo-rec pilots, they knew where all the guns were situated. They also knew that the trip was important – one of those that could possibly shorten the war – and that to provide the army with the information they needed, they would have to make at least six runs over the beach area at different angles. Then they had a look at the forecast. The weather would be clear and perfect – for gunners.

'We couldn't work out how we could survive the first run,' says Bud.

Whichever way they looked at it, it was impossible to even get to the target area without coming within range of the fierce network of anti-aircraft guns that covered the beaches. The flight commander even seemed a little guilty in not insisting he go himself. But, says Bud, he was sticking to the rules, and you didn't tamper with the low-level roster.

'We really thought we had no hope of getting back. It was almost the time to write your last letter to the family before you took off.'

On 29 October 1944, almost sixty years to the day he told me the story, he and Bill took off in their Mosquito from Cairo for the four and a quarter hour return trip to Salonica. They had a feeling in their stomachs that it would probably be their last. The route took them high over Crete and then swooped down to commence the first run at the prescribed operational height of just 300 feet (90 metres). Bud flew the Mosquito into position and braced for a hail of anti-aircraft fire. Then . . . nothing. Not a puff, not a shot, not a soldier visible on the ground. The first run completed, he commenced his second, and was again met by no resistance. Bud was stunned, but as he says, 'it was quite exhilarating'. Bud and Bill, who were still friends until Bill died a few years ago, turned around and headed for home feeling like they'd won a reprieve. 'What potentially was our most dangerous trip, turned out to be the safest,' he said.

The entry in his log book described several long runs along the coast of Salonica, and assumes they took the German defenders by surprise. Today he guffaws at his own entry. 'Taken by surprise? Bullshit!' They later discovered that the German army had evacuated Salonica just one hour before their arrival.

Two days before the end of the year, Bud completed his tour and came home for a stint as an instructor on Mosquitos at Williamtown in New South Wales, where he felt comfortable flying for the first time.

Years later, Bud discovered that none other than Kurt Waldheim, the former UN head plagued by his shadowy Nazi past and lampooned for his 'I wasn't there' mantra had been in charge of that Salonica garrison. Bud wouldn't hear a word against the man!

It's six o'clock and I've kept Bud all afternoon. I thanked him but as I left, remembered something I'd meant to ask earlier. Did he ever catch up with the two mates who went on to train in Scotland, the ones he missed joining because he was late getting back from leave?

'As it happened,' he told me, 'they were both lost over Berlin.'

PRU flying was a dangerous business.

13

Dick Thomas

Pilot

Our job was to generally mess everybody up.

On the night of 14 November 1940, Dick was lying in hospital in Cheltenham having his appendix out. Further north, in Coventry, the German air force was carrying out the most intensive air attack of World War Two thus far, sending 500 bombers to destroy the centre of the city, including the only cathedral Britain lost during the war, the fourteenth century built St Michael's. It was also the first big-scale use of an electronic device to aid in bomb aiming and this night, it worked horribly well. The Germans called the operation Moonlight Sonata – the insult to Beethoven can hardly be imagined.

Although miles away, Dick heard the raid, as he could the shrapnel from the virtually useless anti-aircraft guns raining down on the hospital roof. He determined then and there to join the air force.

After several months of elementary training, Dick found himself on a ship, sailing across the Atlantic to Canada in the middle of winter. The ship had been in dry dock, the air was stale and the sea was rough. In a moment of insanity, he volunteered for cookhouse duties, and found the choice of cuisine, well, not conducive to a rough sea voyage. He is still scarred by the experience.

'The main meal was something swimming in gravy, and then custard with prunes' – just the thing for a stormy Atlantic crossing. As the sea got worse, more and more sailors and airmen left the foetid atmosphere of the mess in a hurry.

'I was literally up to my knees in a mixture of gravy, tea, custard and prune juice,' he remembered.

As quickly as he could, Dick volunteered for submarine watch duties up on the icy deck, and stayed there. For the next fourteen days he survived on All-bran. Years after, he still couldn't go near the stuff.

Via an uncommon arrangement, Dick ended up training not in Canada, but way down south in sunny Florida with the Americans. He found flying pretty easy and ended up graduating with not one, but two sets of wings – the metal badge of the US Army Air Force, as well as the cloth of his own RAF. In fact, Dick was such a good pilot that the Yanks decided to hang on to him and train him up as an instructor, a job for which he had absolutely no relish. Protest he might, but instruct he did, for over six months, clocking up 900 hours before they let him go home. The journey this time was on the *Queen Elizabeth* and took just four days.

In retrospect, the extra training probably saved his life. Most new pilots went into battle with a couple of hundred flying hours up their sleeve. Dick totalled 1,100, an advantage in experience impossible to measure. However, this setback proved to be just the first in a series of unexpected events – some bureaucratic, others just bizarre – which delayed the beginning of his operational flying nearly until the end of the war.

All those hours on single-engined aircraft naturally led Dick to expect a career in fighters, but cue bizarre event number one: during a medical examination, the needle of a syringe broke off in his arm. Very little could be done to retrieve it as it had gone deep inside the muscle, damaging both it, and his hopes of flying Spitfires. So now it was a conversion course onto multi-engined aircraft, namely Stirlings. Having had all his previous experience in small trainers, Dick was now taught to fly the biggest four-engined bomber in the RAF.

Being so experienced, his instructors let him go solo after only a few hours, but coming in for his first landing in the massive Stirling, Dick's new crew could only hope their instructors' confidence had been well placed. Concentrating hard on lining up with the runway, the tension in the aircraft was palpable. Then, just before touching down, the wireless operator broke in cheerily, 'Hey, does anyone want to hear Diana Durbin singing "The Lights of Home"?' Just the kind of guy you want with you flying into Germany in wartime. Dick laughed at it today, but I don't suppose he was then, and was soon looking for new wireless operator.

Dick's story is, in some ways, a sad one. So eminently qualified, so under-utilised – a continual victim of changing wartime parameters. Having trained up on Stirlings to drop supplies to partisans in central Europe, the air force decreed that Stirlings were to be phased out for this role. So Dick retrained yet again on Halifaxes to operate in Italy. Then he was told to his amazement that his crew had been taken off transfer to Italy on account of his coloured Jamaican navigator, Viv Cooper. The Americans, he was told, would not be happy about dealing with black airmen, let alone an officer. Dick and the rest of the crew were disgusted, but from what he'd already seen of how blacks were treated in the Deep South, he reflected that it was probably for the best. Viv turned out to be a remarkable navigator and on one occasion, saved the entire crew. Dick could not be more proud to have served with him.

So now they waited again, went on extended leave and visited family and friends while the air force decided where to slot them. After yet another spot of training, they were finally sent to an operational squadron. But how Dick and his crew found themselves posted there is another peculiar, almost comic, story.

By late 1944, they had just about given up any hope of active service, so when they were issued a railway warrant to travel by train to Wells Next-the-Sea in Norfolk – somewhere, they felt, very close to the end of the earth – they resigned themselves to spending the rest of the war on yet another training or conversion course. Arriving late on New Year's Eve at the little rural train station, they telephoned the aerodrome to arrange transport. A little later a WAAF turned up in a small lorry to take them to the nearby airfield at North Creake. Enquiring as to what sort of establishment they were being taken to, the girl blithely announced that it was a fully operational squadron, flying Halifaxes, and they were a new crew.

Dick was gobsmacked.

'I didn't ask any more because I didn't know what to ask,' he said.

Upon arrival, they announced themselves, were wished a happy new year and handed a drink.

They discovered they had joined number 171 Squadron, part of 100 Group. These 'bomber support' squadrons did just that, assisting the main bombing force with all kinds of interesting and shadowy activities: mounting spoof raids that headed out as if to attack a certain target, then turning away to confuse the German defences, dropping 'window', and even carrying specialised radar equipment and German-speaking wireless operators on trips to verbally confuse the enemy night fighters and their controllers. They had an eclectic array of aircraft at their disposal. Apart from the Halifaxes, Dick saw several other types around the airfield, including an American

B-17 and a couple of Mosquito fighter-bombers that would lurk around German night fighter bases to catch them as they returned. There were also bizarre 'siren' raids keeping an enemy population sleepless by flying low over a city in the middle of the night, blaring sirens. 'Just generally messing everybody up,' as Dick put it.

But initially, it was Dick and his crew who felt they were being 'messed up'. After a week of clearing snow from the runways and waiting to be posted to operations, he felt that old familiar feeling of having been sidelined. Finally, he approached the CO, who told him he couldn't go on ops before he had done the mandatory 'second dickie' trip, sitting next to an experienced pilot.

'Well, when can I do that?' he asked despairingly.

The CO considered. 'Tonight, if you like.'

And this is when it became really Python-esque. A few hours later at the briefing, the CO advised him, 'You'd better have a look at the map.' So Dick went and had a look. There was England, there was Germany, with a red ribbon showing the route in and out. It meant very little to him.

'Do you still want to go?' asked the CO.

'Yes,' said Dick.

'But do you know where you're going?'

'Not really.'

'Go and have another look, then.'

He looked again more closely. The route took them over to the Ruhr, ironically dubbed 'happy valley', and then back again. Dick gradually started to cotton on that this might actually be a little dangerous.

A few hours later, and without a word to his crew, Dick embarked on his first operational mission. Next morning they caught up with him.

'Where did you get to last night?' they asked, and he told them what had happened.

Only two aircraft had gone out on a radar-jamming mission. Without bombs, their only task was to drop the bundles of 'window' from the chute and switch on the electronic devices to confuse the German gun-aiming radar. Dick in his passenger seat saw very little except a raid in the distance. At one stage he asked the pilot about the small cone of searchlights on the horizon. 'Amsterdam, perhaps' was his guess. As it turned out, it was the RAF's own emergency landing aerodrome in Essex and the night was so clear it was visible from well within Germany.

'Well, Thomas, what do you think of the Ruhr?' asked the wing commander at the de-briefing back at North Creake.

'Well, disappointing, sir,' replied Dick, enjoying the standard mug of coffee with a large tot of rum.

The senior officer looked perplexed. 'Disappointing?'

'Well, we didn't see anything.'

'Didn't see anything, eh?'

'No, sir. Bit disappointed.'

The CO looked at him for a moment. 'Well, the other aircraft has been shot down.'

Dick couldn't remember what his reaction was, but told me that the other Halifax would have been either just ahead or just behind his own aircraft. So much for his first, uneventful trip.

Then there was another delay as the weather closed in, blanketing the runways in snow for a month. Training, though, was still on the agenda and Dick's crew were put onto some high-level cross-country navigation exercises. It was on one of these that Dick came closest to killing himself.

After completing the circuit which took them along the route 'base-Spalding-York-Shrewsbury-Hereford-base' at night at 20,000 feet, Dick came in to land. However, the wind direction had changed in the meantime so they were now landing into a dangerous crosswind. Sure enough, just as the wheels were about to touch the runway, a strong gust tilted up a wing of the big Halifax. Dick's experience probably saved them at that instant. The aircraft bounced, then Dick instinctively shoved the throttles forward to increase power, take off and come around again.

A four-engined bomber has, naturally, four throttles, moulded to fit within the palm of the pilot's hand. On the Halifax, they could be clamped into a set position once the desired power to the engines had been reached but if not, they had a natural tendency to creep back when released. This is where the flight engineer came in. One of his jobs was to hold the throttles open, hard up against the stops, giving the engines full power on take-off. This particular night, Dick's bomb-aimer was absent, having scored a lift down to London, and the flight engineer was seeing what life was like from his position in the nose. Dick, in the cockpit, was on his own.

After powering up after the aborted landing, the Halifax once again lumbered into the air. Dick raised the flaps and retracted the wheels but could feel that something wasn't right. His airspeed indicator began to fall. To compensate, he put the nose down to gain speed. Then, in a dreadful flash of realisation, he looked down at the throttles. Without the flight engineer pushing them forward, they had crept back to almost zero and were nearly closed, starving fuel to the engines. The aircraft was on the verge of stalling at low speed, which would have meant crashing into trees and killing the lot of them. It happened all the time.

Dick threw open the throttles and the engines surged. Airspeed increased and the nose came up. He doesn't quite know how close he came to going in, but it was certainly a matter of seconds.

'I literally flew round for a quarter of an hour before my knees stopped shaking,' he said. 'We were near as anything to going into those trees.'

On 14 February 1945, Dick and his crew had their first operation, to Dresden. Quite a debut, but instead of bombs, Dick's payload was not one but three wireless operators and an array of early warning jamming devices. Flying what was called 'the racecourse' – a staggered route across the direction of the main bomber force – Dick changed direction every six minutes, allowing the electronic moles within his aircraft to do their work. In his voluminous and immaculate log book it was described as 'special operations'. Fourteen hundred aircraft were in the air that night and flying his staggered course, Dick felt the buffeting from the hundreds of invisible slipstreams all around at various altitudes, but eerily, saw nothing of the aircraft themselves.

Having waited so long to get started, Dick and his crew proceeded to cram half a tour into just a few weeks, an active player in the shadowy war of measure and counter-measure that was the sub-plot to the Allied bombing campaign of Europe. One of the most significant developments was 'window', the dropping of millions of strips of aluminium foil, cut to lengths replicating the wave-length of German radar and showing up on their screens as dozens, sometimes hundreds of aircraft that did not in fact exist. But the Germans learned fast and introduced ways of their own to counter the effects not only of window, but the various other electronic methods used to assist a bomber to its target, and a cat-and-mouse game was played out, ultra-secret, right until the end of the war.

But on the odd trip, Dick's bomber actually carried bombs. One of the ones he remembers was to Schwandorf, a long flight nearly to the Czech border. Schwandorf was on the verge of being taken by the Russians, who had requested the attack to assist with their advance. Late in the afternoon at North Creake ('Up the creek', as they called it), Dick and his crew ate their standard pre-flight meal of bacon and eggs and then went out to the aircraft and waited. And waited. Eventually, they were told to come back and have another meal, after which they returned to the aircraft and waited some more. An impromptu game of cricket then ensued, doubtless played with the pre-flight knot in the stomach that everyone experienced before an op. There was yet another meal of bacon and eggs until taking off just before midnight.

Having long since learned not to question the vagaries of the air force, and happy never to see a plate of bacon and eggs again, Dick climbed into the pitch darkness and for four hours flew solely on instruments, seeing nothing but black. Then the navigator piped up. Dick impersonated the tones of Viv's Jamaican accent with surprising comic ability.

'Oo er, Skip, can you, er, see anything?'

Dick glanced out into the impenetrable darkness. 'Nothing.'

A slight pause, then his navigator said quite matter-of-factly, 'Thirty seconds to go, port side.'

'Then,' said Dick, 'it was just as if someone had turned a bloody light on.'

The darkness was suddenly split by light, and an entire valley stood illuminated before him as the Pathfinders dropped their brilliant coloured target indicator flares. After four hours flying over a blacked-out Continent, it was some piece of navigation, indicative of the machine into which Bomber Command had evolved by war's end. Four years earlier, it was estimated that on the night trips into Europe, one bomb in fifty came within 5 miles of the intended target. 'We were right up at the head of the stream and opened up and bombed immediately.'

Soon after, Viv came into his own again, this time on a flight over the North Sea. With the aircraft heading in the direction of Denmark, Viv called up to say that he was going down the back for a pee, the Elsan 'sanitary pan' being situated right at the back of the aircraft near the rear-gunner.

Dick reckoned he must have found it hard going, clambering over the main wing spar, then in the freezing temperatures fiddling with leads, cords, zips and several layers of uniform and flying suit and he was obviously away from his desk longer than he meant to be. When at last he made it back to his position, he urgently hit the intercom.

'Oo er, Skip, what course you flying?'

Dick told him the heading he was on, which made his navigator even more anxious. While he'd been attending the call of nature, they had missed a course change and were now heading too far into Denmark. He quickly gave the correct heading and Dick made what he called a 'split-arse turn', whipping the aircraft around on its wing. As he did so, a Junkers 88 night fighter which had been hiding right underneath the Halifax shot out from underneath.

'With the moon in the position it was, we would have been a sitting duck,' said Dick. It was so close that he actually saw the German pilot and reckons he noticed the shock on his face. With their '*schrage Musik*' upward-firing 30-millimetre cannons, Dick estimated the German could only have been seconds away from shooting into the engines and fuel tanks of the Halifax. As it was, Dick turned quickly away, and the fighter did not re-appear.

'I think he may have been tired of the war,' he reckoned.

If not for their navigator spending a little too long at the loo, they could well have been just one of the hundreds of crews that simply vanished in the night.

It was the closest he came to a night fighter, but not the closest to his demise. Even as late as 1945, an average of eighteen Bomber Command aircraft a month were being lost to collision, and Dick nearly became one of them. With six or seven hundred aircraft passing over a target in the course of about 20 minutes, at night with no navigation lights, the figure is hardly surprising.

On the way home one night from a trip at four in the morning, Dick was feeling tired and irritable, a mood not improved by the fact that he could hear the hissing sound of an open microphone in his headphones. Someone in the crew must have failed to switch theirs off after speaking and the ambient noise was annoying.

'Check your mikes,' he announced.

But the noise continued. 'Come on, check your bloody mikes,' he implored the crew, but the noise didn't go away.

He began to feel uneasy and something made him look up. The great black shape of a Lancaster, oblivious to Dick's Halifax just below was moving over his head barely feet away. The gunners, looking not down but up, had missed it completely. 'We were virtually at the same height,' Dick told me. He pushed the stick down to lose height. The hissing noise stopped.

Dick did eighteen trips, then ran out of war. Afterwards, he flew his crew and some of the ground staff over the ruins of 'happy valley', so they too could witness the destruction to which they had contributed.

Dick's was a strange career of stop-start and many unexpected turns but he regretted none of it. He showed me a post-war picture of Viv Cooper, who he kept in touch with for many years after.

'Viv had five boys and a girl. We had five girls and a boy.' As Dick reflects, if not for Viv, no-one would have had anyone at all.

14

Derek French

Pilot

I'm part German. I've still got some shrapnel in me.

Derek completed his flying training, answered a call to volunteer for the Royal Air Force for a five-year stint and arrived in England nearly two full years before war began. Not that his Australian training cut much ice with the RAF at that early stage. When asked where he had undertaken his initial flight instruction, he answered 'Point Cook' and was sent straight back to training.

At least he was able to hang onto his distinctive dark-blue Australian uniform, until such time as it wore out, after which he was expected to buy the sky blue tunic of the RAF. This however, never eventuated. As Derek said, 'Once war broke out, there was always someone getting bumped off, so we just took his.'

When trained up to their liking, Derek was posted to number 50 Squadron, Royal Air Force Bomber Command, which at that stage operated the Hawker Hind bi-plane – a quaint old kite with strings and open cockpits – looking more a part of the nineteenth century than the twentieth. In 1938, at the height of the Munich Conference, when Britain opted to sell its ally Czechoslovakia down the river rather than stand up to Herr Hitler, Derek and his crew spent a day and a night painting their Hinds in camouflage in expectation of going to war. God help them if they had. In any other context the old Hinds would have been delightful and jaunty in a 'magnificent men in their flying machines' kind of way, but at that time they epitomised Britain's total unpreparedness for war with the rising industrialised monster that was Germany.

At last, however, the British government realised the imperative to re-arm and re-equip, so went about replacing one under-performing, outclassed aeroplane with another, the Handley-Page Hampden. At least the Hampden was fast, because that's all it had going for it. A twin-engined medium bomber, the expectations it raised were enormous. Sleek-looking, powerful and manoeuvrable with an all-metal monoplane construction, twin tail and lovely big bomb-load, it more than looked the part of the new-age bomber that would bring His Majesty's air force kicking and screaming into the twentieth century. Then, sadly, it was flown in combat.

I've found it to be a rule of thumb that the more nicknames attributed to an aircraft, the worse it usually is, and the Hampden had more than just about any. Flying suitcase, flying panhandle and tadpole are a few and these tended to flatter it. The design flaws were twofold: firstly, it was woefully under-armed, with nothing but a couple of old hand-operated Great War vintage Vickers guns sticking out the front and back (and these with so many blind spots they were next to useless) and secondly, the fuselage was absurdly narrow – less than a metre at any point – so that you could knock both sides with your elbows. This meant that the pilot was always extremely uncomfortable, couldn't stand up even for a pee and if wounded, was impossible to remove from his seat. Nor could any of the crew of four reach one another.

The Hampden also had a low ceiling – 15,000 feet – and

lacked self-sealing fuel tanks (a rubbery coating which reacted with the leaking petrol to form a rudimentary barrier and plug the holes cause by enemy bullets or shells). This made them burn very easily.

'We thought we had the best aircraft in the world and that we were so well trained,' said Derek reflectively.

Sadly, neither turned out to be the case. The Hampdens were put onto the early daylight raids with catastrophic results, then relegated to night bombing. Enter people like Derek.

'When I started on operations on Hampdens, I'd had as much training for night flying as anyone else on the squadron – 3 hours 50 minutes. That's barely a circuit.'

Derek's flying career was so colourful, so varied and took in such a variety of places, I simply could not keep up. My woefully short interview with him thus became a kaleidoscope of places, people and anecdotes. I soon discovered him to be a highly engaging, well-read and sensitive person of great wit and intelligence.

Derek fascinated me primarily because he was the only pilot I met who had operated during the early, primitive stages of the European air campaign between 1939 and 1941. By war's end, Bomber Command had evolved into a machine of hideously efficient destruction, with the ability to dispatch a thousand aircraft to obliterate an entire city in a single night, aided by the most sophisticated scientific developments of the day. But its early stages were a very different story. On the first day of the war, President Roosevelt urged the warring and soon-to-be warring nations to agree not to bomb areas where civilians might be harmed. Everyone agreed, even Germany. Besides, British thinking of the time reasoned that attacks on German factories were an assault on private property and therefore forbidden, a view expressed by none other than the Minister for Air, Sir Arthur Kingsley Wood, when it was proposed that the RAF bomb the Krupp armament factories in Essen!

Such absurd niceties were not to last long, of course, and in any case were simply making a virtue out of necessity as the inexperienced British crews of the time were just about incapable of hitting anything anyway. Instead, for the first few months of stand-off during what became known as the 'Phoney War', the RAF dropped propaganda leaflets, telling the German people that Hitler was a very nasty man indeed and politely suggesting they all surrender. It had no effect but did gain crews valuable night flying experience over enemy territory.

It all started to change when the Germans bombed ships of the Royal Navy at their home base at Scapa Flow in the Orkney Islands. Some of the stray bombs killed one civilian and wounded seven more in a nearby village. Two nights later, on 19 March 1940, Bomber Command ordered a retaliatory attack on a German seaplane base at Hornum on the island of Sylt, near the Danish border. It was the RAF's largest operation of the war so far: twenty Whitleys and thirty Hampdens attacked a German land target for the first time. Derek French was in one of them.

'We got back and couldn't wait to count the bullet holes in our aircraft. There weren't any,' he said.

Not a great deal of damage was done to the Germans either, but only one aircraft was lost. A notice came down from headquarters to the effect that 'the squadron' had been awarded a Distinguished Flying Cross. A quick toss up decided that Flying Officer J.J. Bennett was the most senior officer on the raid and was therefore given the honour of wearing *the* ribbon on his tunic. A few days later, however, navigation logs revealed that Bennett had been nowhere near Sylt and had in fact bombed Denmark, for which the British government was required to pay substantial compensation. If

Derek felt a little put out by this, he didn't let on. Besides, it was soon his turn to win one all on his own.

A month later on 9 April, Germany struck north into Denmark and Norway. Denmark was gone within hours, but Bomber Command was ordered to try and stem German maritime operations in Norway. Losses were enormous. The aircraft barely had the range to cope with the eight hour, 1,000-mile (1,600-kilometres) round trip across the North Sea and all of them went unescorted by fighters. Added to this, the bizarre restriction on bombing German land targets was still not lifted, so instead of attacking the vital communication centres that were directing the campaign well within range of the RAF in northern Germany, crews were ordered to targets at the limits of their endurance in southern Norway and which were already occupied and well defended.

Derek was given the task of mine laying in Oslo Fjord. Long and narrow, surrounded by mountains and easily defendable, it was highly dangerous, considering the mine had to be dropped at night at a height no greater than 500 feet (150 metres) and a speed not more than 150 miles (240 kilometres) per hour. On this trip, he was led by another Australian, Duncan Good, 'a magnificent character', Derek said. Going in ahead of him, Derek watched as Good's aircraft was picked up by searchlights and anti-aircraft fire, but he continued along the whole length of the fjord and dropped the mine. Derek could see that he was in trouble but he seemed to be occupying the Germans' attention, giving him an easier run. Both aircraft made it home. Only upon returning to his base at Waddington did Derek realise what Good had been through. He had stopped a shell in the cockpit which had shot out most of his teeth as well as badly damaging both his wrists, his second pilot having to sit on top of him to lay the mine and fly home. Good recovered, picked up a new set of teeth (and a new wife as it happened) and was back again flying with his wrists in plaster, only to be killed later, mine laying again south of Brest.

I had trouble keeping up with Derek. Every moment, he seemed to be telling me a new story from a different part of the war, flying a different aircraft. Suddenly we were in Burma, flying Wellingtons with a ceiling of 10,000 feet, negotiating mountain passes of 9,500 feet. Then we were back in Scotland, being greeted by one Winston Churchill just before his ascension to the prime ministership in May 1940 and who was keen to sit down and talk to Derek about operational flying. I asked him for his strongest memory of the man.

'He ate peas using his fork like a spoon,' he told me. 'I encouraged my kids to do the same.'

Once during the invasion of France and Holland, Derek was sent to bomb Dutch railway yards at Eindhoven. His navigator and second pilot had the night before damaged an aircraft in a bad landing and his nerves were probably more fragile than normal. They couldn't find the target. Peering into the gloom of a blacked-out Continent, it was all eerily quiet and they were flying low at 1,000 feet (300 metres) to make out the terrain. All he could see was a big river, bigger than anything that should have been where they were supposed to be. Then everything seemed to open up on them, lights, explosions and red hot lines of tracer coming from all directions, whooshing up to meet them and accelerating as they came closer and flew past into the night. One slammed into the fuselage and exploded inside the aircraft. A few days earlier, a slab of armour plating had been installed behind the pilot's chair. 'That saved me,' said Derek.

Shell fragments left him bloodied, but still able to return to base, where he was abused by the CO for flying too low over enemy territory. As Derek put it, he 'just faded away' and collapsed, spending the next seven weeks in hospital. As it turned out, they had mistakenly flown due east of the target and had been the lone attacker of the mightily defended German industrial centre of Dusseldorf. The river they had been following was the Rhine.

On his recovery, and having completed his first of many tours, Derek was given a special all-black Hampden to test the efficacy of the British night fighter tactics and searchlights. 'None of them could ever catch me,' he said. Once, he was summoned to fly down to Grantham to report to none other than the commander of number 5 Group (and later the Commander-in-Chief of Bomber Command itself) Air Vice-Marshal Arthur T. 'Bomber' Harris, one of the most controversial figures of the war. Derek had no idea what the big chief could possibly want and felt apprehensive about the whole thing.

As it turned out, Harris simply wanted his opinion of the station commander at Waddington, a man Derek disliked and told him so. Harris obviously admired his candour and asked, 'So, what are you doing now, and what do you want to do?' Derek didn't have to think twice.

'I've heard on the grapevine you're getting a new type of aeroplane and starting a new squadron. I'd like to be in it.'

Harris picked up the phone. 'French is joining 207 Squadron tomorrow.'

And it was done. It was the first and last time he met the man.

The 'new' aeroplane was the Avro Manchester and it was yet another unmitigated disaster, primarily because of its ridiculous engine, the ominously named Vulture. Even today the idea seems slightly silly. Rather than have two good engines on each wing, the manufacturers at Avro thought it would be interesting to squash two into one and so came up with the Vulture, in reality two 12-cylinder engines, one atop the other powering a single crankshaft. It gave enormous power to the single propeller, but the concept was in reality beyond the technology of the day and the Vulture was chronically unreliable. They caught fire, the bearings broke, engine oil overheated rendering it useless. The troublesome Vulture became the bane of crews and mechanics alike.

The only positive about operating the Manchester was that you had so much time off, entire squadrons being grounded at a time as the endless problems were rectified, usually unsuccessfully. As Derek told me, not a single person managed to complete a tour on Manchesters, ever. Their loss rate was appalling, up to 6 per cent per raid, compared to the 2.5 per cent of comparable types such as the Wellington.

Then there was the Channel Dash, in February 1942, when two German cruisers broke out of the French port of Brest and raced up the English Channel to their home port of Kiel, one of the war's most daring events. The alert that they would do just that had been on for days and Derek, now a flight commander, had got sick of waiting for anything to happen and had gone to the pictures. Barely had he sat down when a sign came up on the screen summoning him to return to base.

'It was a complete panic,' he remembered.

Everything was thrown against these two ships but the German fighter cover was enormous. Even so, he managed to get near enough to bomb the *Scharnhorst*.

'Did you hit it?' I asked.

'Well, I claimed it,' he answered. He came back with a hole in his wing.

Derek also had a stint in the desert, so close to the enemy lines they often did two trips a night in Wellingtons.

'We'd bomb, come back, bomb up and do it all over again.'

On one of his early desert trips, he was advised to remove the 'Australia' flash from his shoulder.

'If the Italians caught you, they'd cut your throat. Not many people know that.'

I certainly didn't, for one.

Derek's experience and reputation allowed him to become something of a free agent in the RAF, slipping in and out of a variety of jobs in some interesting places. But all he really wanted to do was get back to Australia. Hearing that a Wellington needed ferrying into India, he offered to take it down himself and found his way to Madras, something of a pleasant backwater, but a little closer to home. Finding himself with no further orders, he wandered into the RAF HQ in Delhi and asked if there was anything he could do.

A senior officer told him that the squadron needed to move up to the North-West Frontier. Perhaps he could take a plane up there and scout about for a suitable route. Fine, thought Derek. Could he possibly have a map? 'Sorry old boy,' was the answer, so he went next door and bought an atlas from a newsagent and flew off north with it resting on his knees.

Then one day he found himself in a Blenheim, by this time a wing commander, second in charge of an operation called 'Ferry Wing India', which required him to fly up the Nile to Khartoum and find another route from Cairo to India. He got as far as Luxor when one of his engines fell to bits. He put down in the Valley of the Kings and happily spent the next few days as a tourist before hitching a ride back. He also spent some time training Nepalese paratroops and operating out of an airfield 7,000 feet above sea level in Ethiopia.

Derek's wife, Barbara, was obviously immensely proud of her husband and his remarkable history. She showed me his medals, the Africa Star, Burma Star, Air Crew Europe Star and the DFC with an added bar.

'How did you get it the second time?' I asked.

Derek looked puzzled, his amazing memory stumped for the first time. 'I can't honestly remember. Perhaps I bombed a ship?' he offered.

Later, he confessed that at one stage he was in line for the DSO but blotted his copybook when he disagreed with a squadron commander on his flight plan for the squadron. Perhaps he should go fly it himself, Derek suggested. Not the way to get ahead.

Derek was away for six years and flew an amazing four and a half tours with five different squadrons, at one time or another piloting just about everything there was to fly, including a couple of trips in a single-engined Hurricane.

'Any mug can fly one of them,' he said with a scoff.

It's amazing how he beat the odds, especially in the early stages of the war in Europe. Did he ever think he wasn't going to make it?

'You just couldn't think about it,' he told me. 'If you kept your eye constantly on making it to your last trip, you'd go mad.'

But he recognised fear when he saw it. Derek could go into a briefing room and know whether it was going to be a tough one.

'You could smell the fear,' he said. 'Like a strange, sour smell that hung in the room.'

Everyone had their own way of coping. Derek chewed chewing gum when flying, but when scared, his mouth went dry.

Derek is still fighting, concerned about the way the world is going and in a more local sense, battling with the Canberra War Memorial to have the men he trained and flew with properly acknowledged on the honour roll of the dead. There's definitely a fire still smouldering inside Derek French, but bitterness? I wasn't quite sure. I asked him about his return home.

'They treated us like shit,' was the conclusion of the way many RAAF personnel were received by the authorities upon returning to Australia with a log book of operational flying under their belts.

'They were jealous, you see,' said Derek.

One friend who had gone through Point Cook with Derek, Bob Bungey, flew Hurricanes with number 145 Squadron during the Battle of Britain, commanded the first Australian fighter squadron in Britain and rose to the rank of wing commander. Upon returning to Australia in 1942, he was told to remove his stripes and demoted three ranks to flying officer by jealous RAAF staff officers who hadn't seen a shot fired in anger.

'He went down to the beach and blew his brains out.'

Another friend had served on three separate aircraft types, completed a tour and was awarded the DSO and DFC. The best job he could get was serving behind the counter at David Jones.

'Actually, worse than shit.'

15

Pat Dwyer

Wireless/air-gunner

When we arrived at the station as a crew, we were given two weeks to survive.

The first thing Pat showed me was a picture of himself as a skinny eighteen-year-old, taken at Luna Park in Melbourne, just one face among a group of similar looking eighteen-year-olds, all in rather baggy air force trainee uniforms.

'I was 5 foot 6 and 8 stone 2. More like a fifteen-year-old.'

They all look like a bunch of kids about to get on the Big Dipper. He pointed to one of the faces.

'That bloke there, he got killed on Bomber Command; this one was in the army, then transferred to Bomber Command and was also killed. This one was a school mate. He got the chop over Germany.'

Sitting in Pat's lovely home with a nice view over the Swan River in Perth, well turned out in a jacket and shirt, you'd never guess that he'd been a bit of a stirrer, regularly getting himself into strife. In his words, he was 'a bit young, and a bit dopey'. His first scrape was getting caught eating a pie on parade, being saved from a charge only by getting his orders to catch a ship for England. On ops, he once impersonated an officer at a party at a neighbouring base, then came back late and missed the briefing for an operation. He got strips torn off him, but that was about it.

Pat remembered everything. Absolutely everything. Every name, every place, every tiny little detail in the big picture of his highly eventful tour as a wireless operator in Lancasters over Germany. His reminiscences were many and varied, some dramatic, some poignant, some simply hilarious. While training in Victoria, his pilot had for some silly reason drunk a big milkshake before taking off. It soon went from the bottom of his stomach to the bottom of the fuselage of the small Airspeed Oxford, with Pat having to dance about in the back to steer clear of the sloshing white regurgitation, all while trying to avoid throwing up himself, hit the gunnery target with his machine gun and try to stop laughing.

The Fairey Battles were so rough that on one particular exercise, 90 per cent of the trainees lost their lunches. There was one fellow who had lost his two front teeth in a game of cricket who delicately removed his falsies, handed them to a fellow crew member for safe keeping and then heaved violently over the side.

Pat remembers meeting his crew for the first time. He'd arrived at a station called Peplow in Shropshire to undergo training on Wellingtons. He was early, so dumped his gear in a Nissen hut and went to the otherwise empty mess. An English pilot came up.

'Hello. Would you like to be in my crew?'

Without hesitation Pat answered, 'Yes, I'd love to.'

Nothing complicated, just a question, a reply and the beginning of a life-long bond of affection that lasts to this day, not just for his former crew members but the RAF in general.

'The Australian squadrons were full of bullshit,' he said. It's an opinion I've heard expressed before. Compared to the RAF who, from the word go, were in a shooting war on their own soil, the RAAF was small, provincial and often riddled with petty personal ambitions that thwarted the careers of many a deserving, but poorly connected airman.

With his new crew, all English, he trained on clapped-out Wellingtons. One night they nearly came to grief on take-off. At 85 miles an hour, a strong wind kicked the aircraft out of line with the runway. Rather than run off completely, the pilot, Les Landells, gently applied the brakes as a counter measure, but this just threw the machine into a series of uncontrollable ground loops, spinning around under its own centrifugal force. Pat had just checked the fuel tanks and knew them to be full.

'It was like being thrown about in a dark car from side to side.'

When it stopped, Pat bolted for the nose where the bomb-aimer had just pulled up the escape hatch.

'I just leaped straight through it,' he says.

A fire tender, ambulance and the commanding officer were soon on the scene. The pilot was yelled at for damaging a 'perfectly good' aeroplane, and this was the beginning of a series of black marks and a bad reputation that would dog Pat and his crew throughout their tour.

Next up was a conversion course on Halifaxes at Sandtoft in Lincolnshire.

'We called it Prang-toft,' said Pat. 'Some people said it didn't deserve that name, but gee, the people who flew there did.' On a long cross-country flight one night, Pat woke up to find his oxygen mask dangling off his face. Startled, he checked his watch and log book and realised he'd been out cold for an hour. He told no-one, and simply clipped the mask back on. On landing, he buttonholed another wireless op, and simply copied the radio log for the missing hour from his log book. No-one ever discovered his serious indiscretion.

Still under training, Pat's first flights over enemy territory were 'Bullseyes', diversion flights into France and Germany designed to lure German night fighters away from the main force, but not hang around long enough for them to actually find you. It was a risky business. The early Halifaxes had a bad reputation, but Pat enjoyed flying in them.

'They were much more comfortable than the Lancaster,' he said.

Except for the unfortunate seating configuration in the nose where the wireless op effectively sat under the pilot.

'When he used a can to have a pee, he'd sometimes miss and hit me instead,' he remembered. 'So I really was being pissed on from a great height!'

'This is my squadron badge,' said Pat. 'I put it on today especially.' On his lapel is the 626 Squadron emblem, an ancient sailing ship above the motto: *To strive and not to yield*. There was nothing particularly remarkable about 626 Squadron. It had no famous personalities, no moments of drama, no celebrities that made it stand out from most of the other hundred or so squadrons under Bomber Command. But for people like Pat, it was the scene of the starkest and most vivid moments of their lives.

Number 626 spent all of its brief two-year life at Wickenby, a temporary wartime base carved out of requisitioned Lincolnshire farmlands in 1941. It followed the standard RAF pattern: three concrete runways, three large T2-type steel hangers, technical, administration and accommodation blocks and a long narrow road leading to the bomb dump, which was constructed in a natural depression away from the buildings. It was close to a brace of villages with names such as Rand, Fulnetby and Holton-cum-Beckering, whose publicans, when the air force arrived, must have thought their dreams had come true.

Wickenby was home to another squadron, number 12, which suffered one of the highest loss rates in Bomber

Command, a factor which contributed to that station's grim distinction of being the first to lose 1,000 aircrew, all in just 32 months of operations.

'At one stage, they cut the tour from thirty to twenty-five, just to give people a chance to get through,' remembered Pat.

As wireless operator in a Lancaster, Pat sat at the rear of the large perspex 'glasshouse' under the round astrodome with his back up against the main wing spar, that connected the two wings through the fuselage. In front of him was a big Marconi 1154/55 wireless set with its distinctive red, blue and yellow tuning wheels, a morse key and, at varying times during the war, one or more of the array of radar and night fighter warning equipment sporting code names such as Monica, Village Inn and H2S (so named after 'rotten egg' gas, hydrogen sulphide, by an air ministry official who supposedly declared of the project, 'It stinks!').

He operated the flare pistol in emergencies, sent and received morse signals from the edible rice paper code book – a completely new one for each trip – and kept an eye on the electrical systems. His position had one distinct advantage – he was next to the warm air outlet and was often sweating even when other members of the crew froze.

Pat's first trip in a Lancaster was an easy one, but as far as he was concerned, it was not an aircraft built for comfort. Compared to the Halifax, it was small and cramped. The seats were hard, small and uncomfortable and on a long flight, were literally a pain in the backside. Here Pat's amazing memory kicked in, and he took me on a sort of virtual tour of the aircraft interior, explaining the difficulties involved in moving through it.

'The navigator's seat was a piece of timber a foot across on two poles in the floor. To get past him you needed to squeeze yourself against the internal starboard side of the plane.'

Sometimes, to get the blood back into his nether regions, he'd perform a little exercise, hoisting himself up onto the spar, then sliding across from starboard to port, sitting himself down on a small step, then repeating the operation in reverse. The discomfort also extended to the Elsan toilet, which at 50 degrees below zero (–10°C) was a serious danger to sit on.

'It was like the inside of a freezer,' he told me. 'Your backside could stick to the metal seat.'

In all his flying career, Pat never took the risk of answering the call of nature mid-air.

Trip number one in Pat's log book was a milk run to attack German positions along the Dutch coast. No fighters, light flak, everyone home safe and sound. Enthused in a moment of relief and patriotic fervour, and thinking they'd all be like this, he immediately volunteered for a second tour – 55 operations in all. Then came his second trip. It was a medium-sized daylight raid of 340 Lancasters to Emmerich, right on the Dutch border. Three Lancasters were lost that day, and Pat was witness to the destruction of one of them.

'I was looking out the astrodome. Everything seemed to be OK. Then the Lancaster directly behind us got hit by flak and just seemed to curl over and go down.'

Pat saw an airman attempting to get out of the stricken aircraft but was unable to see what happened, because then it was their turn. Right over the target, about to drop with their bomb doors open, they suffered a direct hit from a flak burst in the open bomb bay. Thirty tons of aircraft lifted upwards in a massive surge, but stayed in one piece, protected, ironically, by the heavy iron casings of the 1,000 pound bombs themselves. The fact that the thinly cased 4,000 pound 'Cookie' didn't explode was a miracle.

'If we'd been hit after we dropped them, it would have been a different story,' said Pat.

Back at Wickenby, the crew inspected the damage. The

shrapnel could clearly be seen to have passed through the bomb doors from the inside outwards. The report said Pat's Lanc had been holed 'from nose to tail'.

Next was Duisburg in the Ruhr, another daylight trip. The group was ringed in a barrage of black explosions. They got through, but not everyone was so lucky.

'I was watching ahead when I saw a massive flash of orange and yellow flame. It was a Lancaster blowing up right in front of us. Shocking sight.'

Their aircraft had to fly through the debris of the stricken aeroplane.

'The windscreen and the bomb-aimer's section – splattered with blood.'

Nothing was said about it over the intercom at the time. What could be said?

'Some things were pretty demoralising. That was a nasty one.'

Not all the dangers came from the enemy. Once on a very cold night trip, Pat checked the electrical systems and found a fault with the generators, one charging at 32 volts, the other at 34. This meant the batteries were being overcharged and were at risk of boiling and releasing inflammable acid fumes into the aircraft interior which could ignite on contact with a flame or spark. To avoid this, Pat switched the generators off, then restarted them when the battery charge had diminished almost to nothing, as registered by the dimming of a globe above his head. All well and good, except for Freddy, the rear-gunner, who relied on his electrically heated suit to keep warm in the minus 50 degree temperatures and protested vigorously.

'Freddy, I can't do anything about it,' Pat told him. 'If I'm not careful I could blow the plane up.'

'I don't give a stuff if you *do* blow the plane up,' was his considered reply. 'It's better than freezing to death back here!'

One night they were flying at 14,000 feet over the North Sea on their way to bomb Wilhelmshaven. In the dark, the aircraft ran slap bang into a huge cumulonimbus cloud and became caught in a thermal. Weighed down with 7 tons of bombs, the Lancaster went into a spin. The pilot, desperate to regain control of the aircraft, put his feet up onto the control panel and attempted to pull the control column back, but to no avail.

'I heard him give the order over the intercom, "Bail out if you want to", but I thought, what's the bloody use?'

They had been told that in the freezing water they would be dead in 3 minutes. In that moment, Pat believed, as firmly as anyone can believe, that his number was up. Bugger it, he though, I'll just go down with the plane.

But up the front, Eric 'Marty' Martinberg, the flight engineer, had got behind Les and he too pulled back on the stick for all he was worth. Between four hands and two feet, it was just enough to pull the nose out of the spin and save the aircraft.

'We were all as happy as buggery in the plane. Chuckling, laughter, all sorts of good humour.' And there was no fear. 'While we were in the spin, everyone was quite calm. No-one screamed. No whinging or whimpering. No-one called out, "Save us". We just shut up and waited for the end. That was the way it happened in those days. You were going, and that was it. It wasn't like on those American shows.'

I knew what he was referring to, the film *Memphis Belle*, made in 1990 and starring Matthew Modine and Harry Connick Junior. For those who haven't seen it, it's the story of an American Flying Fortress on a daylight trip where just about everything that can go wrong, does. In one sequence, a crashing Messerschmitt 109 slices off the tail section of an adjacent bomber and the wireless operator listens in to the doomed crew screaming their heads off as it begins its long plummet to the ground, a hysterical cacophony of 'Oh God, I'm gonna die! Save me!' etc, in typically over-blown Hollywood style. All this is simply laughable to every old bomber crew member I have met who has seen it, and that is most of them (flying films are popular with these blokes). To a man, they tell me that it just wasn't like that. The discipline acquired over years of training and the duress of operations, as well as the desire to stand by your crew stood firm until the terminal moment.

'Death was so close to us in those days,' Pat said without a hint of morbidity. 'You became familiar with it, and in the end, came to expect it.' I told him that I found it a very difficult concept to grasp, and he offered no argument. 'It was just the sort of thing you had to put up with,' he said. 'When we arrived at the station as a crew, we were rated as lasting two weeks. That's it. Two weeks. We were given crappy aircraft, crappy ground crew . . . and if we'd crashed and died on take-off they just would have taken our names off the chalk board and got in another crew.' The RAF were tough.

Only once did the fear begin to get at him. It was in a two-week period in the middle of his tour, and reached a stage where he simply didn't know how he could keep flying. One trip to Dortmund he could only face by taking it stage by stage. He plucked up the courage to go to the briefing, and made it through that. Then out to the aircraft. So far so good. Then came the pre-flight checks and the take-off. At one stage he thought about bailing out over England, but he made it through that too. Then he was over the target with a job to do, and six other people were relying on him. He made it home that trip. It was a turning point – enough for him to regain the strength he needed to keep going.

Other problems included sub-standard equipment and careless ground crews. Once, taking off for Essen, pilot Les Landells found he could barely get enough speed to get off the deck. Just managing to clear the end of the tarmac, the aircraft bounced several times in a field before gradually building up speed and climbing awkwardly into the air. Pat heard the pilot and engineer discuss whether they could make it to the target but did so, and returned without incident. The crew knew their Lancaster was an old aircraft and in peacetime would not be flying at all. The reason they had been relegated what was to all intents and purposes a lemon may have been because Pat's crew were not popular with the flight commanders, nor the CO himself. Pat was a larrikin from the colonies, Marty was the sole survivor of an earlier crash and had his own particular demons regarding drink and Les, orphaned at four and in the workforce by thirteen, had been well versed in the art of standing up for his rights at Hard Knocks College and had thus made few friends among the powers-that-be.

'The next time we had to go up in it, we were going to get Les to put it on automatic pilot, bail out over England and let the bloody thing fly to Germany on its own,' was the general consensus after that incident.

But the explanation for the previous night's events was not as simple as just a dud plane. As Les discovered, earlier that day the aircraft had been prepared for a target somewhere in eastern Germany, a long trip requiring a smaller bomb load but a large amount of fuel. At some stage, the target had been changed to Essen, a much shorter distance, enabling a heavier bomb load with reduced petrol, and requiring the ground crew to make the necessary adjustment. They only got it half right, loading the extra bombs but neglecting to draw off 500 gallons from the tanks. Severely overloaded, it's surprising Pat's Lancaster made it off the ground at all.

And then there were the risks of flying after dark.

'Night flying was dangerous. You couldn't see anything.'

Sometimes that was just as well. On a daylight trip over

Cologne, Pat was in his position in the perspex astrodome when a Cookie plummeted past the starboard wingtip. The Cookie was often the first one to go, so Pat knew what was about to happen. 'Hard port!' he yelled into the intercom, not even having time to look up. The aircraft yawed violently, then straightened. This time Pat looked up to see the entire bomb load from a plane above plummeting towards them.

'We're going to get hit!' was all he could say before instinctively ducking down and, somewhat comically, putting his hands over his head.

Thud, *thud*, *thud* reverberated through the aircraft. Like a startled rabbit, Pat emerged from his hole to see petrol pouring from both wings.

'Prepare to bail out!' came the order from the pilot.

Three 1,000-pound bombs had hit them through the starboard wing, three through the port, another through the tail section and, according to the mid-upper gunner, a second Cookie had passed through the narrow gap between the wing and the tail elevator. Petrol was also being sucked into the rear-gunner's compartment, like a station wagon with the tailgate open.

'With the hot exhaust from the engines, we expected to just blow up at any moment,' Pat said. The rest of the formation, thinking they were doomed and also expecting an inferno, quickly manoeuvred away, leaving them alone in the sky. On the ground, the Germans also watched the Lancaster streaming fuel and concentrated their fire, hoping for an easy kill.

'They were spot on our height, but just a fraction of a second out, and it burst just behind us.'

They had lost about 500 gallons, but by some judicious transferring of fuel from one petrol tank to the other, Marty the flight engineer brought them home safely. Some of the bombs had gone straight through the wing, and some were still lodged in it.

The very next trip was yet another apparent attempt by their own side to kill them. Having been relegated to a second dodgy aeroplane, Les saw that the two inner engines were dropping revs and pulled into Dispersal just before take-off. The commanding officer pulled up in his car beneath them.

'Landells, what's going on here?'

'We've declared the plane U/S, sir. Two inner engines dropping revs.'

'Well, start them up, you're on your way.' So, half an hour behind everyone else, they took off.

In thick cloud over Germany, Pat thought to himself, What the bloody hell are we doing here? We've been hit by bombs on our last trip, sent up on an aircraft that's ratshit, and now we're all on our own for the Germans to make us very welcome. So he made a decision – a brave one – and switched on his intercom.

'Better live cowards than dead heroes,' he said to the rest of the crew, not really knowing what the response would be. There was a pause and then a cheer went up. 'Yeah, yeah, yeah!' they responded. The pilot came on. 'Alright, where do we drop them?' and someone said, 'Right here.' So, somewhere over Germany, it was 'bombs gone' and they headed home. But the ordeal was not quite over.

Coming back to land at Wickenby – 2,850 revs, full flap and wheels down, farmland on one side, the Wragby road on the other, 2,000 yards of runway dead ahead – the two dicky engines again decided to drop their revs. The Lancaster came down in an open field, skidding along the ground, cleaning up a concrete drainage channel and sending a fence flying over their heads. But running into a raised road embankment somehow propelled them momentarily into the air, and the pilot managed to find the runway in a sideways manoeuvre Pat could only describe as 'flying crabwise'. However he did it, he got them back onto the runway. Years later, Les met a woman, who as a five-year-old girl was in a car on that road and was convinced the aircraft was about to hit them.

I was intrigued by the CO who sent them off with a dicky aircraft.

'Funny thing about him,' said Pat. Apparently, after sending them off, the officer in question returned to the mess and announced, 'That crew's got a one way ticket.' Is this really believable? I asked Pat to clarify, but he didn't think it very remarkable. According to Pat's generous point of view, everyone was under strain and the officer had been new to the squadron and under pressures of his own. As it turned out, the officer met Les Landells, the pilot, after the war and apologised, and they became firm friends. In a sense, this near disaster worked in their favour because they were then issued with an aircraft only three weeks old. But then they nearly lost that one too.

Over Dortmund, they had a 'hang-up', a bomb that failed to release. Not just any bomb, but the highly volatile Cookie. Try as Les might to release it over Germany by 'bouncing' the aircraft up and down in the sky, it held fast, and there was no choice but to land with it still attached.

As soon as the wheels touched down, they all felt the thud as it finally decided to release – right into the closed bomb bay. Ordered to the end of the runway and to abandon the aircraft, they parked and bolted to a nearby truck to take them out of there. Looking back, they saw the massive bomb had partially forced its way out of the closed bomb bay and was hanging perilously above the tarmac. The ground crew, it transpired, had attached it to a rack clearly marked 'unserviceable'. Pat just shrugged his shoulders again.

He remembers every trip of his tour: Mannheim, Cologne, Chemnitz, Dessau. But after every one, he would ask himself Why are we surviving? Why us? Hurtling along the runway on take-off, seated under his astrodome, he would say his prayers and wonder, is this the last time I'm going to touch the ground alive? From their respective perspex bubbles a few metres apart, he and the mid-upper gunner would exchange grins and a silent 'thumbs-up' as they lifted off into the unknown.

Pat's encounters with night fighters were limited, but one story stood out. In a rare lapse of memory, he'd forgotten the target, but on the run in, the bomb-aimer, Boris, realised the Germans had set up a dummy target, nothing more than a series of fires lit in the woods outside the town as a decoy.

'We'll have to go round again,' he announced.

They swung to port and into a large cloud, emerging into a clear patch of night sky. Dead in front of them was an unsuspecting twin-engined Heinkel 219 'Owl' – produced only in small numbers but arguably the nastiest German night fighter of the war (on 2–3 November 1944, over Dusseldorf, one downed six bombers in 12 minutes). They could see it clearly in the moonlight. The Lancaster was armed in the nose with two .303 machine guns – described by Pat and others as 'absolutely useless' – but here, it would seem was a golden opportunity to turn the tables.

'Do we have a shot?' asked Les.

No-one wanted to stir up this particular hornets' nest and the answer from the crew was unanimous. 'No, let him go!' For a bomber, leaving well enough alone was always the more popular option.

In spite of all the odds, Pat, for reasons he has long since given up wondering about, got through, finishing his tour with a couple of 'Manna' trips, dropping food to the starving residents of Rotterdam.

'Much nicer thing to do than dropping bombs and killing people,' he said.

The only one of his original crew not to finish was Marty, the magnificent flight engineer who saved their bacon on more than one occasion. Having been the sole survivor of a Halifax crash in training, his nerves were already in tatters by the time he started with ops but he pressed on.

'These days he wouldn't have flown again, but back then they wanted their money's worth.'

Finally, his nerve went altogether and he could take no more, and who could blame him? Facing a charge of LMF – Lack of Moral Fibre – he faced a court martial but the squadron engineering officer would hear none of it and Marty was instead re-assigned to a non-combat role flying in the Mediterranean. He just disappeared from the crew one night, and that was that.

After the war, Pat suffered from stress himself enduring rashes, stomach complaints and bad hearing from the hours spent alongside the spinning prop tips. Pat's affection for his old crew was undiminished, and he was still close to Les, his pilot. He caught up with all of them on a trip to England a few years back. All except Marty, who died some time in the 1980s. It was one of Pat's few detectable regrets. The attitude to death and the men's deep loyalty to one another were evident in one last anecdote before I left.

In his hut, which housed roughly eighteen men of different crews according to rank, lived another Australian wireless operator, Ollie Just. Ollie had survived a bail-out over the French coast and had told Pat the remarkable story of his escape. After being given the order to jump from the pilot, Ollie had harnessed up, clambered over the main spar and stood at the open rear doorway. Standing next to the hatch, but making no sign of moving, was the English mid-upper gunner. Ollie couldn't work out what the man was waiting for and gestured for him to go, but he remained where he was. It was no time for niceties so Ollie jumped and was soon picked up. Both the rear and mid-upper gunners perished in the crash. Pat had thought about this a great deal and reckoned he understood exactly what was going on. For some reason, the rear-gunner in that aircraft couldn't, or wouldn't jump and chose to go down with the aircraft, and his mate, whom he'd trained with, simply chose to go with him.

Pat smiles and shrugs his shoulders. 'That's just how it was back then.'

16

Brian Walley

Pilot

I signed up at seventeen and put my age up. What happened afterwards taught me not to be so impetuous.

Brian joined the RAF on 1 July 1940. Exactly a year later on 1 July 1941 he was handed his pilots wings. There was no ceremony, no passing out parade. He was simply given a list of items to collect from stores with 'brevet, flying' appearing slightly above 'laces, boot'.

In the year since joining up, he had watched the Battle of Britain, been given ten rounds of ammunition to guard an aerodrome in Shropshire against possible German paratroop attack and trained to fly one of the stupidest aeroplanes ever built, the Armstrong-Whitworth Whitley.

It's hard to find much to say that's positive about the Whitley. This twin-engined tub was the first of the so-called 'modern' British bombers, admittedly a step up from the fabric-covered Heyfords and Hendons (which boasted natty features such as 'wheel spats' and 'dustbin turrets'), but only just. It also earned for itself a number of distinctions, such as the first British all-metal stress-skinned bomber, the first aircraft to bomb Germany as well as Italy and the first to be equipped with a power-operated gun turret. But these accolades are misleading. The Whitley first flew in March 1936 and graduated into immediate obsolescence. It was slow, virtually unmanoeuvrable, pitifully underarmed and handled like a truck. It even looked ridiculous, flying with a heavy 'nose down' attitude because of the high angle of the enormous wings which themselves were nearly 300 square feet larger than its far more sensible contemporary, the Vickers Wellington.

'In the Whitley, if you wanted to turn left, you'd turn the wheel, slowly count one-two-three-four-five, then the wing would start to drop, and gradually it would begin to turn,' says Brian. Just the thing to outrun a nimble German fighter.

Brian joined 51 Squadron, operating from Dishforth in Yorkshire, a short runway aerodrome right on the A1 Great North Road, which had to be closed to traffic whenever the bombers took off, 'otherwise we'd have taken off the roofs of the cars with our wheels'. He arrived in the winter of 1941 – indeed, the winter of Bomber Command itself – when barely a crew lasted beyond five trips.

'There were six of us and we put in a pound each to buy a little Austin 7, on the strength that it would pass down to the last man. My share went very quickly,' he says.

With the war nearly two years old, it had become obvious to many that the capacity of the British bomber to hit targets inside Germany was severely limited. Just how limited was not appreciated until a civil servant, D.M. Butt, decided to actually examine over a thousand aerial photographs taken of targets after a raid. The resulting 'Butt Report' presented in August 1941 exceeded everyone's worst fears, concluding with the startling statistic that just one third of all bomber crews were dropping their bombs within *5 miles* (8 kilometres) of the aiming point. It was the nadir of the wartime fortunes of Bomber Command, and resulted in a significant review of policy.

But not before the night of 7 November 1941 which saw a

series of disastrous raids costing thirty-seven aircraft out of nearly 400 dispatched, including a particularly foolish attack on Berlin that achieved little materially, but changed the direction of British bombing policy for the rest of the war and ended Brian Walley's brief wartime flying career.

Brian's first three trips were relatively uneventful: Stettin, Le Havre and Frankfurt. Stettin, on the Baltic in Germany's far east, was a trip lasting 10 hours 40 minutes (he remembered the flying times off by heart) and at the absolute maximum endurance of the Whitley's range. On his return, the ground crew looked at the fuel tanks and told them they'd have been lucky to do one more circuit of the aerodrome.

Then, over Hamburg, he was given a taste of things to come when caught in the master beam and 'lit up like a Christmas tree' by a cone of searchlights. With the Whitley's maximum speed a dismal 192 miles per hour, the anti-aircraft gunners on the ground could take their time. One engine was hit, but a corkscrewing dive to 8,000 feet shook them free and got them momentarily out of trouble. On the way home, the damaged engine blew up, but they made it back to England, landing at Driffield in East Yorkshire.

The trip to Berlin was one that should never have taken place. Air Marshal Sir Richard Pierse has become the forgotten head of Bomber Command, and justifiably so. Having taken over the job in October 1940, he did little to remedy the situation of high casualties for little results, becoming a pollyanna insisting the current policies would eventually yield results, despite all evidence to the contrary. Eventually he was sacked and sent packing to South-east Asia, where he later brought his air force career to an abrupt end by eloping with the wife of General Claude Auchinlek!

Frustrated by recent bad weather, Pierse was anxious to prove his critics wrong with a spectacular strike on the Nazi capital and other major centres with every plane he could get into the air. His aim was to set a new record for aircraft dispatched in a single night. This, despite persistent forecasts of atrocious weather: storms, hail and ice along the routes and over the targets. The commander of number 5 Group rebelled, refusing to send his squadrons all the way to Berlin, insisting they venture no further than Cologne. But number 4 Group was more compliant, and so on the evening of 7 November 1941 Brian, as second pilot in Whitley 'F' for Freddie, took off from Dishforth into the face of an ice storm.

'It was one of the worse gales I'd ever taken off in,' Brian recalled.

They didn't even get close to Berlin. Dreadful at take-off, the weather proceeded to get worse, although there was some talk of it improving for the return journey. Climbing through 15,000 feet of solid cloud, a 40-knot tailwind increased to 60 and began blowing them south of their track, directly over the heavily defended German port of Kiel. At least they were travelling fast, but in the wrong direction.

'The enemy guns were on target,' Brian said. A burst of flak set the port engine on fire. The extinguisher, thank goodness, worked and the pilot immediately jettisoned the bombs. 'Retribution for such an unfriendly welcome.'

All there was left to do was head for home. Brian had made it back on one engine before, perhaps he could again. Clinging to the hope of an improvement in the weather, they turned the Whitley around and headed for home over the North Sea. But instead of a lessening of the storm, it had swung around to the north and was now an 80-knot head wind blowing straight down from the Arctic.

From 15,000 feet, a power glide on one engine would normally have got them home, but in the prevailing conditions with the risk of the wings icing up in the clouds, the pilot had no choice but to get below them, and quickly, eventually breaking cover at just 1,500 feet. It was time to jettison everything that was not bolted down. Making his way to the front turret, Brian opened the escape hatch and threw out everything he could get his hands on: equipment, ammunition trays, even the big gas-operated Vickers machine gun (a useless antique at the best of times), which he lifted off its mount and hurled through the hole in the floor. On the way through, it became entangled in the intercom cord dangling from his helmet and as he put it, 'There but for the grace of God went I along with helmet and gun.'

The wireless operator managed to contact base, inform them of their predicament and get a rough bearing before clamping down the morse key to relay their own position, somewhere in the middle of the ocean on a very inhospitable night.

Knowing they were soon to be afloat on the North Sea, Brian had the wherewithal to stuff thermos flasks full of coffee and the crew's sandwiches into a duffle bag, and leave it by the open rear hatch, to be thrown into the dinghy as soon as possible after impact. The last thing he remembers saying is, 'Don't forget the duffle bag.'

Back in his position, strapped in the cockpit, he watched vast waves rise and fall like black foaming mountains illuminated in the Whitley's landing lights as they approached the surface. 'The sea,' wrote Brian, 'was in a malevolent mood.' Then *bang*. As the aircraft hit a wave like it was a brick wall. It slid down a second, then crashed through a third. 'The whole front of the fuselage disintegrated with most of it wrapped around my legs.' Trapped in his seat, water surged up to Brian's chest, forcing him to half-swim, half-scramble out of the canopy escape hatch above his head. Losing a flying boot and injuring his knee, he scrambled along the rapidly sinking fuselage and made for the dinghy, which rose above his head, then fell below on the surging sea. In shock, whimpering like a 'whipped schoolboy', Brian in that moment 'grew up from a nineteen-year-old teenager to manhood'.

He was the last into the dinghy, hauled in by the four crew before the Whitley sank. Twenty feet below them, they watched the still shining landing lights recede and disappear forever. 'The sheer sense of desolation was terrifying,' he said.

For the next two days Brian endured a nightmare that can scarcely be comprehended. With a broken knee cap and lacerations to both thighs, he and his four crew faced the full force of a North Sea storm that for an entire day did not even begin to let up. The grey dawn that eventually broke the gloom revealed to Brian nothing but 'a scene of utter desolation'. With the birth of the new day the storm increased.

'We would rise slowly up the face of 20 foot waves, hang for a moment on the crest, then shoot down into the trough.'

Sodden, exhausted, with freezing water sloshing around at their feet, violently seasick and nothing to relieve the thirst or hunger – in the rush to leave the aircraft, the duffle bag, with its potentially life-saving provisions had been left behind – they simply faced the day as best they could.

'The skipper suggested we pray to God for succour. We did so most fervently, each quietly in his own way.'

The rear-gunner and the wireless operator went first. Atop one peak, a savage gust tipped the tiny dinghy over, spilling them all into the sea, and washing away their few meagre rations. Brian never saw the two men again.

'They just vanished beneath those great grey ugly breakers.'

In the water, lacking the strength even to climb back in, Brian had a notion he could swim to safety, but after a few yards he says, the voice and prayers of his mother came to him across the water, making him turn back to the dinghy.

Another night seemed to extinguish the possibility of rescue. The battered dinghy sprung a slow leak which had to be attended to with what little lung power the three men could muster. Still the storm refused to subside, and ice flecks formed on their clothing. In sublime understatement they faced, wrote Brian, 'a doubtful future'.

Then the navigator went. Showing signs of hysteria, he terrified them all by standing up, risking what in their condition would be a fatal capsizing. The other two settled the man down, got him off to sleep and he simply froze to death.

Then, in the small hours of the night, they heard a plane. Brian and the skipper waved and shouted but never saw it, and soon its engines faded into the night. Afterwards, they remembered the distress flare, still lashed to the side of the dinghy and 'we could have wept at our stupidity'.

The dawn of the second day was as bleak as the first. The two remaining men were now in appalling shape. Brian, almost too weak to top the dinghy up with air, used his remaining flying boot to bail out water. In his exhaustion, his mind began to play cruel tricks on him, making him believe he could see land just over the wave crests. That afternoon the skipper went, leaving him all alone in the dinghy with the bodies of his two comrades, sensing his own end could not be far off. The storm was at last subsiding, and with it the pain in his numbed body. At dusk, as the night came on once again, he began to settle into a sleep he knew would be his last.

Then, from nowhere, an aircraft roared low overhead. Brian looked up. It was German, a Heinkel 59 seaplane with its front gun trained right on him. 'No! No! No!' he yelled, expecting at any moment a burst that would put him out of his misery. Instead, the big seaplane banked, circled and touched down on the water just yards away from the dinghy. One of the crew climbed down onto the port float and threw Brian a rope, which he secured to the side.

'They hauled me on board, then the bodies of my crew and finally the dinghy.'

Inside, he discarded his sodden, freezing clothes and was

wrapped in a blanket. A couple of swigs from a Schnapps bottle and he was unconscious.

It would be three and a half years before Brian would alight from another aeroplane at Westcott in Buckinghamshire in England, get down on his knees and pat the ground of his homeland, 'giving thanks for my deliverance'.

He was incarcerated in a number of POW camps around Germany, finally enduring a forced march in the winter of 1945 from Poland to the outskirts of Berlin as the Red Army neared. Among his experiences he had been part of a failed escape attempt and beaten up for his troubles, and had discovered a love for working with soil that would last him his life.

When his liberation came, it was in the form of a Russian tank that crashed through one end of the camp and out the other. 'They didn't even stop to open the gate.' But still he had to wait, as the Russians showed little interest in their repatriation. Eventually he took matters into his own hands and walked back to the American lines, passing through bombed-out cities where the rubble was piled up to the windowsills.

For all his trials, Brian seemed to bear little ill-will towards the Germans. The air–sea rescue Heinkel that picked him up took him ashore at Norderney, an island just off the German coast near the Dutch border, and put him in hospital where, as he says, 'they could not have taken more care of me had I been one of their own'. His two crew members were buried with full military honours and now lie side by side in the war graves cemetery in Sage in northern Germany.

He was however, another one of those subjected to the line that was probably a cliché even then, when the commander of the air–sea rescue base stood at the foot of his hospital bed and told him, 'For you the war is over.'

In camp, he managed to befriend an Austrian guard, an elite alpine trooper convalescing after thrice being wounded on the Russian front and in dread of being sent back there. He and Brian were the same age, and 'got on like a house on fire'. The Austrian's only ambition was to join his friend, happily sitting out the war in style in Canada as a POW. Brian wondered if he survived the war.

In his story, he related his disgust at witnessing an American GI urinating on the face of a dead German soldier, reflecting that 'some mother had lost a son and no-one ever deserved such treatment'. Not a bad show of compassion from a bloke who spent over three years locked up by them.

Half a century later, Brian sat down to dinner, a guest of ex-Hauptmann (Captain) Karl Born, the man who had told him his war was now over, and former commanding officer of the Luftwaffe air–sea rescue base at Norderney. He had been wary of the invitation at first, but his apprehension was soon eclipsed by a warmth born of a shared experience.

His pilgrimage to Germany included a visit to the last resting place of his crew where he lay a single rose on each grave. He also stood on the same spot at Norderney where he was taken ashore half-dead on a stretcher.

'There is nothing left of the seaplane base now, and the hospital where I languished is now a kindergarten.'

He even managed a toast to the German air–sea rescue service without whom he would not be there.

After the war, Brian flew again in the RAF Volunteer Reserve, had a go at farming in Western Australia and ended up with his own mining exploration company, spending much time in the outback. During our candid discussion, I discovered a distinctive sense of humour, albeit as dry as a bleached branch out in the opal country.

It takes courage to reveal the most traumatic moment of one's life to a stranger, even an interested stranger, but Brian did so calmly and unflinchingly, and I can only guess at the horrors still inside in his head.

He told me those words 'for you the war is over' haunted him for many years until he once again faced the man who had first uttered them.

Postscript: Brian fought a long battle with the British government to be awarded the air crew service medal, the coveted Air Crew Europe Star. Unbelievably, despite his travails, he was refused on the grounds that his time on active service fell short of the required minimum by two days. But Brian wasn't the type of bloke to roll over to an underhanded piece of petty bureaucracy such as this. He fought them and won, receiving his medal fifty years after earning it.

'I think I deserved it,' he said.

17

Ken Fox

Spitfire pilot

I saved his bloody life, actually, which he was very grateful for.

Ken Fox loved flying and happened to be very good at it, a natural, in fact, which is what you had to be to achieve the dream of nearly every trainee pilot – selection for training on single engined aircraft to become a fighter pilot. Ken joined up in Sydney at the height of the Battle of Britain, went through initial training at Bradfield Park and earned his wings at Amberley in Queensland. His parsimonious instructors gave him their highest accolade, 'above average'. So far, so good.

I met Ken through Peter Forbes, a World War Two aviation nut who had heard about my project and came along with me to the interview.

At the end of training, bored but tense young airmen would wait inside the sealed embarkation camp for the ship that would take them overseas. Often they would try their luck at gaining a final, brief couple hours on the outside. Usually, the excuse was something like, 'my grandmother died'. Sometimes it worked, sometimes not. Then one day, Ken's grandmother died. For real. The adjutant was sceptical but gave him two hours to see Grandma off to the next world. Hopefully, he wouldn't be following her too closely.

Ken's next temporary escape was on the very day of his departure, at Circular Quay. The boat was ready and sailing time was an hour or two away. A wire mesh fence running down the wharf separated the departing airmen from their families and loved ones but Ken's fiancée, Joan, was nowhere in sight. Laid up with a broken ankle, the unhappy girl was being looked after by an aunt in nearby Elizabeth Bay, as her beloved boy in blue prepared to sail. A friend of Ken's on the outside had an idea.

'If you can talk your way past one of the guards, I'll run you up there to say goodbye.'

Ken talked his best talk, and promised to be back in half an hour. The mate had the car ready, and a few minutes later he was at his fiancée's front door, giving her the surprise of her life.

'It was a romantic touch – she thought I'd already gone.'

Ken sailed to Europe in a massive convoy of over a hundred ships. Orange flashes on the horizon at night dampened the excitement of the new recruits as U-boats picked off their unlucky victims. The convoy at least offered protection but as everyone knew, if any one ship got into trouble and lagged behind, they would be left on their own.

At Brighton in England, Ken was given just about the best news a pilot could ever hope to hear. He was to become a Spitfire pilot. I asked Ken how he felt.

'Magnificent!' he said, as if the news come just yesterday. 'Best thing that could have happened to me!'

I am quite certain that there is absolutely nothing left to say about the Vickers-Supermarine Spitfire, and yet the books still roll out, the documentaries continue to be made, and this remarkable little aeroplane continues to make people swoon the world over, and I confess I'm one of them. Considering some of the rubbish that was rolling off British production lines at the time, it's a wonder something as brilliant as the Spitfire ever managed to be made, but made it was and in amazing numbers. Over 20,000 were produced, and it was just about the only aircraft on the production line on the very first, as well as the very last day of the war. This, despite its many intervening transformations, leaving it almost unrecognisable from Reg Mitchell's original design.

As he was soon to discover at his Operational Training Unit at Hawarden, near Chester on the Welsh border, the Spitfire's greatest attribute was that it was amazingly easy to fly. Its equally iconic adversary, Germany's Messerschmitt 109, was a thoroughbred also, but a forgiving aeroplane for a pilot it was not. As has often been said by those who flew them, 'Anyone can fly a Spitfire.'

The English weather was, however, anything but easy and as many Australians found, the difference between training over the open expanses of the outback and the close-knit fields of England was all the difference in the world. From horizon to horizon, Ken was presented with every conceivable permutation of the colour grey.

'By the time you'd taken off and bumped your undercarriage up, the only way to find your way back to the aerodrome was to do an immediate 180 degree turn and land again.'

Then there were new hazards such as the dozens of barrage balloons that floated above every English city (a protection against low-flying enemy aircraft) and the thick steel cables that tethered them to the ground. In bad weather, you had to know where you were, or you risked shearing off a wing.

After a couple of hours in a Miles Master trainer seated next to an insouciant ex Battle of Britain pilot, Ken was given his first flight in a Spitfire, albeit a fairly clapped-out example, a retired Mark I which had worn itself out a year before in the skies above Kent. There were no dual-control Spitfires, so your first flight in one was taken alone. 'Magnificent' was how Ken remembered it, eyes sparkling.

In November 1941, Ken was posted to an operational squadron, the well-established number 124, flying out of Biggin Hill, then the best known airfield in Britain. I suggested that the atmosphere in this RAF bastion must have been stuffy, but was quickly corrected. 'It was great,' Ken said, a multicultural melting pot: four Norwegians, four Czechs, a Pole, a Frenchman, a Dutchman, a New Zealander, a Canadian and a couple of Belgians. Ken was the only Australian. 'At one stage there were thirteen nationalities flying, including a chap from Mauritius.'

Starting operations at the beginning of winter, flying for 124 was fairly limited by the weather. During this time the RAF were restricting themselves to what were really only nuisance operations over occupied France, luring the Germans up for a fight or strafing their airfields with various combinations of bombers and fighters. The casualties were high, and the results limited at best. In six months, no fewer than ten of Ken's fellow pilots were killed on these types of operations, which were given fittingly ineffectual codenames such as Rodeo, Rhubarb and Circus.

But then, in February 1942, something very dramatic happened in the English Channel. Three big German warships, the *Scharnhorst*, *Gneisenau* and *Prinz Eugen*, had been docked in the French port of Brest, and regularly attacked from the air. At some stage, the British knew, they would need to return to Wilhelmshaven to be re-equipped and re-fitted to then go out and wreak havoc among the Atlantic convoys. Everyone expected them to take the long, safe route back home, around Ireland, across the top of Britain and down through the North Sea. Instead, they decided on a shortcut.

The weather was so dreadful that day that most fighter squadrons, including Ken's, had been stood down. But late on the morning of February 11, the pilots were assembled and told that 'something was up' in the Channel. Under cover of filthy weather, and escorted by a small fleet of destroyers, mine-sweepers, flakships and fighters brought in from as far as the Russian front, the three ships had decided to make a dash for it, up the English Channel, an incident the papers quickly coined the 'Channel Dash'. Incredibly, and to much subsequent scandal and inter-service recrimination, the ships nearly made it through undetected, only being sighted by chance just off Dover. But then, it was as Ken put it, 'On for young and old.'

The squadron was ordered to rendezvous with a formation of Fairey Swordfish torpedo bombers and escort them to their target, the big ships right at the centre of the convoy. The cloud was dark grey overcast with visibility down to 300 feet (90 metres). The squadron CO looked up into the murk and turned to Ken, the new boy.

'Right. You're my number two. Stay on my tail.'

Ken had undertaken a couple of bomber escorts into France, but had never seen anything like this. Then again nor had anyone else. What he did see, however, and for the first time, were lots of aeroplanes with black crosses on the wings.

It was chaotic. Visibility was so bad they never even saw the Swordfish and Ken immediately lost his CO as well.

'It was impossible to maintain any sort of formation at all. Aircraft [were] coming from everywhere,' he recalled. He got his first real taste of combat, in the form of a bullet in his engine head. It was all a melee of confusion, aircraft appearing and disappearing inside a great grey soup. Shaken, he made it back to base, only to be yelled at by his CO: 'I told you to stick to my bloody tail!' He didn't seem to care that he'd brought back a bullet in his engine.

In retrospect, Ken was probably grateful for the bad weather that day. With his lack of experience, separated from his formation and in the face of so many of the enemy, he would under almost any other circumstances have been an easy target.

At least Ken had the advantage of an excellent aircraft. Spare a thought for the crews of the Swordfish. Yet another in the pantheon of second-rate Allied aircraft, these slow, ungainly and truly antiquated bi-planes should have been retired long before the war, and had no chance whatever against such concentrated defences as they met that day. Not only did they never reach their target in this heroic, tragic engagement, but not a single Swordfish returned that day and a VC was won, posthumously.

Ken is a widower now, but it seemed life has been kind to him nonetheless and his mind was sharp and clear. I was keen to know if the mythical image of the cool and collected fighter pilot stacked up against reality.

'Often it was just a shambles,' he told me.

Flying in formation of 'finger four', the mutually dependent system whereby each aircraft looked after the other ones' tail was one thing; being attacked by German fighters was another. When that happened, the system tended to break down somewhat. In seconds, the formation was gone and it was simply a matter of wheeling the aeroplane around the sky and shooting at anything that passed in front of you (hopefully the enemy) or being shot at yourself. Sometimes you didn't even know you were being attacked. Then, seconds later, you'd look around and the sky was suddenly empty. The 'dogfight' was it seems, a term that largely expired with the First World War. A more appropriate term for fighter engagements of the second was usually 'melee'.

On one occasion, Ken's squadron was visited by the king, and Ken handed me an old cutting to prove it.

'What did he say to you?' I asked.

Nothing profound, just mumblings about 'good luck' and 'safe return', etc. But the effect on the men's morale was astonishing.

'After meeting the king, you'd go out quite happily and die for king and country,' Ken told me. 'Incredible, isn't it?' he added, slightly astonished. Then he smiled. 'I'm not sure if the present royal family would have the same effect.'

Peter and I quizzed him about what it was actually like flying a Spitfire on a patrol over German-occupied France. 'What did you do when attacked?' I asked.

Ken went into the role of instructor: 'Always turn into the attack. Never try and outrun or out-dive a Messerschmitt in a Spitfire – your advantage is manoeuvrability. When he tries to follow you into the turn, he'll either overshoot or black out.'

You had to be constantly on the alert, one hand on the throttle, the other on the control stick. Constantly looking around, sweeping every possible corner of the sky from inside your cramped little cockpit.

'That's why we had those silk scarves. It looks like a bit of an act, but it wasn't,' Ken explained. In the forties, men wore shirts with starched, detachable collars that would chafe the neck. In life or death situations neck rash was the last thing you needed to worry about. The scarves not only eased the problem, but added a touch of élan to the fighter pilot image as well.

'What about formation flying?' asked Peter.

'If you're under attack, forget it. You didn't fly in any pansy formation any more, you broke up. You're on your own and the fight is on.'

On one sweep into France, Ken was in a section of four, and three of them were shot down.

'I was the only one to make it back that day. Just luck.'

'Did you ever encounter the Abbeville Boys?' asked Peter,

referring to the nickname given to two famous German fighter units, JG (*Jagdgeschwader* meaning fighter squadron) 26 and JG 2, stationed around Abbeville in northern France. They were the only two German units to fly exclusively in the west for the entire war. They painted the noses and spinners of their aircraft yellow and were regarded as an elite unit, boasting such famous commanding officers as Adolf Galland.

While the Messerchmitts and Focke-Wulfs of the Abbeville Boys commanded a good deal of respect, you also had to watch out for your own side. This was a theme that was to recur again and again throughout my interviews with aircrew of all types and in all theatres. That is, no matter where you were or at what time of day or night, some American would probably be shooting at you. Towards the end of his European tour, Ken was escorting Douglas Bostons, an excellent American medium bomber flown by the RAF, and later the B-17 Flying Fortresses of the United States Army Air Force. The difference in approach between the British and the Americans says it all. With the British-operated Bostons, Ken would be just a couple of wings' lengths away, but when flying with the Americans, the Spitfires would quietly fan out to a mile or more once over the English Channel. If you were within range of the Fortresses'.5-inch guns (and the Fortress was bristling with them), you could expect to be fired at by trigger-happy gunners whose talent at aircraft recognition left a great deal to be desired.

Once, escorting B-17s over France, a lone Focke-Wulf 190, high above the bombers, swooped down on the formation, firing as he went. Not one of the escorting Spitfires moved. Instead, in his headphones, Ken heard the Spitfire pilots chuckle, then, amazingly, cheer the German on with a 'Go get 'em!' It's a wonderfully black story. Ken still laughs at it today, although somewhat guiltily.

'That was just how we felt,' he admitted. 'It was bloody terrible for a while there.'

Often, the Americans' penchant for self-aggrandisement left a cold taste in the palate of the British and Commonwealth pilots as well. On the first raid by the Americans Ken escorted, the target was Brest, just across the Channel.

'They dropped their bombs right on the coastline then came back and were all awarded DFCs!' he said with a hint of bitterness, but was quick to acknowledge the dreadful casualties the Americans subsequently sustained over Germany.

In early 1943, Ken came home and joined number 452 Squadron about a month after it had settled into its new base in Darwin. This was a wholly Australian unit originally formed in England, in fact, the first RAAF squadron in Fighter Command. To meet the Japanese threat, however, it was brought home, together with number 457 and an RAF squadron, 54, in June 1942 to form a new larger unit, Number 1 Fighter Wing. Its job: to repulse the Japanese air attacks on the north coast of Australia. Ken remembered mixed feelings about his transfer back home. Europe, it was felt, was where the important work of winning the war was really happening, and morale at his old squadron was, despite the casualties, sky-high. But come home he was ordered, and come home he did, to the most dramatic day of his life.

The wing leader of this all-new, all-Spitfire unit was none other than Group Captain Clive Robertson Caldwell, Australia's number one fighter ace and already a legend. Caldwell was truly one out of the box. Born in Sydney, he learned to fly before the war, and at twenty-nine was officially three years too old to be trained as a pilot, so he forged his birth certificate to get in.

Later, in the Western Desert, flying P-40 Tomahawks, he devised his own brand of deflection shooting by firing at the ground shadows of the low-flying aircraft in front of him. He quickly learned how to shoot down real aeroplanes. Lots of them. On one occasion, in December 1941, he tore straight up and into a formation of Junkers 87 Stukas, clipping the wings of several, and shooting down five in about a minute and a half. On his way back from sorties, he acquired a taste for shooting up any ground target that looked like an enemy and usually came home with his ammunition boxes empty.

By the time he was posted to Darwin, Caldwell had already accounted for twenty of the astonishing total of twenty-eight enemy aircraft he would eventually destroy and had acquired the nickname Killer, which he detested, but which for obvious reasons, stuck.

On 2 May 1943, Caldwell got to meet a new enemy for the first time. Flying with him that day was another pilot, Ken Fox, also on his first trip in the Pacific. It was an active time up north, with the Japanese air force although passed its zenith, still a formidable force.

Prior to Ken's arrival, 452 had had some awful luck, losing its commanding officer, Ray Thorold-Smith, on March 15, killed in an earlier action over Darwin. His replacement was inexperienced on Spitfires and so this day Caldwell, as the overall wing leader delegated him as his number 2 wingman to gain some valuable experience. However, engine trouble forced the new CO to drop out of formation and return to base at Strauss. Ken was called into the now vacant position as Caldwell's number 2.

High over the Arafura Sea, about 50 miles off Darwin, the wing had scrambled to intercept a formation of eighteen bombers and thirty fighters on their way back from a high-level attack on Darwin. The first two attacks were made from positions of height, but by the third they were mixing it with the Japanese Zeros on their own terms and it was not a good idea. The Spitfire, brilliant in its conceived role as a short range defensive fighter over England, was often found to be wanting in the thick tropical skies of northern Australia. It tended to overheat, and mechanical failures increased dramatically. And although it could out climb and outrun a Zero, it was no longer the most manoeuvrable aeroplane in the sky.

Two Zeros now attacked Caldwell's Spitfire. Ken, as his wingman, moved in and fired at one of them. Then he himself came under attack as the Zero turned. At this point he made a fatal mistake. This was not Europe, and these were not Messerschmitt 109s, and the Spitfire couldn't outturn the very light, very nimble Mitsubishi Zero.

'I used the wrong tactics,' he admitted. 'I should have half-rolled away and joined the fight later.' However, in doing so, he had diverted the enemy's attention away from Caldwell. I saved his bloody life, actually, which he was very grateful for!'

Ken knew he had been hit, but didn't know where. Then the whole aircraft began to shudder like a stalling car and the temperature gauge soared. He knew then what had happened. The glycol engine coolant had been hit and was now smoking inside the cockpit. Then the engine stopped, and the propeller windmilled to a halt.

He remembered what he'd been told about how to get out of a doomed Spitfire: undo the safety harness, roll and just drop out. The forward thrust of the prop will carry the aircraft away and you'll be free to deploy your 'chute. All very well, provided the propeller is still turning, but with the engine seized the aircraft was simply a dead weight with no forward momentum, falling at the same rate as its pilot towards the surface of the ocean.

'I had to push the aircraft off me,' he recalled. In mid-air, he bumped his way along the fuselage to the cowling and literally pushed himself off one of the now motionless propeller blades. Man and machine at last parted ways. Free, Ken now pulled his ripcord and watched his aircraft fall into the sea below.

I have to pause for a moment to consider this truly surreal scene: in mid-air, miles out to sea, an air battle raging above, watching the aircraft you have just left hit the water, knowing you would soon be floating in it yourself. Peter and I are silent as Ken tells us his story in a detached, strangely serene voice, as if describing the most beautiful scene he had ever witnessed. Perhaps it was.

'You don't notice the rate of descent, you're just sort of floating around. But the last 50 feet or so rushed up towards you.'

'What was the water like?' I asked him.

'Warm. Fortunately.'

There was no seat as such in a Spitfire. The pilot instead sat in a scoop that in flight was filled up with his parachute pack and inflatable dinghy. Once in the water in his Mae West inflatable life jacket, Ken turned the cock on a little bottle of carbon dioxide and the one-man inflatable boat opened up. He was now in the water, alone, and the silence was deafening.

It was about 11 am, and Ken was in for a long wait. At the time, he had no idea how long. All he could do was to sit and watch the hours pass by and hope.

At one stage, he saw a fin go close by. As warm as the water was, his blood ran cold. Then he saw it joined by another, then a third. Then, a flood of relief. They were porpoises. He strained his ears for the sound of an engine.

'I started paddling, but gave that up very quickly.'

Ken knew he was being looked for. Number 2 Squadron operated Hudsons, which he could see doing large circuits around him. At one stage, one was heading straight towards him but turned 90 degrees away about a mile off. Ken had done plenty of air–sea rescue flying himself in England and knew just how hard it was to spot a lone man in the water even when nearly on top of him. Eventually, however, one went right overhead and dropped a smoke marker nearby.

It was just on dusk when he was rescued, seven hours after being shot down.

'It's a long time when you don't know you're going to be picked up,' he said.

A week later, Ken was back flying and continued to do so until the completion of his second tour. He then did a stint with transport aircraft and finally enjoyed a long post-war career as an airline pilot.

Before leaving, Ken drew our attention to a big aviation art painting. The scene is of a Spitfire Mark VIII in Australian livery, with a parachute floating down below while an air battle with Japanese Zeros rages around. Ken points to the small figure in the 'chute.

'That's me,' he said. 'This is my Spit.' It's the very scene of his most dramatic day, lovingly depicted by a dedicated aviation artist, and a source of immense pride for Ken.

'What do you think?' he asked.

In truth, I've never been much of a fan of these types of things, having always found them rather gaudy.

'Wonderful, Ken. Just wonderful,' I replied.

18

John McCredie and Lewis Hall

Pilots, brothers-in-law

The flak was heavy enough for you to wonder if you were wise to be doing this sort of thing.

We never felt it was hopeless or that they were going to win.

I stood outside a very smart inner-suburban house, about to conduct my first double-header interview with two blokes who had flown against the Japanese. I was thrilled.

John McCredie and Lewis Hall were brothers-in-law and were delighted to talk, but not half as delighted as I was to hear them. It had proved hard to track down men who had served in the Pacific, and I was lucky to catch Lewis as he was visiting from interstate. I was excited to learn that he had started operational flying in January 1942, in the very trough of Australia's fortunes against the seemingly invincible Japanese tide running from the north. John, intriguingly, had flown in India.

One morning in Darwin in February 1942, Lewis Hall was going down the steps to the shower wrapped in nothing but a towel. He was tired, having just brought his 13 Squadron

Hudson back from Timor with a load of exhausted evacuees; having avoided capture by the Japanese in the nick of time.

Outside, the noise of aeroplane engines could be heard circling the harbour. Nothing too unusual, thought Lewis, glad that some of his fellow pilots were getting in a bit of low level practice. Then he heard, and felt, a massive blast from the direction of the harbour and, as he puts it, 'things rapidly changed'. He learned later that it was the explosives-laden merchant ship *Neptuna* blowing up 5 miles away in Darwin Harbour, taking forty-five crew with her and raining white hot pieces of metal over the town.

It was the morning of 19 February 1942, and the aircraft he had heard were Japanese conducting their first, and by far their biggest raid on Australian soil. Many were the same pilots who had taken part in the attack on Pearl Harbor six weeks earlier. As on that day they had taken off from aircraft carriers several hundred miles away. Some pilots were flying so low that in between strafing runs over the town, they could be clearly seen in their cockpits waving to people on the ground.

Lewis had already been posted to England and had just settled into his cabin on the boat, when 'some clever person thought there might be a chance of Japan coming into the war' and he was taken off it again. Although saved from the very gloomy prospect of flying in England in late 1941 (where, as he put it, 'my expectations would not have been very great'), he was soon to find himself not in the least bit out of harm's way.

In January 1942, Lewis arrived by plane on the island of Ambon to Australia's north in the Dutch East Indies, just in time to be evacuated.

'We were lifted out by flying boat in the morning, and the Japanese landed that same afternoon.'

Back in Darwin, he found himself helping others avoid a

similar fate of death or capture in the face of the relentless Japanese advance into the south-west Pacific.

On February 18, his was one of six aircraft sent to Kupang in Dutch-controlled Timor to evacuate ground staff. The Japanese arrival was imminent, so they were told they would be taking off at first light. Then, realising the enemy was even more 'imminent' than previously thought, the flight time was brought forward to 2.30 am. In the middle of a warm tropical night, twenty-six people packed into Lewis's cramped Lockheed Hudson bomber designed for a crew of four and took off for Darwin, 517 miles (830 kilometres) away.

'[There was] no chance of falling over, because they were all packed in like sardines,' he said.

The decision to go early saved them all. At first light, the Japanese landed at Kupang. Lewis had slipped the noose again.

A few hours later, early on the 19th, all six aircraft arrived safely back in Darwin. Lewis was debriefed, had some breakfast and then went to have a shower, just in time to witness the aircraft with big red circles appear over the town.

From a slit trench, still not properly dressed from his attempted ablutions, he counted three separate Japanese dive-bombers descending on three separate hangars.

They know exactly what they're going for, thought Lewis and watched the bombs actually leave the aircraft.

Overall though, he thought the Australians hadn't got off too badly as many of the fighters on the ground escaped damage in that first attack. After making himself a little more decent, Lewis went over to the mess to join a group of rather shaky looking officers standing around outside. Then someone rode up on a bike. 'They're coming over again!' Lewis looked up and saw two perfectly formed high-level flights of twenty-seven Japanese bombers, which seemed to converge directly over the airfield. This second raid by land-based medium bombers occurred just before midday and pattern-bombed the aerodrome. Even so, Lewis still reckoned it could have been much worse.

'The papers said the airfield was destroyed. [Yet] I can remember we ate in the mess that same night.' I wonder what the dinner conversation was like that night.

The Japanese only mounted one really heavy raid on Darwin, but continued to visit it on a daily basis for some time. Several weeks after that attack, a number of Zeros got into the habit of appearing over the end of the runway at Darwin aerodrome every afternoon and shooting up anything they saw, roaring along low at about 100 feet.

'There wasn't much opposition,' said Lewis, 'so these blokes were having the time of their lives.'

Then one day an army convoy appeared, fresh from the Middle East, sent straight from Adelaide without leave as soon as they got off the boat. At the intersection of the two runways, a Bofors anti-aircraft gun was set up and dug in overnight. Fresh from a couple of years' experience shooting down Stukas, the two-man gun crew were no mugs.

The next day, they waited patiently for the Japanese to arrive. As usual, three Zeros appeared and the gunner calmly fired the big gun, distinctive with its deep *woomph-woomph-woomph*. One aircraft went straight into the ground. Then another, and then the third.

'The Japs kept it up for about three days and after that, we never saw another one.'

Lewis stayed in Darwin until June, when 13 Squadron was brought south to re-equip on Beaufort bombers. These British-designed medium bombers were built under licence in Australia, at a time when it produced not so much as a bicycle on its own. Virtually overnight, from plans that arrived on microfilm, we began turning out highly complicated weapons of war like the twin-engined Beaufort. There's a famous, horrific piece of wartime news footage of two Beauforts in a display for the cameras over Jarvis Bay. The wing of one clipped and sheared off the tail of the other. No-one from either crew survived the subsequent crash. I had always thought them to be a bit of a lemon, but Lewis would have none of it. He flew over 1,000 hours in them, he reckoned, and never had a problem.

'I once flew in a tropical storm so severe it would have torn the wings off other aeroplanes,' he told me in a tone that left little to doubt.

It was in a Beaufort that Lewis had his real moment of glory or, as he would put it, his moment of near-glory, during one of the most important (and today largely forgotten) air engagements of the war in the Pacific: the very dramatic, very bloody Battle of the Bismarck Sea.

Lewis' brother-in-law, John wasn't pulled off the boat to England, but ended up fighting the Japanese anyway. About the time he was completing his training at Point Cook, Messrs Churchill and Roosevelt were meeting in Casablanca. Very, very low down on the agenda was a request by President Roosevelt for Britain to kick in a few more airmen to man some of the hundreds of aeroplanes the Americans were churning out of their factories and sending to the Far East to attack the Japanese in Burma. It was a conversation that probably lasted two minutes, but it decided the course of John's life for the next three years. First, though, he would have to survive training.

Flying in the crowded skies of wartime England was a very different experience to the open spaces of outback Australia. Instead of the flat open vastness and clear skies of their training areas, pilots now had to contend with the crowded patchwork of densely populated Britain. Everywhere they looked was another identical village, church steeple or neighbouring aerodrome. Many felt they had gone back to the drawing board. Concentrating hard on his instruments in a night landing, John's instructor suddenly grabbed the controls and pulled the Wellington around. Another aircraft, probably from the adjacent aerodrome, was coming in on John's beam. He'd completely missed seeing it and so nearly did the instructor. I ask him what was said.

'Something profane,' he told me.

On his first ever training flight in 1943, John delivered a Christmas message to the citizens of Paris in the form of leaflets assuring them their day of liberation was now a little closer. Unfortunately, the very much clapped-out Wellington 1Cs they were flying, barely capable of making 10,000 feet at the best of times, and now weighed down with thousands of paper leaflets and ice forming on wings and carburettors, refused to budge above a pitiful 8,000 feet in the freezing December sky. And then there was a problem with the navigator.

Officially a training flight, it was supposed to be an easy run. Paris, an open city, was left undefended and the route there and back was chosen to avoid the flak. The run-in was perfect and they reached their dropping zone 20 miles from the city and began tipping bundles of leaflets out of the aircraft to be carried by the wind to fill Parisian hearts and gutters alike. All they had to do now was make a quick exit across the quiet Normandy coast and home. The Germans, however, tended not to distinguish between Allied aircraft carrying bombs and leaflets and when John felt 'a bit of a pitter-patter of the flak on the fuselage', he knew something was not quite right.

The navigator was a lovely chap, but his inexperience had taken them off course and over the heavily defended town of Lisieux. Everything started coming up at them.

'It was only two holes, but they sounded like a lot more.'

They got through it, and were over the English Channel into safety. The navigator set a course for home. A few minutes later, they were over their own coast, and then suddenly they were caught in a web of searchlights. Yet another dodgy route had taken them directly over the Royal Naval home base of Portsmouth, one of the most heavily defended targets in Britain, and as dangerous for friend and foe alike. After the second panic had subsided, John's rear-gunner came in over the intercom in a timid voice.

'Can I come out now, Skipper?'

Lewis, meanwhile, chuckled at this, then pitched in with his own story about taking off at 2 am for a regular first light appearance in New Guinea.

'It was so cold I had to take a blanket off the bed,' he remembered.

I loved this image: flying to war with a blanket over your knees.

The Beaufort had no heating and, amazingly, no oxygen even at heights of up to 20,000 feet (6,000 metres). Surely this was highly dangerous I asked, but Lewis assured me that's how it was done. There was a limit, however, to just how much oxygen the brain can be deprived of, and by 1945, if he ventured even to 14,000 feet without oxygen, he was violently ill.

When John arrived at his Operational Training Unit, whatever glamour there had seemed to be in flying bombers over Germany had been evaporated by the blowtorch of statistical reality. Survival, said John, was 'not the most likely of prospects'. But, unbeknown to him, he had already been earmarked to pack his things and head to Blackpool, then via ship to Bombay. I imagined it to be an exotic Far East journey, but the reality was somewhat starker. John was crammed onto a 'mess deck', directly under the two curve-shaped upper decks with overflowing latrines positioned at either end. This, combined with a very rough Mediterranean crossing, gave the word 'mess' a whole new meaning.

'One was glad to be at the end of it,' he said.

Feeling rather ludicrous in his enormous government-issue 'Bombay Bloomer' shorts, he was posted to number 355 Squadron, flying the second most famous American bomber of the war, the Consolidated B-24 Liberator. His job was to fly it from a place called Salbani in India's east, near present-day Bangladesh but then known far more romantically as West Bengal. In late 1943, 355 began bombing Japanese targets behind the battle area in Burma and Thailand: airfields, harbour installations and also the infamous Thai–Burma railway. He also carried out air–sea rescue ops, criss-crossing endless stretches of ocean for hours at a time, dull but necessary work, especially if you happened to be the one bobbing up and down on the ocean in a life jacket. But as far as flying was concerned, it was 'like mowing a lawn in the air', said John.

'We had an utter drongo as a CO,' he told me in a way that suggested he was winding up to something important. In such a remote theatre of war as India, getting fuel to the big, thirsty Liberators was a constant supply headache, and all RAF squadrons were under pressure to reduce consumption.

Some 355 Squadron pilots had even landed at forward bases when their Liberator's glass tube-type fuel gauges showed empty, and had been berated for it. 'The fuel gauges are unreliable!' was the angry response from the flight commander and John's skipper, Joe Morphett, who instructed his pilots to henceforth fly 'on the step'. This was a way of edging back the throttles to reduce power – akin to easing one's foot off the accelerator on the highway to achieve the same end in a car. In an aeroplane, however, a reduction in power usually means a reduction in height, and one clear night on the way home from bombing Mandalay, John's skipper almost paid for his efforts to reduce the petrol bill with his life.

As second pilot, John sat beside Joe as the Liberator made its way home from Burma, when suddenly ahead of them loomed an enormous black shape, blacker even than the black tropical night which surrounded it.

'Jesus Christ!' said Joe, 'we're going to hit a mountain!' Mount Victoria was 10,000 feet high, and flying 'on the step' had cost him the height he needed to get over it. What happened next sealed the aircraft's fate. To quickly gain height, Joe pushed the throttles forward through an emergency 'gate' of copper wire, increasing boost from 48 pounds to 60 in a surge of power to the engines. They climbed fast and cleared the mountain, but the drain on the fuel was irreversible, and fatal.

Coming in to the Indian mainland over the Bay of Bengal, and only 20 miles from base, the first engine conked out over the Indian coastline. John switched on an emergency fuel pump and it came back to life. 'Only a blockage,' he thought. But he was wrong. Immediately, an agitated flight engineer appeared.

'The fuel gauges are empty, Skip!'

The same fuel gauges the skipper had earlier deemed 'unreliable'.

'Jesus Christ!' exploded the skipper again, just as all four engines began to die.

There was no choice for the crew but to bail out while the pilot held the spluttering Liberator as steady as he could. The flight engineer had to be pushed out of the bomb bay, and broke his leg in the process. John was last out, bar the pilot, who would have to take his chances in the crash-landing.

'We all landed 50 yards apart,' said John. Half a mile away from them, the Liberator went down. With no fuel left in the tanks there was, luckily, nothing to burn, so the chances of Joe surviving the crash were relatively good, provided they could get to him.

The men made their way in the dark to a small village, looking very out of place in their flying kit. There they used desperate hand signals to ask the bewildered inhabitants for a guide to take them to the crash site.

At four in the morning, they made it to the downed machine. The fuselage, they saw, was largely in one piece and Joe was alive, sitting dazed under a mango tree. His scalp was severely lacerated, and later a metal stake had to be removed from his right thigh and another from his left calf. He suffered an agonising day being pulled along in a bullock cart while his crew trudged beside him. Late in the afternoon, they reached a town where he was picked up by an ambulance and hospitalised.

John put in a report of the accident, but the essential reason for the crash was ignored. Joe was awarded a bar to his DFC and his citation stated simply that the engines had failed, and that he held the aircraft straight and level in order to assure the safety of his crew, at risk to his own life.

'It's obvious to anyone that four engines don't fail for any other reason than running out of fuel,' said John. For all that, Joe was still a hero, according to him. 'A hero, in my opinion, was one who put themselves after the lives of other people. This is certainly what Joe Morphett did, and I tell his story as an example of true heroism.'

Lewis was also awarded the DFC but was a bit vague as to why.

By the beginning of 1943, the Japanese had been bloodied but not defeated in New Guinea and decided to make one last big effort to reinforce and retake areas lost along its northern coast, then regroup and take the rest of the island. Radio interceptions determined that a large convoy was planning to steam out of their New Britain base of Rabaul to the stronghold of Lae.

Convoys had been attacked before, but piecemeal, and the bulk of troops and reinforcements had made it ashore to make life hell for the Australian soldiers fighting in the jungles and mountains of New Guinea. As recently as January, one such convoy had made it through with relative ease. The new head of American air power in Australia, General George C. Kenny and Australia's Group Captain William 'Bull' Garing determined that the next one would not.

Garing was one of those figures made for command in wartime. He was short, stocky, had nothing that bore much resemblance to a neck, his manner was blunt and his nickname entirely deserved. He was tough and determined, and hated the Japanese.

One of those rare individuals lacking any sense of physical fear, Garing had already earned a DFC in Europe, piloting Sunderland flying-boats with number 10 Squadron when he single-handedly broke up an attack on a ship by five Junkers 88s. Upon his return to Australia in mid-1941, he was convinced war with Japan was inevitable and helped organise the air defence system of northern Australia. He lived well into his nineties, dying in 2004.

Later, he convinced General Kenny that the only way to attack a convoy successfully was by large scale coordinated, multi-pronged attacks from many angles by different aircraft, and went about developing the means to do it. The Bismarck Sea would be his magnum opus.

Lewis Hall, the man who sat opposite me enjoying some fine cake baked by his sister, Allison, had been away from New Guinea, as far away in fact as Nowra in New South Wales, acquainting himself with the fine art of dropping a torpedo from an aeroplane. But by March 1943, he was back in the tropics, with number 100 Squadron at its base at Number 1 Strip, Milne Bay on the island's eastern tip, otherwise known as Gurney Field.

This strip of mud bulldozed out of the jungle the previous year was little more than a quagmire of black overlaid with perforated steel mesh. Even so, during the Battle of Milne Bay in August 1942, the Japanese tried desperately to take it as a base from which to attack Port Moresby. The fighting had been so close that the former footballer and famous Spitfire ace Keith 'Blue' Truscott and his 76 Squadron Kittyhawks took off and began strafing the Japanese in the surrounding jungle even before their wheels were retracted.

Intelligence knew a convoy was coming, and a big one. Its eight merchant ships, eight escorting destroyers and several smaller ships had left Rabaul on 28 February, headed for Lae on the east coast of New Guinea to reinforce their undersupplied army. But to intercept them at the precise moment when maximum strength could be brought to bear, their exact location had to be determined, and this was proving difficult.

The Americans had spotted them, then lost them again, and continual rain storms had, for a few days, thrown a cloak over their presence altogether. On 2 March, they were seen again and a high level attack was made by American B-17s. A Cairns-based 11 Squadron Catalina flying boat had been shadowing the convoy earlier in the night, and was told to continue to do so until it could guide the Beauforts in at first light. For a coordinated attack to proceed the next day, their exact location needed to be known.

Someone had forgotten to wake Lewis Hall, and he wasn't happy about it. During the early hours of 3 March, the rest of 100 Squadron had taken off with their torpedoes to find the Japanese convoy and attack it. Eventually someone noticed him, and shook him awake with an abrupt 'Get up!' He didn't need further encouragement.

The torpedo was actually too large for the Beaufort's bomb bay and so, in the true spirit of wartime innovation was slung underneath the fuselage. Lewis had taken off at Nowra in such a configuration, but never from the small, muddy airstrip at Milne Bay and certainly never in darkness. 'I didn't think we were going to get off,' he said.

Earlier, the Catalina had dropped its four bombs, missed, decided that was enough, and headed back to Cairns. The Beauforts would have to find the convoy on their own.

Just before 5 am, Lewis wobbled into the air with his heavily laden Beaufort, facing filthy but intermittent weather. He had been told, as far as was known, the approximate position of the convoy – somewhere between the western tip of New Britain and the New Guinea coast in the Vitiaz Strait.

His CO, Squadron-Leader Smibert, was already up, dropping flares over the sea in the hope that other aircraft closer to the water would be able to make out the vessels' silhouettes.

'I was in rain and cloud nearly all the way,' Lewis remembered.

Then he caught sight of his CO's flare in the distant sky, and realised he was in an entirely different position. Another flare went down, this time a different colour. The weather had started to clear, but it was the signal to break off the attack and head back to base nonetheless. No-one was finding anything in this tropical gloom.

The first faint glimmers of a pink dawn began to edge out the blackness, 'Piccaninny Dawn we used to call it,' said Lewis. Having slept in and arrived late, he was in no mood to simply head home again, break-off flare or not. He thought to himself. I'll just go and have a look.

With the darkness behind him, Lewis swung the Beaufort

around and came down low to the water. And there, outlined against the first pink blushes of the day, he saw the unmistakeable outlines of ships.

'I could see every one of them, in three neat lines, all spread out and stationary,' he said.

Flying down the line of the assembled ships he thought to himself, all my birthdays have come at once, and selected the largest cargo ship he could find.

'I aimed to put the torpedo under the bridge of the ship and break it in half.'

He swung around into a turn, so low he needed to virtually leapfrog over the first line of vessels. It was a beautiful morning, calm and still. Then a small escort vessel opened up with a machine gun, and the eerie tranquillity was broken.

'Everything that was around the place opened up,' he said.

With a torpedo attack, it was essential to fly straight, steady and slow. Lewis ignored, as best he could, the fire coming up at him, kept one eye on the ship and another on the airspeed indicator, which to make his attack needed to read 150 knots, making him a very tempting target.

With the ship's hull looming in his windshield, Lewis hit the electric switch for the torpedo and heard a wire cable release its grip, but the torpedo didn't drop. Then he tried a manual release – and still it stuck fast. Disbelieving that he could have been given such luck only to have it snatched away was almost too much. All he could do was open up with the two front machine guns for a belated strafing attack before flying away. The rear-gunner called up, 'They're trying to get a shell over us.' One of the escorting naval vessels was attempting to fire over their heads to send up a wall of water in their path. Lewis, alone against the now alerted convoy with a torpedo that would not drop had no choice but to 'up and off'.

'It was a perfect opportunity but nothing came of it.'

Back at base, he taxied in and informed his armourers who

quickly placed a cradle under the belly and examined the weapon. One of the men put a screwdriver up to the release mechanism and the torpedo instantly fell into the cradle. A small stabilising pin, designed to stop the thing from rolling in flight, had been incorrectly machined. For Lewis, it would simply have to go down as the one that got away.

'We were all pretty dejected,' he remembered. The CO came up and asked why the long faces. They told him, and he offered his condolences. 'A jolly good try,' he said cheerily. It was little consolation.

But, as he said, 'I was unlucky and I was lucky.' Although he missed the ship, he was able to report the exact location of the convoy, and a few hours later, roughly 100 aircraft assembled over Cape Ward Hunt on New Guinea's north eastern shoreline and proceeded to tear it to pieces.

At around 10 am, the 30 Squadron Beaufighters went in, armed to the teeth with 4 cannon in the nose and .5-inch machine guns in the wings. The Japanese thought they were torpedo planes and made the mistake of turning their ships head-on to present less of a target. The Beaufighter pilots couldn't believe their luck. Roaring in at mast-height, they raked the ships from stem to stern. Cargo, decks, gun platforms and even superstructures were splintered, the officers on the bridge instantly decapitated.

Then the A-20 Havocs arrived, skip bombing from zero feet and tearing out the hulls, and the Americans attacked from high above. The Japanese put up fighter cover, but they were kept busy by the American P-38 Lightnings above. It was a massacre. All eight cargo ships were sent to the bottom, as well as four of the eight destroyers. Out of the nearly 7,000 Japanese troops desperately needed in New Guinea, a pitiful 800 made it ashore to Lae. Estimates vary, but over 3,000 Japanese soldiers and sailors are believed to have lost their lives.

Then, to make assurance doubly sure, orders went over the next few days to strafe the rafts and the lifeboats, crammed with the survivors of the initial carnage. Many pilots were nauseated at having to do it, but carried out this grim task nonetheless.

Bismarck Sea finished the Japanese as far as New Guinea was concerned. Generals Kenny and MacArthur were delighted, of course, despite exaggerating the extent of the victory and leaving the Australian participation out of their official reports. Even today, American histories of the engagement give the RAAF scant regard for their efforts.

19

Marcel Fakhry

Spitfire pilot

I'm so anti-war these days, it's just unreal. And I think most of us who have been through a war are.

With a name like Marcel Fakhry (pronounced 'fayk-ree'), you're almost obliged to be a little larger than life and Marcel didn't disappoint. He was a big man with a big personality and a round, rollicking voice to match. Meeting him at his country property just outside Melbourne, I kept thinking I was in the presence of a well-known actor, or perhaps a barrister. He had a big laugh and seemed as amazed as I was that he had flown Spitfires in Africa, Malta and Italy during the Second World War.

The name, he told me, originated in Lebanon, 'way back in the dim dark ages', when his grandfather made the trip to Australia in 1888. 'Why he came out here I've no bloody idea.'

As with a number of the airmen I'd met, Marcel started off in the army, or more precisely the militia, and when war was declared in 1939 expected to be offered a commission in the regular AIF. He waited and waited, and nothing happened. So, almost in a fit of pique, he simply joined the RAAF, hoping to realise his long-cherished ambition of flying. His

CO in the militia was not happy, and an almost comical conversation ensued.

'You can't!' said the CO.

'Well I have!' said Marcel.

'Well you can't!'

'Why not?'

'Because you can't resign your commission in wartime!'

'Well, if you'd given me a commission in the AIF I wouldn't have had to, would I?'

'Well you still can't!'

And so it went on in circles for some time, until the CO became sick of the sight of him, decided in fact that he could and signed the necessary paperwork. So, in January 1941, Marcel swapped his officer's khaki for the dark blue of a regular airman. But it was worth it, because he became a Spitfire pilot.

Flying a Spitfire for the first time, even the old Mark I that Marcel trained in at his OTU in the north African desert, was, he said, a 'wonderful, wonderful, adrenalin-pumping experience. All that power!' He still seemed amazed by it.

Marcel arrived in North Africa by ship via training in Rhodesia – 'Now, sailing up the Red Sea on the *Queen Elizabeth* at 32 knots, *that* was fun!' – and, landed a job with number 92 Squadron, RAF. This squadron had only wanted one Australian pilot, so Marcel and two mates were told to go and decide among themselves. Someone produced a deck of cards.

'They drew nine of spades and eight of clubs. I drew eleven of diamonds. Goodbye fellas!' he recounted.

It all sounded very democratic. He was told to hitch a ride to Algiers on any army vehicle he could find, and get to a place called Ben Gardane, south of Tripoli. It took him two days to find it.

Marcel joined 92 at the end of 1942 just after the Battle of

El Alamein, on a makeshift aerodrome that kept moving as the advancing Eighth Army pushed the Germans westwards along Egypt's Mediterranean coast. Everyone slept in tents, it was hot, there was little water and no facilities of any kind, and little distinction between officers and sergeants.

'We all ate in the same mess. That would never have happened in England. The desert air force was not very big on discipline,' he tells me. He's not referring to the fighting spirit, but the spit and polish, the saluting and the highly structured, largely class-based regimens that characterised life in the RAF in England.

The situation was often so fluid that they would take off from one spot in the morning and be told to land at their new location later that day.

In November 1942 alone, Marcel moved no less than five times from one patch of the Egyptian desert to another, places with names such as Sidi Heneish, M'sus, El Nogra or simply 'Landing Ground 21'.

Marcel arrived thinking he knew just about all there was to know about flying a Spitfire. 'I knew nothing! Just a bloody novice!' he soon realised.

Straightaway the skipper took him aloft to see whether the new boy could pass the basics. Ordered to stay as much as he could on his tail, Marcel started to realise it wasn't as straightforward as he had thought. The skipper was a highly experienced veteran and did everything humanly possible to shake him. Marcel did as best he could. Then the order came, 'OK, Red Two, back home.' Back on the ground he wasn't certain how he'd gone, and he'd even made a rotten landing.

'Right,' said the CO perfunctorily and to Marcel's amazement, 'first op tomorrow morning.'

Marcel was one of those pilots who loved the flying but hated the fighting. I asked him to tell me what it was like flying into combat in a Spitfire. Your left hand was permanently on the throttle, he told me, your right on the stick. You made constant adjustments in speed and height, while at the same time, trying to see where you were, where you were heading and where everyone else was, friends and enemy.

In the beginning, he was number two to a more experienced pilot and would weave in, around and slightly behind him to protect his tail from attack. Marcel initially found over-correction a problem.

'If you weren't careful, you'd suddenly find yourself leading when you were supposed to be following.'

A dogfight would start when one group of aircraft spotted another and would turn in to face them. In theory, you were supposed to be looking after your number one but in a few seconds the system broke down.

'You would start weaving and dodging and darting, and doing all kinds of strange things,' Marcel said. Perhaps an enemy would cross over your sights and you'd get a shot at him, but more times not. They sound more like sudden, all-in brawls than any kind of strategic encounter and I asked him whether it was possible to think clearly when engaging the enemy. He assured me you could.

As the desert campaign began to dry up, 92 Squadron turned its activities toward the impending campaigns in Sicily and Italy, but not before a stint in Malta. Malta occupies a unique place in history as being the only country ever to be awarded a medal – the George Cross. In 1941 and 1942, this tiny place earned the distinction as 'the most bombed island on earth', when the Germans tried to eliminate it once and for all as a staging point for submarine and bombing attacks on their supply routes into Africa. This thorn in the Germans' side was bombed for over 150 consecutive days and lost 1,500 of its civilians and thousands of buildings.

An English pilot who was stationed on Malta once told me that on still mornings, he could actually hear the German bombers warming up their engines in the pre-dawn on their airfields 58 miles across the water in Sicily before taking off to attack. After the king awarded the medal to its battered, diseased and half-starved population, the decoration was ceremonially taken from village to village to be inspected by all. People who were young children at the time never forgot the occasion.

Marcel was stationed in Luga, the airfield that had been all but obliterated a few months before.

'Whatever you do,' he was told, 'don't fly over the harbour.'

If Malta was the most bombed place on earth, Valletta Harbour was the most defended, and its gunners would open up at any aircraft of any nationality that came anywhere near it. An astonishing 455 German aircraft (and quite a few Allied) fell to the gunners of Malta and every pilot made a point of giving them a very wide berth as they came back and forth from their targets in Sicily.

At that point in the war the German air force had been largely suppressed in the Mediterranean. With appearances by German fighters becoming more infrequent, 92 began to transfer to strafing and dive bombing roles. It was very crude, and not at all what the Spitfire was designed for but by slinging a couple of 250-pound bombs under the wings it became an extremely effective weapon: a dive bomber, then, once the bombs were released, a fighter.

'You'd get over the target with your left wing and just drop straight down,' Marcel said.

For this purpose they'd been issued with a new type of Spitfire, or rather a new type of an old Spitfire. By 'clipping' 2 feet off each wingtip the aircraft became very manoeuvrable at low-level, although less efficient higher up.

'You could spin them on a threepenny bit but above 15,000 feet they'd fall out of the sky.'

Once again, Marcel followed the Eighth Army on its advance, this time north on its slow, tortuous climb through the mud and mountains of the Italian peninsula, bombing and strafing troops, flak concentrations and anything that moved that looked suspicious.

'The firing button had three positions: top for machine-guns, bottom for cannon and what we called middle for diddle – the whole bloody lot!'

It was in Italy that Marcel was shot down not once, but an amazing three times, and twice in two days. He still marvelled at his survival and even today is a little angry at the German gunners.

'Twice in two days! Bloody unreal! I was called Flak Fakhry on the squadron. The German gunners seemed to like me. Bastards! Ha!'

The first time he was hit by flak over the Anzio beachhead. This was the scene of the botched Anglo–American amphibious landing on the Italian coast in January 1944 that was doomed as much by squabbling between its commanders as it was by the Germans. Marcel came down for a rough landing in a paddock.

'I thought I was behind our lines but wasn't certain. As soon as I landed I hid behind a bloody bush!'

Then he heard an unmistakeable American drawl.

'Are you okay, British boy?'

They'd watched him come down, gave him a lift to the Anzio airstrip and he was back with the squadron the same day.

The next day, again at 15,000 feet over Anzio, he was hit a second time, again in the engine. Having seen enough of paddocks, Marcel thought he'd try and get down at the Anzio airstrip. With smoke pouring out of the aircraft, however, he presented a marvellous target for the 88-mm gun the Germans had ranged on the runway. Just as he came in, about to touch down, a shell landed on Marcel's port side. The aircraft swung around violently but remained intact as it came to a stop on the runway.

'So what did I do?' he asked rhetorically, 'I got out and hid in the shell hole, didn't I?'

The Germans kept up the shelling for an hour or so until he was rescued by an American jeep and put up for the night, rejoining his squadron the next day, but having to endure the nightly air raid on the airfield in-between.

But, as Marcel found out a couple of weeks later, luck, both bad and good, comes in threes.

On a shipping reconnaissance over an Italian harbour, flying number 2 to his CO, Marcel broke through a thick overcast base at 1,500 feet, not a wise move, as the German gunners would often find their range by firing on the cloud base and simply wait for an aircraft to pop out. He was hit, once again, right in the engine, by 88-mm anti-aircraft fire. In a now familiar scenario, smoke and glycol began to pour into the cockpit, the oil pressure dropped, the engine temperature rose and 'everything else just went off the dial'.

He knew he had to bail out and was preparing to do so when 'a voice in my head said, *no, stay there, Marce. Put the bloody thing down.*'

Hitting the silk this close to the Germans would mean becoming a prisoner of war, so he headed south. Marcel didn't remember how far he got in his crippled Spitfire, as its engine began to seize, but he remembered his amazement, and frustration, at not being able to find anywhere to land. All he could see were hills. He had no engine and no power and was gliding close to the ground, about to bring it down at the point where it wanted to go when, still flying, he blacked out. He remembers nothing except waking up in an army casualty clearing station behind the lines.

The skipper who'd followed him down and seen the crash thought there was no hope for Marcel. He'd watched the Spitfire hit the ground, then skid along for 100 yards or so before hitting a tree. This sheared off one wing and flipped the aircraft upside down. It continued to skid until a second tree was struck, which turned the Spitfire right side up again. I asked how badly hurt he was.

'I had a broken bloody this and a broken bloody that and a God knows what else!'

Not surprisingly, Marcel was posted 'missing, believed killed', only to come back from the dead, rejoining his squadron with a hero's welcome after three weeks in hospital.

'You know,' he told me as I was about to leave, 'the whole game was ludicrous. You're fighting these Germans and Italians that obviously love flying as much as you do. Bloody good blokes – same as us – the type of blokes you'd like to make friends with, and there you are trying to kill each other. War is stupid. Stupid and sad.'

20

Trevor Trask

Bomber pilot

It wasn't like a car ride. Every trip was different from every other trip.

Having lost my tape recorder, I'd resorted a very old dictaphone with sticky tape around the bit where the batteries go and the 'play and record' button missing, operable only by sticking a biro into the slot, and holding it there to record my conversation with Trevor Trask, 514 Squadron Lancaster pilot.

After the break-up of his family Trevor's early life was spent at a boarding school. Although a prominent establishment, it doesn't sound like a pretty place. 'If you can survive that, you can survive anything'. It gave him a toughness which, he said, prepared him for life in the services.

With a pedigree that included a father having flown in the Australian Flying Corps in World War One, there was never any doubt he would join the air force. However, the taxation office, his employers at the time, had other ideas. Apparently, separating working citizens from their hard-earned cash was even then considered an essential 'Reserved Occupation' and his bosses refused to let him go. So, in the true spirit of the public service, one morning he just didn't turn up. Instead,

Trevor had joined number 31 Course at Bradfield Park Initial Training School, RAAF.

Did he possess any natural ability for flying? Absolutely not, he said adamantly. 'There was no logic whatsoever to the way they chose us, except if you went to a private school you had a better chance of being a pilot' – something to thank his nasty old private boarding school for after all.

We spent a lot of time talking about his training, both in Australia and England. Trevor remembered it as being nearly as dangerous as operations. Once, when waiting to catch a bus at Banff aerodrome in Scotland to join his OTU he stood with a group of fellow trainees to watch a Wellington take off along the long runway. Starting seemingly on the horizon, it took the entire length to get airborne, its outline rushing nearer before taking to the air.

'We all stood and watched. It got to about 500 feet, then just turned over on one wing and crashed. Five people killed. As easy as that'.

Later, hurtling in a similar fashion down the runway himself in a Wellington on his first ever night circuit and landing flight, Trevor had reached flying speed when one of his tyres burst. Instinctively, he pulled the stick back and they were airborne. 'However,' as he put it, 'my main aim in life was to be on the ground.' Landing a large aircraft like the Wellington with a burst tyre was a virtual impossibility. In an impressive feat of memory, he remembers the ensuing conversation with the tower.

'Hello Bluebottle, this is Rasher-Zebra. I've just blown a tyre on take-off!' he called up to the tower in an excited voice.

'Stand by, Rasher-Zebra, stand by,' came the cool calm tones of the 'little girl on the radio'. He stood by, and did a couple of circuits until the voice of the CO came on. He was ordered to attempt a belly landing, but any of the crew who wished to bail out could do so. There was a deathly silence until Bill, the rear gunner said dryly, 'It's fuckin' dark down there, I think I'll stay with you', and all of them followed suit. Without the usual drag of the lowered wheels, Trevor's first approach overshot, but on the second he eased it down onto the ground and 'we just slid along' to a stop. Rather proudly, he shows me a letter from a senior officer praising him for his careful handling of the aircraft and the minimal damage caused, enabling it to soon be airworthy again.

Apart from his training, we discuss many things: his stint as an instructor after completing his tour and his preparations to become part of 'Tiger Force' – the proposed RAF plan to finish off the Japanese, rendered unnecessary by the dropping of the atomic bombs and Japan's subsequent surrender.

Finally, I open his log book, point to his first trip as the obligatory 'second dickie' pilot with an experienced crew and ask him to tell me about it.

'Yes, I remember it,' he tells me. 'I had to stand all the way there, and all the way back. I was exhausted.' There were no spare seats in a Lancaster for an extra bod and it was an uncomfortable ride. Trevor also remembers the briefing that night.

' "Well gentlemen, tonight is the night we visit Russelsheim: the Opel manufacturing works", he mimics the clipped tones of his English CO. "The Opel manufacturing works make Flying Bombs. Flying Bombs can't fly without wings!".' It's a memory that makes Trevor chuckle just a little.

This first attack on Russelsheim, near Frankfurt, on 12 August 1944, was not a success. Twenty out of the 297 aircraft despatched were lost, and the factory was barely damaged. It was not one of the air forces finest moments.

'We arrived at the station on the Thursday. On the Saturday four of us flew our first trip as second pilots. By the Sunday, I was the only one of them left alive.'

Trevor had joined number 514 Squadron based at Waterbeach, a few miles out of Cambridge, but on this first trip, his aircraft landed at an emergency strip at Woodbridge because of hydraulic troubles. This, after becoming disorientated and flying on the reciprocal (or reverse) compass bearing over the North Sea in the wrong direction. He was the one who realised what was happening and got the message back to the navigator. 'Everyone was just exhausted,' he remembered. It was not an auspicious debut.

We moved on from target to target: his first trip as captain of his own crew, a big raid on a German night fighter airfield at St Trond, in Belgium, then Kiel where, in a co-ordinated attack, the Halifaxes came in low to drop mines to catch the ships as they fled their anchorages to be bombed by the Lancasters high above.

His course home that night took him over the northern German island of Sylt. He remembered watching the gunners on the ground emerge from their bunkers and scatter like ants in the still-blazing lights of their barracks.

His account of his life on ops is candid and extremely interesting, revealing such things as the strain of operational flying on some of his own crew. 'My navigator went ga-ga', he told me somewhat matter-of-factly. I asked him to elaborate but he simply said that the fellow 'went off his rocker and was taken away'.

Then, one day when on leave after completing their first twelve trips, his rear gunner casually announced that he wouldn't be flying with them any more. Slightly dumfounded, Trevor asked, 'How are you going to arrange that?' How he arranged it was by deliberately contracting venereal disease, an instant disqualification from flying and a way to avoid the dreaded stigma of cowardice, LMF – Lack of Moral Fibre. This was the classification meted out to those men who simply could not bear the tension of living under the shadow of probable annihilation. Trevor seems to bear him no ill-will.

'Calais,' I asked him and he shook his head and told me the story of fellow pilot, Len Arkless.

The Calais attack was one of a series low-level sorties carried out in the latter part of 1944 on the French coastal town the Germans had yet to relinquish as the Allies pushed beyond them. It was an important port close to England and needed to be taken. On 20 September 1944, 646 aircraft attacked. Visibility was good and the bombing was accurate and concentrated. Only one Lancaster was lost.

Trevor explained that 'Len was the sort of Englishman that would end up running the MCC. He was good at everything.' For several months, Trevor and Len had trained together, become friends and squash partners, even though Len usually won. 'He was that kind of bloke.'

Trevor remembers that one Lancaster lost that day, as well as the warning the crews received at the briefing. 'Whatever you do, turn to port after you bomb'. A right turn would bring the aircraft right on top of the heavier defences of the town.

Trevor explained how 'out of 1,000 aircraft, 999 dropped their bombs and turned to port. Len Arkless' turned to starboard.' The last Trevor saw of the aircraft, it was alight from one end to the other. 'It was only small arms fire that got them, but it was deadly. They were probably the most competent crew that had come through Bomber Command,' he said.

On another occasion, the cloud base over a German town was down to 3,000 feet, with the raid being directed by the master bomber, a solitary aircraft with an experienced officer whose mission was to circle and direct the main force over the radio. 'It's quite safe down here,' announced the guiding voice from under the cloud base. 'You can come down below this and bomb from 1,200 feet.'

At this height, there was a risk from being blown up by your own bombs – nevertheless down through the overcast the rest of the force went. 'When we broke cloud,' said Trevor, 'there was just one crashed aircraft on the ground on fire, it was the master bomber.'

Trevor was full of stories like these. He remembered how in a surreal moment on one trip, he watched a bomb that had just left his aircraft appear to follow the line of a small path that led up to a concrete pill-box on a ridge somewhere in France. 'Like in slow-motion,' he told me, the bomb slowly descended towards the pin-prick target then slammed into it, obliterating it in an instant. Trevor is still amazed at this chance moment of freakish precision.

On 14 October 1944, Bomber Command chief Arthur Harris decided to try out a novel tactic on Duisburg, the port of the Ruhr River in the industrial Ruhr Valley. 'You've heard of the Ruhr Valley?' Trevor asked. The appropriately named 'Operation Hurricane' was an entire day and night of almost continual RAF raids, with 9,000 tons of high explosive being dropped on the unfortunate residents of Duisburg in just 48 hours. Trevor was on the first raid just after dawn, then went back to the same target for the night operation.

The next day, his crew appeared on the battle order for Wilhelmshaven that night, but enough was enough. Whether it was his established skill as a pilot, or just his pluckiness that carried the day he wasn't sure, but Trevor's decree that he and his crew were all exhausted and would not therefore be taking part in the Wilhelmshaven trip was accepted by higher authorities. They would sit, or rather sleep this one out. I had never before heard of a bomber crew deciding to simply opt out of a trip without extremely serious consequences but Trevor reckons he did it, and I believe him.

On the 29th and penultimate trip of Trevor's tour, to Koblenz, one engine failed close to the target. Engine failure was always a legitimate excuse to abort a mission, but Trevor decided to carry on, not he insisted through any desire to hit the enemy but being so close to the end of his tour, he really just wanted to get the thing over with. Turning back would simply mean the trip was aborted, and he would have to do it again.

A few months later, when instructing on an Operational Training Unit, Trevor received a rather important-looking letter. It was from Bomber Harris himself, and he had been awarded the DFC. Trevor had kept very quiet about this, and it was not until I found a copy of the citation among some other odds-and-ends documents he had dug out that I even realised he had one.

21
Norman Robertson
Catalina pilot

I never even bothered to put a parachute on. If you were shot down in the jungle 1,000 miles behind the Japanese lines, well, what were you supposed to do?

'The best of air over the sea and over the bush,' is the poetic way Norman Robertson described his country idyll, situated on the fringes of bush, bay and ocean in Victoria's south. We sit, surrounded by birds, fruit trees and his very own organic vegetable and beef cattle farm, a picture of enlightened self-sufficiency.

Norman was a flying-boat pilot and had begun his tour in the Pacific early in the war. Just how early became apparent when I asked which of the thirty or so RAAF wartime training courses he had been assigned to.

'Number one,' he said. Hitherto, the earliest I had met was a fellow who went through course number six.

'What was the organisation like at that early stage,' I asked. I imagined it to be somewhat shambolic. To my surprise, Norman told me he felt part of a well-oiled machine, even when some of the wheels started to wobble a bit. At Point Cook, one unfortunate attempted to take off in an Anson without unlocking the flying controls.

'He sped across the aerodrome, crashed through several fences, over some vegetable patches and finished up somewhere down near Werribee.'

The CO, on loan from the RAF and extremely British, lined everyone up and dressed them down. 'I would rather lose ten of you men than one aircraft!' he told the chastened group of young men.

Norman took the remark to heart, and 'I spent the rest of the war trying not to lose my aeroplane'.

Did he feel he was a natural pilot?

'Yes,' Norman answered emphatically. 'When I was three, my aunt told me she would make me a suit of feathers so I could fly.'

His youth was spent constructing flying model aeroplanes out of doped paper and balsa wood. At seventeen he entered a competition for 'Freda Thompson's Flying Scholarship' at Essendon Airport, coming sixth out of a field of ninety. The next year he came third. The year after that came the war.

Although its armies were fighting Italians in North Africa, its navy was active in the Mediterranean and some RAAF units had begun to arrive in England, the antipodes felt very much a backwater to a distant conflict. At the end of his training, and after a minor incident with a vindictive warrant officer that cost him an on-course officer's commission, Norman was assessed as being 'a good type in some respects but not amenable to discipline'. It was the beginning of 1941. Where else to send such a miscreant but to a backwater within a backwater? A sleepy hollow – 'as far away from the war as they could possibly send us' – Port Moresby. Nobody at that stage, however, had counted on the Empire of the Rising Sun.

Far from being disappointed at being assigned to the less glamorous flying boats, Norman was delighted. The American-built twin engined Catalinas were the RAAF's only aircraft to be in service on both the first and last day of the war. It was enormously popular with its crews of nine, had incredible endurance of up to 20 hours in the air, a 3,000 mile range and was immensely robust. It was, however, terribly slow, with a cruising speed that hovered just above 100 miles (160 kilometres) an hour.

Although they were safe to fly, you had to know what you were doing.

'There were very very strict rules, and if you didn't obey them, you were dead.'

According to Norman, the secret to handling a flying boat was attitude. The attitude, that is, in the aviation sense, of the nose in relation to the water from which you were taking off or landing. Unless it was level, the aircraft could 'porpoise', becoming sucked down into the troughs and thrown up over the peaks eventually becoming overwhelmed.

'We lost three aircraft this way as soon as we began operations,' Norman told me.

If in open water, the pilot would have to ride the swell like a surfer, avoiding the troughs in-between. If it was too rough for a normal landing, Norman would slow to the point of stall just above the surface and let the aircraft simply fall out of the sky.

'It made a hell of a noise but we never broke one.'

It all sounded extremely difficult and nefarious, a strange fusion of aviation and seamanship, subject to the laws of both sea and air.

I enquire what Port Moresby was like in the year before the beginning of the Japanese war. 'A hell hole,' he replied instantly. He remembered iron huts, illnesses and herrings in tomato sauce in the heat of a tropical day. All in all, it was 'no place for a white man to live in'. Life was nevertheless interesting. At that time it was not the Japanese but the Germans, who were sending armed merchant ships to patrol the sea lanes of the south-west Pacific and Indian oceans.

In November 1941, one such raider, the *Kormoran*, sunk HMAS *Sydney* along with all its 645 hands in Australia's most infamous naval engagement off the Western Australian coast. A few months before this, a Catalina in Norman's squadron reckoned they had spotted the *Kormoran* but by the time permission came through to bomb, night was falling and the aircraft was forced to break off. 'Who knows if we had managed to get a couple of hits on it,' he mused.

Japan was a topic of conversation in those long lazy months before December 1941, but common belief, supported by government literature of the time, assured the men that the Japanese air force consisted of nothing but antiquated bi-planes, flown by pilots with bad eyesight and whose rice diet prevented them from flying higher than 10,000 feet. How this piece of absurd logic was reached was never apparently questioned. Soon enough though, Norman and his fellow airmen would get 'the shock of our lives'.

When Pearl Harbor came Norman, somewhat anti-climactically, was in Melbourne on a shipping navigation course. But by January 1942 he was back in Morseby, no longer a dead end but a town in the front line of a new war that was going very badly indeed.

In his absence, the Catalina's lack of speed had showed them unsuitable for daylight operations, so a decision was taken to paint them all black and send them up at night, as bombers. The very next night after returning to work, Norman was taking off on what could be considered his first serious operation of the war, a night attack on Japanese ships in their newly occupied harbour base of Rabaul on the island of New Britain.

This night, flying over Rabaul harbour, searchlights, as well as night fighters (a rarity in the Japanese air force) concentrated all their attention on an adjacent Catalina, giving Norman his chance to swoop in and make his run. At this stage still a second pilot, he doubled as bomb-aimer and crouching in the nose, lined up on the searchlight that was now illuminating them.

'Where there's a light, there's got to be a ship underneath it,' was his reasoning. Looking through the bombsight, about to release, the searchlight suddenly went out, blinding him and spoiling his aim. He asked the skipper to go around again.

'This time, I thought I had a ship in the sight, but apparently I bombed a sandbank,' he said.

It was a less than auspicious debut. As a testament to the Catalina's durability, however, the aircraft that had taken all the attention of the Japanese defences limped back to New Guinea on one engine, riddled with 150 bullet holes and having been in the air for 7 hours.

With only a handful of aircraft during this desperate time, some ingenuity was needed to make the most of the small force.

'We'd go over to Rabaul with five planes, drop half our bombs, go away and rest for an hour, then come back and deliver the other half, making the Japanese think we had twice the number of planes than we actually had.'

I'd heard of General Rommel doing something similar in the desert by driving his tanks around in a circle to increase the appearance of their numbers, but this was a revelation.

From here on, Norman and his 11 Squadron Calatinas became 'lone wolves', given free rein to attack the Japanese in whatever manner they saw fit. One suspects this was a reflection of the desperation felt in the face of a competent and grossly underestimated enemy, but if people like Norman reckoned they could get at the enemy, the air force was happy to let them have a go.

On one trip to Rabaul, Norman still wondered at his own success. On a night hampered by stratocumulus cloud and murky visibility at the designated bombing height of 6,000 feet, Norman and fellow pilot Terry Diugan decided to feign breaking off, then double back and descend through the cloud for a low-level attack, skirting around an extinct volcano for cover. The ruse worked perfectly, and Norman operating as bomb-aimer in the nose, lined up his sixteen 250-pound bombs in the sight.

'Our first bombs hit the living quarters, then the workshops, then a fuel dump on one side of the airstrip. Across the strip was a line of nine fighters parked wing-tip to wing-tip. The first one was well ablaze and the second catching alight.'

At first, he thought that the flashes and commotion coming up at him was the Japanese returning fire, but it was only the mayhem caused by his own bombs. The Japanese had been caught napping. His pilot was so excited he started to come around for a closer look, but Norman, not one to push his luck, performed a minor mutiny and wrested the controls away, steering the Catalina into the safety of the night. Seventy minutes later, they could look back and still see the orange flashes of explosions on the black horizon.

When the United States Fifth Air Force began to arrive in Townsville, Norman was sent down to guide the raw American B-17 pilots north to the battle zone.

'Say guy, I don't like this one little bit,' protested the nervous American captain he was accompanying when flying into a thunderstorm on their way to Rabaul, feeling anything but comfortable in this new tropical theatre.

Norman assured him it was standard procedure to go straight through it, but the pilot was unconvinced.

As it happened, this flight was one of the first attacks mounted by B-17s from the Australian mainland. Over the target, endeavouring to line up a row of ships, Norman looked down and saw the shapes of three Japanese fighters coming up to meet them. When he informed the edgy American, 'the cigar dropped out of his mouth'. In a panic, the bombs were jettisoned in the jungle, throttles pushed up to 300 miles an hour, and according to Norman, 'he just ran'.

Later, the entire crew went to sleep, leaving Norman to fly the B-17 back across New Guinea to Port Moresby. Over the base, the bleary-eyed captain emerged. 'We're here,' Norman told him. 'He took a look at the fuel gauges and saw they were on empty. He panicked and yet again got her down as quick as he could.'

As Norman tells me, one contingent of American P-39 Airocobras were instructed to make their way to New Guinea by flying up the east coast, 'keeping Australia on your left'. They followed their instructions to the letter, making their way up Cape York then, still with Australia on their left, they proceeded around the tip down the west side of the cape into the Gulf of Carpentaria, strangely oblivious to the fact that their compass read south instead of north. They arrived at Mornington Island, ditched the aircraft and headed out to sea in inflatable boats, believing themselves to be behind Japanese lines. By luck, a Catalina found them paddling madly out into the middle of nowhere, and picked them up.

I asked Norman if his opinion of Americans had cause to improve over the duration of the war. He took a long pause.

'I'd have to think that one out. Let's say we had a healthy disregard for them.'

For better or worse, the sense of having been saved by the Americans in our darkest hour is a sentiment singularly lacking in Norman's recollection of the period.

Norman continued on night operations for the rest of the war. There was one trip, though, that he felt was a blot on his copy book.

The squadron had been told to be on the look-out for a huge, troop-carrying submarine the Japanese were using to re-supply Kokoda. One night, Norman spotted the solo, first on radar, then visually on the surface 'going at a hell of a speed' on its way to the north coast of New Guinea. He knew exactly what he was looking at, but any suspicious vessel had to be positively identified before the commencement of an attack. Norman dutifully radioed the signal for the letter of the day. He didn't expect a reply, and none was received. The Japanese submarine, thus alerted, began to dive.

'I quickly went straight in, made too hurried an attack, missed, then it dived and it was all over.'

Had he disobeyed instructions, he said, and made his usual stealthy approach, he might just have prevented 1,000 extra men landing at Kokoda.

I could see he still felt bad about it, but not nearly as bad, I would guess, had he mistakenly sunk a friendly submarine.

Norman and his 11 Squadron Catalinas became the night-time specialist 'black cats'. The Japanese, frustrated at these 'hit and run' tactics, complained loudly via their propaganda radio services that 'American bombers' had once again attacked Rabaul harbour (though the enemy claimed they had hit nothing). This, despite the nearest American bomber being 10,000 miles away. In a moment of mistaken patriotic fervour, the Air Minister and member for Maribyrnong, one Arthur S. Drakeford, stated publicly that these attacks were in fact being carried out by our own Australian flying boats from Port Moresby.

'Uh-oh, it won't be long now,' was the reaction from Norman's CO.

'At nine o'clock the next morning, over they came' – an entire squadron of high level Japanese bombers, escorted by five Zeros, which came in low over the harbour.

And, 'At that stage, I think we had five Catalinas left. They got three, and the fourth was badly damaged.'

Not that Norman was witness to any of this, because his Catalina, number 5, had left on a patrol two hours before the attack and returned that evening. His was now the sole aircraft left in the squadron. He was told to fuel up immediately and head to Cairns.

'It's not safe here any more for Catalinas.'

Norman was happy not to argue the point and headed south.

Much of the astonishing total of over 3,000 operational hours flown by Norman was spent mine-laying in harbours between New Guinea and the China coast. Once, when mining Rabaul at night, Norman was so low he could see the Japanese soldiers loading the anti-aircraft shells in clips of six rounds.

'One clip went over the wing, the other went under.'

The Japanese were completely baffled by the magnetic/acoustic mines that could be detonated by the vibrations of a ship's propeller, and their only recourse was to stop sending ships over 1,000 tons to resupply their armies. This was considered a very reasonable outcome.

His other major activity was supply dropping to army units operating behind Japanese lines. On one occasion, after making such a drop, he proceeded to the nearest occupied town and dropped a couple of bombs, just to make a nuisance of himself. He had no idea what he had hit until six months later, at Young and Jackson's Hotel in Melbourne, he met some soldiers just out of Heidelberg Repatriation Hospital, recovering from myriad tropical illnesses after a long stint in the jungle.

'You know what you did when you dropped those bombs?' he was asked rhetorically by a group of mates in khaki who all eagerly shook his hand as Norman could not possibly have any idea. 'You hit the dog kennels!'

The story told to him was that the Japanese had just imported a pack of hounds to flush out the remaining men from the jungle. 'Apparently I cleaned up the lot,' said Norman.

Another story is not quite as cheery and, I suspect, one that still haunted him. A radio signal had been received from a coast watcher operating behind the lines. The Japanese were closing in, and a supply of tobacco to coerce the natives, as well as some pistols were urgently needed.

'I was given the job and left in the dead of night.'

Norman's instructions were to watch for three separate fires burning on the beach, which would be the drop zone. When he arrived, engines plugged back and flying as quietly as he could, no beach fires could be seen. Knowing the Japanese were close, he surmised that the men had headed inland for their own safety, a theory supported by the sighting of three small fires in some nearby hills. He came in and made the drop. Heading home, he flew back over the beach and the gut-wrenching sight of three large, blazing fires came into view. He immediately realised his error: the fires he had seen were simply native fires up in the hills. To make matters worse, the crew had missed seeing one of the packages in the darkened fuselage – the one containing the guns. It remained unnoticed until their return to Cairns.

The next day, Norman's squadron commander made a trip in broad daylight to try and pick them up. As he got there, a Japanese ship was leaving the island. They had found the coast watcher, and he was executed soon afterwards.

'With no charts, it would have been suicidal to try and land to pick the fellow up in the dark, but it did cross your mind.' It was an understandable mistake, but it still bothered him. 'It puts a sour thing in your mouth.'

Norman saw more of the war in the Pacific than anyone I had met. Despite many near-misses, he finished the war intact, but not without several doses of malaria and dengi fever.

I left Norman as I had found him, happily in his chair on the porch surrounded by the beauty of the birds in his garden. His daughter Heather shows me the large vegetable farm behind the house and gives me a generous bag of produce to take away. I thank a now tired-looking Norman, and make my way to my car, receiving a warning. 'We had a snake over on the path there yesterday. I think he's still there. When you hear the blue wrens twittering, you know he's around.' I vow to tread carefully.

22

Ron English

Navigator, Dakotas

Transport Command, we thought. That doesn't sound too risky!

Coming down through the cloud towards the surface of the Mediterranean, Ron English lay flat on his belly in the nose of a Hudson bomber, listening intently to the wireless operator calling the range of the contact he had picked up on the cathode ray oscilloscope of his radar set. 'Half a mile . . . quarter mile . . .' In fact, all the w/o could see was a sliver of green light, indicating an object of indeterminate size on the surface of the water ahead. What it actually was could be anyone's guess: battleship, submarine, fishing boat. 'Two hundred yards . . .'. Ron peered through the perspex but the cloud was unbroken. Then, feeling he must be right on top of whatever it was, there came a break in the overcast. Then he spotted a dark shape below. He hit his intercom button.

'It's a bloody whale!'

Sadly – for the whale – the anxious pilot didn't quite get the end of the sentence. On the word 'bloody' two depth charges were released from underneath the aircraft. The automatic stereoscopic cameras later confirmed the accuracy of the attack.

This turned out to be the most eventful day in Ron's twelve-month career as navigator flying anti-submarine patrols with number 48 Squadron, Coastal Command. By February 1944, with the U-boat war largely in hand, the emphasis began to shift to the impending invasion of Europe, and 48 was incorporated into Transport Command. Ron was given the choice of becoming an instructor or training up on the military version of the legendary DC-3 passenger liner, the Dakota.

'Transport Command?' we thought. 'That doesn't sound too risky!' Time would prove this a hasty assessment.

A staggering total of over 10,000 DC-3s were made between 1935 and 1946, with several military variants being utilised all over the globe in a wide variety of roles: airliner, cargo transport, glider tug, air ambulance, paratroop platform, etc. They were rugged, carried a huge load, were cheap to make and easy to fly: the perfect aircraft for hurriedly trained wartime pilots and crews. After 1945, hundreds of surplus Dakotas formed the basis of the international airline industry well into the 1950s and a few still fly today in exotic places like Haiti, Chad and Burkina Faso. Around the world, no aircraft museum worth its salt does not sport an example or two.

I am rummaging among the many pieces of memorabilia Ron has dug out for me: telegrams, letters, and some souvenir German currency from the pre-Hitler years such as a bank note for fifty million marks, not worth the paper it was printed on, and material evidence of the economic collapse that aided the rise of the Nazis. I start to ask him how he came by it, but my eye is caught by a photograph of an extremely attractive girl, taken during the war. I look up and Ron's grinning at me from ear to ear.

'I was down staying with her family in the south of England and got a message that I was needed back on the squadron. Immediately.' It was a couple of days before D-Day, as it happens sixty-one years to the day we are talking in his and his wife Joy's tidy suburban unit.

Upon returning to his base at Down Ampney in Gloucestershire, all the Dakotas in the squadron had been painted with large black and white 'invasion' stripes on the wings and under the fuselages applied to all Allied aircraft involved in the imminent invasion of Normandy to aid in identification.

Ron knew the invasion was coming. He'd been training in parachute dropping and glider towing for months. But on the day itself, Ron's job was towing into battle one of the enormous wooden Hamilcar troop-carrying gliders.

'We took off at a rate of three gliders every 20 seconds,' he said, the idea being to keep them as close as possible, providing a concentration of troops and equipment on the ground in a very short space of time.

Ron took off at night, the glider releasing at the appointed place over Caen just before dawn, and headed for home. The entry in his log book for the momentous day simply read *three bullet holes in aircraft*.

'One of them came up through the bottom, passing between myself and the wireless operator, out the top of the aircraft and exploded. You could hear it quite clearly.'

Had it done so a nano-second earlier, he would certainly have been a goner. On the way home in the first light of D-Day, he was able to gorge his eyes on the amazing sight of a 5,000+ ship invasion fleet heading for France.

He had survived the big day unscathed. For Ron, the moment of truth was to come later, at Arnhem.

All in all, he decided, his earlier prediction was proving right, and flying transports was turning out not a bad way to spend the war. After D-Day, he became part of the supply build-up in Normandy, sometimes dropping into a different forward air base every day to unload the cargo needed to supply an army. It was not very glamorous, perhaps, but he enjoyed the company of his largely Canadian crew and casualties were light. At Arnhem, however, the fun stopped.

If you've seen the film *A Bridge Too Far*, you've got the general idea about Arnhem: Operation Market Garden was the ambitious plan to drop a couple of divisions behind the German lines in Holland, open up the bridges across the Rhine, hurl the Allied armies into the industrial heart of Germany and end the war by Christmas. It was the sort of immensely complex military operation requiring months of planning. Market Garden was thrown together in a week, and it all went badly wrong. The paratroops were landed too far from the objectives without the element of surprise, resistance proved stronger than anticipated, communication was lost and chaos and confusion ensued.

Ron never knew exactly what was contained in the panniers being parachuted from the aircraft to the men below, but assumed it was important enough not to be simply handed to the Germans. So when, on 21 September 1944, four days into the battle over his designated drop zone, he spotted a German anti-aircraft gun sitting in a field supposed to be held by the British, he and his pilot made what he calls their 'fatal mistake' and turned the Dakota around to look for some friendlier recipients for their delivery.

'As we came out, we got caught between two anti-aircraft batteries,' he recalled.

The Arnhem battlefield was so turgid and confused, that a matter of a few hundred yards could be vital. From his low altitude of 600 feet, Ron felt the impact of small arms and light anti-aircraft as soon as the Dakota made its turn. First, the starboard engine caught fire. The pilot switched on the internal fire extinguishers but to no effect.

'It was burning like a bloody big glow-lamp,' he said. On the other side of the aircraft, the petrol tanks, holed by bullets, began trailing plumes of fuel. With one wing ablaze and the other streaming petrol, they were seconds away from an inferno.

The pilot headed for the nearest field, cheerily called out, 'Hang on fellas, here we go,' and hit the ground, ploughing through a hedge that sheared off the burning wing completely. After sliding for 100 yards that seemed like 10 miles, the Dakota came to a stop.

'We thought it was going to blow up so we just got up, got out, and hid in a nearby ditch.'

After a minute or so, it became obvious that the aircraft was not in fact about to catch fire, so Ron went back into the fuselage to collect a first aid kit to assist a wounded crew member. Emerging, he was confronted with a sight he will never forget.

'When I turned around to get out of the aircraft, there was a German standing there with his revolver pointed at me. Not being Errol Flynn, I decided to go quietly.'

After several hours with a gun shoved in his back, confinement at the local headquarters, and a day or two in solitary confinement, Ron and the rest of his crew were interrogated by another German. He was, 'an officer, very pleasant, who spoke perfect English'. Although he was asking the questions it soon became apparent there was little the officer didn't already know. Ron was blandly informed on which day he had arrived on squadron, its location, the name of his commanding officer and several other pieces of information, all accurate.

He could only think that one of the other crew must have talked, until he realised he was the first one in. Unable to resist, Ron asked the smooth-talking German how he came by such information.

'The British intelligence is the finest in the world,' he was told, 'but the German is a very close second.'

Ron and the crew were sent to a POW camp on the Polish border and managed to keep a diary on scraps of paper. After four months at the camp, they were ordered onto the road with an hour's notice on 25 January 1945. So move they did, on foot in mid-winter to another camp many miles away, just south of Berlin. On the way, in temperatures reaching thirty below, escorted by Germans soldiers with dogs on leads, many of his fellow prisoners stumbled, and dropped out of the line. What became of them, Ron was unsure.

On the march, he witnessed the bizarre landscape of a country in disintegration: lines of high tension cables flattened as if by a giant, cities of rubble and pine forests showered in golden strips of radar-blocking 'window', dropped by the bombers high above.

'It made them look like Christmas trees,' he remembered.

Ron's liberation and repatriation to Australia came soon enough after the war. He had no desire to stick around. He has never joined a returned serviceman's organisation, and is slightly contemptuous of the notion of sitting around endlessly reliving the past. He has marched but once on Anzac Day, and only under sufferance.

'It's something that is finished as far as I'm concerned,' he said.

I suspect though, that sometimes the winter of 1945 is not quite finished with him.

23

Tom Trimble

Fighter pilot

That's a photo of me the day we arrived. They have to photograph you on the day you arrive because you mightn't live much longer.

Coming from a humble family and with only a high school Leaving Certificate under his belt, Tom didn't really think he was much of a show to be selected for aircrew training, but nonetheless pestered his reluctant father into signing the forms allowing him to apply. As an eighteen-year-old he didn't know much about aeroplanes, but from his home above Balmoral Beach in Sydney, he would witness the arrival of the great air races from England. Then there was Kingsford-Smith, and the Australian National Airways Ford Tri-motors making their regular service up to Brisbane in the years before the war. And what about that bloke who cut such a fine figure in his blue uniform walking into the hotel (he forgets the name) near the corner of Pitt and Bridge Streets? That, decided Tom, was the fella he wanted to be.

So, on the last day before the application cut-off, Tom handed his in. It was 2 September 1939. The very next day, the Second World War started.

'Geez, I wish I could withdraw that application,' was his initial reaction. 'This could be dangerous.'

Then one afternoon in mid-December, his sister appeared at his desk in the Queensland Insurance office building. 'You're in,' she said, handing him a big, fat, official-looking envelope. 'You have to be in Brisbane in a fortnight.' He was soon on his way to number 2 Elementary Flying Training School at Archerfield, Queensland.

'The worst aeroplane I have ever flown in my life!' is how Tom forcefully describes the aircraft he went on to train in at Archerfield in Queensland, the legendary Tiger Moth. After hearing endless lyrical stories about the simple but sturdy virtues of this famous bi-plane, his passionate (albeit negative) opinion comes as refreshing. 'Crude' is the word that sums this little plane up for Tom – pure and simple. 'An aeroplane made *by* a farmer, *for* farmers!' Adding to the insult, the uniforms had at that stage yet to arrive and the trainee pilots had to make do with overalls and civilian hats and shoes. 'We looked bloody terrible,' says Tom. 'Some of the lads learned to fly in socks!'

Tom passed the course and was selected for fighter pilot training at Pearce, Western Australia, although his career very nearly never made it past a small dirt aerodrome in Kalgoorlie. Ferrying his brand new Wirraway from the factory at Fishermans Bend to their new home, Tom came in to refuel at Kalgoorlie. Taxying, he misjudged an outback fence post, collecting it with his right wing. With some sympathetic local help, he patched up the damage with butchered bits from another plane and a piece of timber, and took off the next day, not at all sure how his makeshift repair job would be received.

Hours later, taxying onto the bitumen at Pearce, his worst fears were realised as a flight commander jumped up on his wing with an urgent message. 'You're in trouble, Trimble. Black Jack [the squadron CO] has you up on a court-martial.' Tom felt slightly sick, but the grin on the man's face told him there was more. 'But you're lucky,' he added. 'At the same time a signal's come in posting you to the Middle East!'

Shortly thereafter, on a Sydney Harbour crowded with boats of all description amid a poignantly carnival atmosphere, Tom boarded the gigantic four-funnel White Star liner *Aquitania* and sailed out of his home town on a warm Sunday morning. The next desert he would be looking at would be a dusty Egyptian airstrip as the newest member of 3 Squadron, RAAF.

By the time Tom arrived, 3 Squadron was already on its way to building its reputation as one of the toughest units in the desert air force. It had been the first RAAF squadron to leave Australia for the front, in July 1940, and since November had been operating from its base near Cairo as an army cooperation unit flying bi-planes. Solid and respectable, but bi-planes nonetheless. These Gloster Gladiators – tough, well armed and highly manoeuvrable – were in fact one of the last and most advanced bi-plane fighters ever built, but their lack of speed kept them well and truly locked into the previous generation of aerial warfare, closer to the Sopwith Camels of the trenches than the Spitfires and Messerschmitts of the 1940s.

But that's what they flew and on 19 November 1940, 3 Squadron's Gladiators went into action for the first time, engaged by nine Fiat CR42s (another bi-plane but much faster) of Mussolini's air force, the Regia Aeronautica, and destroyed three of them for one loss of their own. A year later, still in the deserts of North Africa, the pilots of number 3 squadron would have amassed a total of 106 enemy aircraft destroyed, making themselves the first desert squadron to crack the ton, but not without considerable losses of their own, including their blackest day of 22 November, when five pilots were lost to the Germans and two captured.

To get his flying hours up, Tom was made to train on the Westland Lysander, a curious high-wing monoplane, developed in the mid-thirties as an army cooperation aircraft with several unusual features such as an extremely narrow overhead wing root to afford the pilot greater visibility, and an ability to fly at amazingly slow speeds as well as an impressively short take-off and landing distance – a true STOL aircraft before its time. Its slowness, however, saw it decimated in France in 1940 but it later found fame as the ultimate cloak-and-dagger aeroplane. Painted black all over, it took off from England in the dead of night to drop off and pick up spies and agents from fields and roadsides across occupied Europe. 'A magnificent aircraft, but bloody hard to fly,' says Tom.

Ironically, 3 Squadron's success at this stage of the desert war contributed to Tom spending a lot of time on the ground. 'They'd only lost one person,' he says, and flying against the lacklustre Italians morale was high. As a replacement, there was initially no-one for him to replace.

With his feet feeling extremely itchy, he was at last given a Gladiator, and made 'weaver', or squadron look-out. As such, he was not required to formate with the rest of the group into the V or 'finger four' formations, but swing in and out, looking for the enemy. 'I was a free man, you might say,' but not permitted to engage in combat. 'I was once told off by the commanding officer, "Your job is to weave and look out. Don't you dare come into a fight unless you're called in!" He really had a go at me.'

Re-equipping with Hawker Hurricanes ('my favourite aircraft,' he says wistfully) and then in May 1941 the American built Tomahawks, Tom spent the bulk of 1941 on the move with number 3 as it moved with the ebb and flow of the desert campaign, patrolling over the sands of Syria, Libya and Egypt.

On one patrol he became caught in a terrifying 'defensive circle'. Like wagons circled by marauding Indians, two squadrons of Tomahawks and Hurricanes formed a 'cone' as Messerschmitt 109s criss-crossed and attempted to break them up. The trouble with such a formation, said Tom is that it's very hard to break out of it once established. 'It was a stupid manoeuvre. The only reason it broke up was because the Germans ran out of fuel,' he said still with a touch of exasperation.

Often with the fluid nature of the campaign, the pilots would take-off at one strip and land at another, the whole squadron having moved in the meantime, or run so low on fuel that their engines would stop while still taxying after landing.

Peter Forbes, my aeroplane enthusiast friend and the man who put me onto Tom, has been sitting quietly beside me, letting me get on with things, but then smiles slyly and asks a question.

'Tell us about your little meeting with Yellow Fourteen, Tom.' Tom gives a knowing laugh and Peter joins in. Tom then patiently begins to recount the most dramatic day of his life, 13 December 1941.

At its desert airstrip of Madalena in Egypt, 3 Squadron, short on pilots as well as aircraft, was no longer riding the high of a year before when Tom joined. 'We were in a pretty parlous situation,' he says. Having spent all day on the ground sitting in his cockpit with everything switched on and ready to be off in 2 minutes, Tom had been finally stood down and so after some lunch retired to his tent to write letters.

At about three o'clock, Bobby Gibbes, the 5 foot 4 flight commander and former salesman (as well as future squadron commander) appeared at the flap enquiring, in that wonderfully insouciant fighter pilot way, whether Tom would be interested in leading a section in a short patrol later that afternoon, provided they could scratch together the requisite number of aircraft. Nothing special, just a short patrol out to the German aerodrome at El Matuba to look after some returning bombers. They were not to go looking for a fight, and it was to be the last patrol of the day.

'Oh . . . alright,' was Tom's non-committal reply.

They took off and flew out towards the west. Bobby had asked Tom to lead the left-hand section. Underneath them, Operation Crusader was in progress, one of the large set piece engagements of the to-and-fro motion of the desert campaign, this one having begun nearly a month earlier, an attempt to link up with the besieged garrison at Tobruk and force Rommel's Africa Korps to the west. As usual, Rommel had an agenda of his own and, just to keep things interesting, counter-attacked into the British rear before being forced to retreat and re-group. All the German fighters, Tom had been told, had been withdrawn east to their centre at Benghazi and would present no trouble.

But it had been raining, and when it rains in the North African desert, sand and dirt turn into a rich desert glue and very little moves in the quagmire.

'I can see all of this in my mind's eye.'

The day was dull and humid, just after rain. At about 4,000 feet, Tom crossed the Gulf of Bomba and started to run into broken cloud. Over the supposedly empty El Matuba aerodrome, Tom and his small formation turned to head home. But looking down, he could not believe his eyes. 'I had never seen so many Me 109s in all my life.' The scheduled German withdrawal to the west had been held up by the rain, and their aircraft were only now, beginning to take off, right into Tom and Bobby's modest patrol in aircraft of an indisputedly inferior quality. 'There were masses of these bloody things,' he said.

The uneventful patrol suddenly became a mayhem of wheeling, dodging aeroplanes. Tom saw one Tomahawk with a German right behind it and fired, having no idea if he hit anything. Another two were so close together that he could not fire on one without risking hitting the other. Then he looked down. A single 109 was pulling up strongly towards him like an enraged, determined animal. Standing out in the humid, late afternoon gloom, Tom remembers 'two beautiful silver streams', emerge from the German's wingtips. These were simply the Messerschmitt's wingtip vortices standing out against the dull of the afternoon, but it's an image forever frozen in his brain.

Like a spectator transfixed, he continued to watch as another stream of 20 millimetre cannon fire – this one gold in colour – emerged out of the German's propeller hub. 'You won't get me,' he thought to himself, strangely calm in the surreal moment of battle. Tom swung his head around to follow the German's path as he flashed by, then placed a thumb over his gun button ready to fire on another target that had emerged out of the melee. It was then he felt the impact of cannon shells as they hit his plane.

Thump, by his left foot, then two more – *thump*, *thump* – and another one on the port side under the tailplane. An explosive round hit under the thick armoured glass of the windshield and blew off the top of the canopy. Then, suddenly, in front of his face, flames.

'I realised I had to get out,' Tom tells us, his eyes shut. He undid his harness, oxygen tube and radio/telephone and blacked out, but not before one calm and uncomplicated thought. 'I'll be dead before I hit the ground.'

It only lasted a moment. Seconds later he woke up to find the aircraft in a spin. 'Then I was dead scared,' he said. The flesh of his eyelids, he could feel, were closed, having cooked in the heat. Once again the notion that he was about to die entered his brain, and this time he was not quite so sanguine about it.

The flames, however, were just about gone. As he has since deduced, the shell which had exploded near his foot had ruptured the fuel lines feeding the engine, and only that small amount in the lines had ignited, but quickly died back. The tanks themselves were undamaged. Through an extraordinary feat of flying, he managed to bring the aircraft out of its spin, and opening one eye ever so slightly, saw the waters of the Mediterranean on his left, and knew he was heading south, away from the German aerodrome.

At only 4,000 feet and in a dive, with no power to his engine, he expected at any second to plough into the ground. But having flown over the country previously, he knew it to be flat enough to at least attempt a landing. Sightless, he pulled the nose back and felt the speed fall away, then dropped the nose again. Repeating this undulated movement three times he felt the airscrew bite the ground and the Tomahawk skidded, then stopped.

'I was really panicky now,' he said, but eventually got out. Badly burned and in shock, standing next to his aircraft, Tom leant forward to peel off his helmet, and 'a firehose' of blood poured out the top of his head. One of the explosive shells had peppered him with metal fragments, some chipping his skull and lodging in his body. Some of them are still in him. 'Veterans Affairs took X-rays of me a few years ago – they're still there!' he says, laughing about it.

He had landed a couple of miles to the south of the Germans at their airfield at Martuba, which, Tommy could see, was laden with 109s. But with the British army fast advancing on them, they had more important things to do than go chasing after a downed Australian airman. In a story reminiscent of Lawrence of Arabia, Tom thought of two good reasons why he should walk east. Firstly, it was the direction from which the advancing British army would arrive, and secondly, the cool easterly breeze soothed his scorched and agonised face.

Searching for water, he came across a trio of Bedouin Arab tribesmen, for whom he promptly produced his 'blood chit', a printed card in Arabic issued to all Allied airmen in the desert, promising a reward in gold of one hundred guineas for the safe return of the bearer. He was put on a camel, fed, and native herbs were found to soothe his burns. That night he slept in a tent, a guest of the local chieftain who placed Tom on one side, his wife on the other and lay down in between them with a loaded rifle. It was hardly needed.

'The last thing I remember before going to sleep was being bitten by fleas,' he said.

After a few days, troops of the 7th Indian Division came from the west and Tom approached a British officer in a staff car.

After an almost surreal dinner that night on white tablecloths in the middle of the desert seated next to a general, Tom found his way back to 3 Squadron a week later, which by this time had moved to a new airfield at El Adem. His injuries properly attended to for the first time, Tom could hear the metallic 'chink chink' of the shell fragments falling into a steel basin as the orderlies washed his scalp and hair.

Yellow Fourteen, as Peter informed me as I drove him home, was the call sign of the German ace Hans-Joachim Marseille, the playboy Berliner with the French name who grew his hair long, listened to banned American jazz records, hated discipline and who once shot down seventeen Allied aircraft in a single day, contributing to his astonishing total of 158 aircraft.

Marseille was a true one-off, whose freakish flying and fighting ability had allowed him, by twenty-one, to have rewritten the book on aerial warfare.

'There it is, you see,' Tom points to the entry in a large book about Marseille's short life, listing every one of his kills. And there is Tom. Not by name, but he's definitely on the list, same date, time and location. He wears it as a mark of some pride, and I get the feeling he would liked to have met his nemesis, but it was not to be. Nine months later, Marseille was dead. Photographs of his young handsome face taken a few weeks before his death show him pale, his eyes sunken, evidence of the depression he is said to have experienced at the continual strain of fighting, and the recent death of yet another colleague.

Tom was repatriated back to Australia to fly Spitfires later in the war, but nothing was to match the drama of his last day in the desert.

24

Arch Dunne

Bomber pilot

The Japanese didn't like coming near the Liberators very much. They had guns sticking out all over them.

Sydney had turned on one of its brilliant afternoons the day I spoke with Arch Dunne. As I stood in his living room, overlooking one of those breathtaking vistas of sun-sparkled water the locals seem to take in their stride, Arch's two adoring daughters, Mel and Trudy, prepared just a fraction of their dad's extraordinary collection of photographs and memorabilia, including some prints of pre-war New Guinea that looked like they were taken yesterday. Pre-war, because Arch Dunne began his flying career not in the air force, but as an airline pilot in the late 1930s, flying the routes from Australia to sleepy New Guinea backwaters like Wau, Salamau and Port Moresby – places soon to be thrust onto the world's stage as battle zones.

'I had a licence to drive an aeroplane before I had one to drive a car,' Arch told me, having graduated as a pilot from the Australian National Airways Flying School in Geelong in 1931 at the very young age of seventeen. Soon after he began co-piloting the elegant de Havilland 86 'Express' four engine bi-plane for the now long-gone ANA.

Arch spent an idyllic few years flying in and out of the New Guinea goldfields, but in 1937, with world peace fast diminishing, the air force wrote to all qualified pilots enquiring as to their willingness to join up in the event of hostilities.

'I had no ties, and figured it was better to offer to go in voluntarily, rather than be dragged in later on,' said Arch, and so duly put up his hand for the RAAF Reserve. After standing in line at the recruiting depot, a surly officer gave him and his tally of hundreds of hours flown the once over, and offered curtly, 'Yes, I think we might be able to use you.'

When war broke out, he was one of the first to receive his call-up papers but disappointed to be sent to Point Cook to train as an instructor. Such were the pitfalls of overqualification, and definitely not how he had envisaged offering his services to his country in time of need. But Arch dutifully began life as an instructor at number 2 Elementary Flying Training School at Archerfield, Queensland, settling in for a long and most unexciting war.

Then, on 13 August 1940, a Lockheed Hudson medium bomber crashed into a hill 8 miles from Canberra airport, killing all ten people on board including three federal cabinet ministers and the newly appointed Chief of the General Staff, General Sir Brudenell White. The cause was determined to be a fatal stall on approach to land – simple pilot error. The air force had a quick rethink, and decided that experienced pilots like Arch could perhaps be more purposefully employed.

The RAAF had only recently taken delivery of the modern, powerful Hudson and compared to the aircraft most pilots at the time were used to flying it was, as Arch puts it, 'very much a horse of another colour'. American-built, the Hudson was converted from a Lockheed airliner, the Type 14 Super Electra, commissioned by the Royal Air Force to replace their fleet of ageing fabric-covered Avro Ansons.

The Lockheed Hudson remains one of the truly unsung

heroes of Second World War aviation. Nearly three thousand were built, nearly all finding their way into the RAF and Commonwealth air forces performing a variety of roles including bombing, air–sea rescue and maritime patrol. It was a squat, slightly comic-looking aeroplane, with a twin tail and a large, distended belly making it look like a porpoise about to give birth.

His qualifications reassessed, Arch was plucked out of instruction and put into active service with number 2 Squadron at Laverton, Victoria, flying the Hudson on maritime reconnaissance patrols into Bass Strait.

Combing the featureless expanse of the ocean for anything suspicious was usually uneventful, but on one memorable patrol, Arch spotted the silhouette of a large ship in the distance. Right on the edge of fuel range, he could afford to make just one pass to identify some of the features before heading back: approximately 45,000 tons, twin funnels, and steaming west towards Port Phillip Bay. He radioed in the details and a short time later received the reply, 'attack – immediate'. But with his fuel low, all he could do was confirm the position and head home.

As Arch flew back to Laverton, the rest of the squadron passed him on their way out to attack the suspicious vessel. He had barely arrived back when an urgent recall was issued. 'Squadron return – do not attack.' After some frantic radio transmissions, the identity of the mystery ship was discovered to be the *New Amsterdam* which had left Wellington the previous day, but neglected to inform anyone of its intended passage through Bass Strait. Had Arch's tanks been slightly fuller that day, he could well have been responsible for attacking a friendly, and very much unarmed passenger ship.

With the prospect of war in the Pacific looming, Arch was posted to number 13 Squadron and on the day before Pearl Harbor, 6 December 1941, arrived at his new home at Laha airfield on the Dutch-controlled island of Ambon, two hours flying time from the Australian mainland. The army was also there in the form of 'Gull Force', an 1,100-strong bastion of men largely from Tasmania expected to halt the as yet unchecked Japanese. For all of them, the situation was entirely hopeless. Gull Force's commander, Lieutenant-Colonel Roach saw what was coming and pleaded to be either reinforced or withdrawn. Instead he was sacked, withdrawn to Melbourne and drummed out of the AIF.

For fighter protection, 13 Squadron could rely only on two hopelessly inadequate Brewster Buffalos of the Dutch air force. The senior RAAF officer on Ambon, Wing Commander Scott, warned in a signal to the Melbourne war room that 'with present equipment, Ambon could not resist for one day'. Arch's war, so far relatively uneventful, was about to change dramatically.

'Just a little strip with a little bay along the waterfront,' is how he describes Laha. 'Certainly nothing too big.' From this tiny outpost, Arch and 13 Squadron's dozen or so Hudson bombers set out on daily patrols to report the inexorable southward march of the Japanese to a stupefied world. On 10 December, he entered history, being part of the first attack by an Australian squadron in the Dutch East Indies in the Pacific war.

'It was a little place out in the middle of absolutely nowhere called Tobi Island,' he recalls. On the map, it's barely a speck in the ocean north of the western tip of New Guinea, but the Japanese were using it as a base for their Kawanishi flying boats. Six aircraft were detailed to attack, led by 13's recently arrived Commanding Officer, Wing Commander McDonald. 'A nice fella,' says Arch, 'but without much experience on the Hudson', having only just completed the conversion course. Arch was McDonald's number 2, and he was worried about him from the beginning. 'He really didn't understand the differences between the old bi-planes and a modern aircraft like the Hudson.'

Taking off in darkness for Tobi Island, 13 Squadron were scheduled to arrive over the target at first light. McDonald proposed to lead off and then slow down to 120 knots to allow Arch and the rest of the squadron to catch up. 'No, don't do that, whatever you do!' Arch warned his CO when told the plan just before take-off. 'At 120 knots with a full load, these things just won't stay in the air!'

But above the island a few minutes later, Arch peered into the night sky and saw the pre-arranged glow of an Aldis lamp being flashed from the turret of his CO's aircraft ahead. He caught up quickly, then overtook McDonald who appeared to have almost stopped in mid-air. 'Holy smoke, he's going too slow!' Arch said to his co-pilot, and then both witnessed a sudden swirling of lights, and a sheet of flame exploding on the ocean below. Like the similarly inexperienced pilot in Canberra the year before, Arch's commanding officer had stalled the Hudson at low speed from an irrecoverable height. Another pilot in the squadron called up, breaking radio silence. 'What's going on?' he said. 'The CO's gone in. I'm taking over,' was Arch's cursory reply. It had been his very first trip and they had been in the air barely 10 minutes.

Unwilling to return and attempt a landing back at the small island airstrip at night with a full bomb load, Arch led the squadron to the target, and bombed the area around a small jetty at dawn as planned. Arch noticed one poor fellow dash from the end of the jetty where he had been fishing into a nearby building which was then torn apart by a bomb. They hit what they were supposed to hit, but what that actually was they were never quite sure. 'Let's piss off out of here,' Arch called up to the squadron and they headed home. The trip back was flown with a sour taste in their mouths.

A few nights later, it was the Japanese who, as Arch put it, 'welcomed us to the war zone', when three flying boats appeared over the airstrip, dropping fragmentation bombs. No-one was killed but bits of metal were sprayed everywhere, imbedding themselves into buildings and aircraft alike. It was to become the pattern for the next few weeks.

One night, Arch took a replacement Hudson from Darwin to neighbouring number 2 Squadron who were based at Namlea airfield on the nearby island of Buru. It was to be a quick stop, and a plan had been put in place whereby the island's natives warned of Japanese aircraft coming from the north, but the pilots had been told to stay close by the aircraft when on the ground, just in case they needed to get off quickly.

This morning, upon arriving, Arch was greeted by a jeep and one of the 2 Squadron pilots, future BHP director Bob Law-Smith carrying a breakfast-laden tray. The five men sat under the wing in the tropical morning enjoying the service, but the distraction was short-lived. Mid-mouthful, Law-Smith paused.

'I can hear aircraft,' he said. Everybody was on their feet in an instant, looking for some kind of shelter. Desperately, the men threw themselves down into the lip of a newly-cut gravel road, trying as best they could to force their bodies into the ground. 'Here they come!' shouted a voice. Arch looked over his shoulder to see two Japanese Zeros roaring towards the end of the runway, 10 feet off the ground.

'All I could feel was my bottom sticking into the air,' he said. 'And Bob's was even bigger!' The strafing bullets sent flying gravel everywhere, and all were lucky to receive only cuts. The aircraft didn't fare so well. Four out of the five Hudsons on the strip burned immediately, the survivor flew again but was so full of holes that the pilot who brought it back to Darwin felt the wind rushing past him all the way.

But 13 Squadron hit back when they could. Ambon, they

knew, was soon to be invaded, but from which direction? With replacement aircraft, Arch was part of a formation sent to intercept a convoy that had been spotted to the north. Seeing smoke down below on the water, they assumed it was just a few ships. But emerging through a haze, was the panorama of a complete Japanese invasion fleet stretched across the ocean beneath them. 'We didn't know what we'd let ourselves in for,' said Arch. 'The whole damn fleet was there.'

Arch dived and dropping his bombs one after the other, came close to hitting something, but missed. Then the sky was full of black smoke. A whole clip of eight or ten shells exploded, each at the exact same place relative to the moving aircraft, right underneath the Hudson's nose, just to the left. Arch has often thought about that Japanese ship's gunner, just a fraction too eager traversing the anti-aircraft gun. 'If he hadn't been just a little too anxious, I wouldn't be talking to you now,' he said.

Ambon itself was spared until the last day of January 1942, when another convoy of twenty-two ships was spotted to its immediate north by Arch's mate from Laverton, Bill White. Arch first became aware of this startling fact when on the runway at Darwin about to return to Ambon, having just brought in a load of evacuees from Babo on New Guinea's western tip. 'I'll bring you back another lot tomorrow,' he radioed to the controller. 'Well I hope you can, mate,' came the reply. 'The Japanese fleet's just been spotted north of Ambon.' Arch's return flight to Laha was scheduled to include a wide reconnaissance arc to the island's north. Instead, he went straight to the airfield.

Arriving at Laha in the dark, the squadron with its few remaining aircraft and its entire personnel were on the ground in an atmosphere of subdued desperation, evacuation plan in place, all expecting the Japanese to adhere to their usual pattern and arrive with the dawn, just a few hours away. 'We knew we couldn't take everybody,' says Arch. The squadron's Hudsons began loading up. 'I had twenty-seven people on my aircraft which was built to carry four,' he remembers. Everything not bolted down inside the aircraft was thrown out and the fuel tanks filled with just enough petrol to get to Darwin and no more.

One by one, the over-laden Hudsons took off. With not an inch to spare inside, Arch prepared to depart. Then he spotted the long face of a friend, the squadron intelligence officer. He was a big man, and Arch had no room for him, but reckoned he'd be able to get back for at least one more trip before the inevitable surrender. The officer was not so sure.

'You know, I'm starting to think of my wife and three daughters,' he said to Arch. 'Any chance of getting on your aircraft?'

'Sorry, I'm loaded to the hilt,' said Arch, and the officer took it well. Then Arch remembered the small cavity of the bomb-aimer's position right in the nose of the Hudson, occupied only on the run into the target. 'Get yourself in there and don't get in the way of anything,' he said. A few minutes later, Arch Dunne's Hudson lumbered into the air carrying twenty-seven passengers, plus one.

He can't quite remember if he was third or fourth off the runway, but just behind him was Bill White, ready to go in his aircraft as soon as the squadron headquarters staff had made their way down to the airfield from the other side of the bay.

Considering its load, the Hudson handled pretty well. 'I didn't feel like making any steep turns, though,' says Arch. Just after dawn, he arrived back in Darwin, immediately unloaded everyone and frantically prepared to head back. 'Just slow down, Arch,' he was told. 'It's too late now. We've managed to get all the aircraft off, except one.'

Bill White's was the last aircraft to be refuelled, and as the other Hudsons flew off, the petrol was pumped into his tanks, but simply poured straight out through the undercarriage and onto the ground. According to Arch, 'Bill was the sort of bloke who had to have a crack at somebody.' When he had spotted the Japanese fleet earlier that day, he couldn't resist dropping his bombs on something, but in the process, must have collected some stray pieces of lead from the Japanese gunners. Nobody noticed the main fuel cock had been mortally damaged. Bill had made it back to Ambon, but his aircraft would never fly again.

Bill and the stranded party made their way up the coast, but were captured and beheaded by the Japanese a few days later. The airfield at Laha became a killing ground. Of the more than three hundred army and air force men who surrendered to the Japanese at Laha airfield, not one of them was to survive, butchered in four separate massacres over two weeks.

Of the 1159 men in Gull Force, only 302 would survive the war. Ambon saw one of the worst death rates of Allied prisoners in Japanese captivity.

'Where were you when Darwin was bombed?' asks his daughter, Mel. Arch grinned a little.

'In Darwin,' he said. The Japanese military code had been broken, he explained, a fact which was itself kept secret, lest the Japanese changed it. The press though, ever eager for a story, or any word on when Darwin would be attacked, began to badger Arch for anything he might be willing to divulge. 'They probably thought I was the weak link in the chain,' he said. He feigned ignorance but was in fact privy to a great deal more than he let on.

'For goodness sakes, stop bothering me!' he said to a group of reporters one day, and then proposed a picnic atop the platform of a water tank stand overlooking the city.

'What if something happens while we're there?' they enquired.

'Well, you'll be able to watch it, won't you?' said Arch. Just in case, the press brought their movie cameras.

Intelligence had warned of a Japanese air raid at 2 pm, and the Japanese were very punctual. At precisely two o'clock, they appeared over Darwin, flying in perfect high-level formation of eighteen little white crosses standing out against the clear blue sky heading in from the east. From their vantage point, Arch directed the reporters, at one point urging one cameraman to lower his camera to capture the strike of bombs along the harbour. The result is a famous piece of footage familiar in many documentaries.

Soon he began to hit back, flying supply drops to those soldiers still harassing the Japanese from behind their lines. He also began bombing newly occupied islands including Timor, and his old home, Ambon. Arch knew just where to drop.

Eventually, Arch would fly again, training on the Beaufort, and then operationally with the B-24 Liberators. Big, heavy but reliable, he says. He would get to know the Liberator, and also the Americans he frequently flew in formation with.

'They're a funny lot, Americans,' he said. 'But then again, they thought we were funny.' On one occasion, Arch was flying with an American squadron as the combined group of eighteen aircraft were returning to Darwin after a raid to the north. Arch's navigator, John Jamieson was exceptionally talented and fazed by nothing. When the American formation began to prematurely turn left and break away on their own, Jamieson, sitting up with Arch, simply leaned across and opened the microphone, saying 'So long, fellas', then hung it up. After a pause, the American lead navigator replied warily, 'Too soon, huh?', and straightened up again to rejoin the formation.

Despite a slow start, Arch Dunne went on to a have a long and eventful war, becoming one of the youngest squadron leaders of the RAAF and earning the first Distinguished Flying Cross of the Pacific theatre. Post-war he resumed flying for the airlines, operating some of the great aircraft of post-war civil aviation such as the Constellation, DC-6 and perhaps the greatest propeller-driven airliner of them all the Lockheed Electra.

For sheer drama though, nothing would, or ever could come close to the day he flew out of Ambon for the last time, with the one lucky, eternally grateful extra passenger he managed to squeeze into the nose.

25

Walter Eacott

Beaufighter pilot

I called out to the wireless operator, 'Dinghy, dinghy, prepare for ditching!' And then down we went, smack!

One day in the late 1960s, Walter Eacott opened the paper at his home in London and noticed an ad calling for experienced air force officers to make their way Down Under to join the RAAF.

'Look at this, dear,' he said to his wife, Jean. 'They want old men for the air force in Australia. Let's go!'

At age forty-five, Walter, with Jean in tow, said goodbye to England and boarded a ship to start a new life as an administration officer with the Royal Australian Air Force. They liked what they found, and settled here for good.

'It's taken thirty years,' says Jean at their home near Melbourne, 'But we've nearly been accepted.'

For Walter, this was the start of his second air force career. His first began a quarter of a century earlier in the backyard of his home in the village of Chingford in Essex, when as a seventeen-year-old, he had a first class view of the Battle of Britain and the London Blitz.

'The glow in the sky the night they hit the docks was so red we thought the whole city was being destroyed,' he remembers.

Not that this experience was needed to shape his already keen desire to fly. At sixteen, Walter had joined the Air Defence Cadet Corps, a kind of air force Boy Scouts, and completed a rather terrifying-sounding glider course.

'It was completely primitive,' he said. 'We sat open to the elements in a tiny wooden glider which was launched when the other boys grabbed one end of a bungee rope and ran as hard as they could!' The only instruction Walter can remember receiving was, 'If you stop hearing the sound of the wind rushing past your ears, push the stick down, because it means you're stalling!'

So, one Friday in December 1940, when Walter walked into the RAF recruiting office at the Air Ministry in the heart of London, the crusty old gentlemen on the interview board sensed they had a keen one. 'We're going to take you on as a trainee pilot,' they told him. 'Now, you can go home and wait for your course to be ready, or if you like you can join up straightaway.'

'I was eager and stupid and joined up straightaway', he said. He signed on the dotted line and spent the next five months paying for his enthusiasm by filling sandbags in a gun pit on 'ground defence duties' until the trainee bottleneck had cleared and the RAF were ready to take him the following May.

With his training finally underway, Walter found his way to number 6 Initial Training Wing at Newquay in Cornwall, where he imbued himself in trigonometry, geometry, meteorology, and flying the Miles Magister, a smart little training aeroplane with spats covering the wheels and a 130 horsepower engine. From the start, he knew he was a natural.

'I didn't have any trouble with my flying at all,' he said matter-of-factly, as if discussing riding a bike. His instructors obviously agreed, and selected him to fly the magnificent twin-engined Bristol Beaufighter.

'There were two wonderful sensations in my flying career,' Walter told me. 'The first was going solo for the first time in the Magister, the second was flying the Beaufighter.'

In 1938, during the belated scramble to re-equip before the Second World War, the British government woke up one day to realise it possessed not one heavy fighter aircraft which could perform long-range interception or escorts. Enter the Bristol Aeroplane Company which quickly knocked up a proposal to adapt just such an aircraft from their Beaufort torpedo-bomber, then in the final stages of design and testing. The Air Ministry hastily approved the proposal, and the 'Beau-fighter' was born.

This new hybrid fighter took barely eight months from drawing board to first flight and was an amazing success story of wartime cooperation and expediency. It borrowed its wings, control surfaces, undercarriage, as well as half its name from the Beaufort, but the result was a far superior aircraft. Rugged, powerful, and with four 20 millimetre cannon in the nose as well as six machine guns in the wings, the Beaufighter was the most heavily armed Allied fighter of the war and a hit from the start.

Beaufighters flew as fighter, night fighter, strike and torpedo aircraft in all major theatres of the war and were adored by their two-man crews. It's 14-cylinder 'Hercules' sleeve-valve engines – itself an invention of the Bristol company – made the Beaufighter not only powerful, but remarkably quiet. The RAAF liked them so much they built 365 of their own 'Mark XXIs at the Commonwealth Aircraft Corporation factories at Fishermans Bend in Victoria for use against the Japanese in the Pacific. Here they performed ground-attack and ship-strafing duties, coming to grisly fame in the Bismarck Sea battle.

One of the Beaufighter's enduring legends was the name 'Whispering Death' supposedly attributed to it by the Japanese as they cowered from its raking fire in jungle or island bunkers and ships' holds. But, as formidable a weapon as it was, the story, which remains firm in the minds of some today, was in fact a myth born of colourful wartime propaganda.

Taking off for the first time in a Beaufighter was an experience Walter has never forgotten. After the briefest of introductions from an experienced pilot, he sat in the cockpit on the runway threshold and received permission to take off. 'I eased the throttle forward and felt this surge in my seat. I've never felt such power in my life,' he says.

The Beaufighter began to come off Bristol's production lines concurrently with the development of the first airborne 'AI' radar, and so leant itself to becoming the first truly effective night fighter of the war. But all this was very 'hush-hush'.

At his OTU at Church Fenton in Yorkshire, Walter trained in an atmosphere of complete secrecy. 'We were more or less threatened not to talk to anyone about what we were learning, and forbidden even to take notes in the classroom.'

In March 1942, Walter was posted to the famous Battle of Britain aerodrome at Tangmere on the south coast of England to number 219 Squadron to begin prowling the night skies of Britain, hunting for German raiders.

'This was the time of the carrot nonsense,' he tells me a little wearily. I'd always known about this famous wartime ploy – still folklore today – to disguise the advent of airborne radar by exaggerating the eyesight-enhancing properties of carrots. The Air Ministry insisted their night fighter pilots eat them by the bucket-load. 'I've never liked them since,' Walter tells me.

In the daylight hours, Walter and the Beaufighter crews would wear dark glasses to protect their vision, then take off in darkness to make standing patrols, flying large figure-of-eight circuits between radar beacons on the south coast of England. Being the most junior pilot on the squadron however, he never got to see much of the action. 'As soon as a German was detected, we were recalled to the ground, and one of the aces was scrambled to fly up and deal with it.'

But just a few weeks after arriving at Tangmere, Walter's night flying career was cut short. After all the months spent in night training, all 219's fifteen aircrews were assembled and informed that they were being transferred to the Middle East as day fighter pilots. 'Such a waste of money,' thought Walter.

From his Mediterranean base in Misurata in Libya, Walter began a very different kind of war, protecting convoys (often the trigger-happy Royal Navy gunners were as dangerous as the enemy) and attacking German ships in harbour or at sea. With a photo reconnaissance picture of a Greek or Italian port, Walter would often fly for several hours skimming the wave-tops under the German radar at no more than 20 feet. Dangerous enough with any aircraft, this was particularly hazardous with the Beaufighter, as it had a tendency to undulate or 'hunt' slightly in level flight. At 20,000 feet, it didn't matter, but at just 20, it could be deadly. Hands-off flying was therefore extremely dangerous. 'We had a couple of quite experienced pilots who just hit the water. They were gone in a second,' he said.

And then there was the German air force. As powerful as the Beaufighter was, it was never as nimble as a single-engined fighter, and pilots had to be very careful about who they tangled with.

'We would go after the Junkers 52 transports and the twin-engined 88s, but we never had the speed to outrun a 109. I should know. That was my downfall,' Walter said with a slight chuckle.

By late 1943, the Germans had been forced out of Africa and most of Walter's squadron had completed their obligatory tour of 250 operational hours. Everyone was about to pack up and head home to England.

On what was supposed to be one of his last trips before the move home, Walter, flying with his wireless operator, Bob Pritchard ('he was about eight years older than me,' said Walter. 'So I called him Grandad'), was detailed to escort a group of American torpedo-bombers attacking German supply ships near Rhodes. He made the rendezvous, met the Americans, and headed onto the target. Around the small convoy, two German Arado 196 seaplanes were circling.

'One of them dived down towards me, firing, so I flew up to meet it,' he said. Walter made a climbing turn heading straight for the German aircraft, firing short bursts from his cannon and machine guns. It was a case of who would pull away first and the German lost. Peeling away, the Arado passed over Walter's head, giving him a view of the damage he had caused to its underside. 'There were bits coming off it everywhere,' he said. Turning again, he watched it hit the water. He then gave chase to the second Arado, fired a few shots but broke off to return to the convoy. Later, he learned that it too crashed.

Back at the airfield after the mission, he discovered that the Arado he had brought down had made a better account of itself than first realised. In the brief and one-sided skirmish, one of its bullets had severed an aileron cable in Walter's Beaufighter, rendering it unserviceable.

The next day, 10 November 1943, Walter was sent to fly another trip, again a bomber escort, almost an exact re-run in fact, of the day before. Today though, things would be different: he would be flying an unfamiliar aircraft, and this time, the Germans would be waiting for him.

'We were immediately jumped by a flight of Messerschmitt 109s at the same spot as the previous day,' he said. It was no contest so the Beaufighters immediately turned and headed for home. But when Walter applied full power he watched in horror as his comrades speed past him. 'I was sitting there, banging away at the throttles wondering why this thing wouldn't go any faster!' he said. The engines on his replacement aircraft, a brand new machine, had not been properly tuned and the Beaufighter was underpowered, a lame duck in the middle of the Mediterranean surrounded by the enemy.

Walter knew immediately how it was going to end. 'There were six of them and they just sat on my tail and used me for target practice,' he said. He tried manoeuvring as much as he could, and Bob retaliated as best he could, firing the sole gas-operated rearward-firing machine gun from a blister positioned half way down the fuselage, but the fighters were not shaken. The chase went on for a seemingly endless 10 minutes, the German aircraft toying with him like a cat with a mouse.

Walter reckons a couple of the German aircraft were actually out of ammunition, but used him to practice attack manoeuvres, coming up close on his tail, then changing place with another aircraft. One engine was hit and caught fire, and Walter hit the automatic extinguisher switch. It seemed to work for a while but then flames flared up again, licking all along the starboard wing. Smoke began billowing from the cockpit. 'I called out to the wireless operator, "Dinghy, dinghy, prepare for ditching!" And then down we went, *smack*!'

Walter knew he had only a few seconds on the surface before the aircraft would start to sink. Water rose quickly around his feet. The aircraft had an automatic dinghy release and he could only hope it had deployed properly. Still strapped in the cockpit, he saw the light fade to green, then darkness as the aeroplane went under. He opened the escape hatch above his head but something held him in his seat. With every second seeing him deeper underwater, he frantically searched around with his hands. In the panic, he had forgotten to release his seat harness.

'Once I remembered the harness, I popped out like a cork,' he said.

On the surface, the dinghy had released, but it was upside down and only half inflated. 'That's when I thought I was going to drown,' said Walter. He and his wireless operator struggled, but eventually righted it and forced what breath they could muster into the mouthpiece. Quietly, he thanked the time he had put in to the dinghy drills at the base.

It wasn't cold, at first, but with the night the temperature dropped. Walter kept a lookout for the lights of Allied submarines, one of which had recently picked up a couple of downed airmen from the squadron in similar circumstances, but this night it was not to be. When the sun came up the next morning, the two men made a decision: they would paddle to neutral Turkey, just 60 miles away. They reckoned they could make it.

It was a short-lived ambition. Soon after, the unmistakeable shapes of two German Arado 196 seaplanes, the same type Walter had shot down the previous day, appeared overhead, circled and touched down on the water a short distance away. The German observer emerged and crawled out onto the wing.

'How long you schwimm?' he called out.

'Since yesterday,' replied an exhausted Walter.

'Ah, for you the war is over!' Walter has heard this cliché recounted by so many captured servicemen, he is convinced the Germans were trained to say it.

'We were bitterly disappointed,' he tells me. 'I was sure we could have made it to Turkey.'

Walter was taken to Crete, fed a meal of spaghetti and flown out at 3 am on a Junkers 52 to Greece, then on a twelve-day trip by a very cold train to Germany.

Walter spent sixteen months as a prisoner of war at the large Stalag Luft 4B camp near Muhlberg in eastern Germany.

From the beginning, his mind was set on escape. Airmen were notorious escapees, and so were put into a separate, and very secure barbed wire enclosure in the middle of the camp. 'The soldiers seemed to accept their lot more readily,' said Walter. 'The air force fellows had a more restless spirit.'

A compound within a compound was no place from which to attempt escape, so Walter teamed up with a fellow 'restless spirit', navigator George Lloyd, who had been shot down over Europe some months before. The two men swapped identities with a couple of soldiers in order to be assigned onto the work parties, where opportunities for escape were more likely to present themselves.

Englishman Walter Eacott became Irishman Fusilier James Leslie and spent twelve hours a day outside the camp working on the German railways, repairing bomb damage, and waiting his chance to abscond. His first attempt was bungled. Four days after doing a runner, he was discovered sheltering in a disused air-raid shelter, recaptured, and put on bread and water in solitary confinement for seven days.

Walter settled down to incarceration with his fellow prisoners, a diverse mixture from every service and nationality. From what clandestine sources they could glean pieces of information, everyone followed the war's progress as best they could.

Food was another obsession. As the war became more desperate for the Germans, the men noticed the vital Red Cross parcels, an essential supplement to their meagre diet, become scarcer. In the beginning they were given one per man, but by war's end, a single parcel would be divided between up to a dozen men, if they turned up at all. Everyone became very thin. But as harsh as life was for Walter, it was nothing to how he saw the Russians being treated, he said. 'They were kept like animals. It was terrible.'

He made more of his second chance of escape when towards war's end, the Americans bombed a nearby town and the men were made to shelter in a nearby forest. Walter and George wasted no time digging a hole, hiding themselves in it and covering it over with branches till the others had returned to the camp.

With a nation collapsing in chaos around them, the two men began an odyssey that Walter relates in sometimes bizarre snatches. Travelling west towards the advancing Allies by night and sheltering by day, he once hid in a ditch by the side of a road as an entire German column made its way along the road a few feet away on the other side of some bushes. 'Tanks, armoured cars, everything,' he remembered. 'It took about two hours to pass.'

On one extraordinary occasion, the two men turned a corner to find a group of German soldiers resting in a laneway. To run would probably guarantee a bullet in the back, so with nerves of iron, they didn't break step, strolled past, and gave a casual 'Guten Tag' and a smile. 'Guten Morgen,' came the reply from a German. Had he looked a little closer, he would have noticed the poorly doctored army uniforms the strangers were wearing.

While I spoke with Walter about this event, his wife Jean stood stock still in the living room on her way to the kitchen, plate of cake in hand, as absorbed as I was in her husband's story.

'I'm going to have to ask you to start from the beginning,' she said, 'because I don't know any of this.'

One freezing morning, after sixteen days and nights on the run sleeping in barns, railwaymen's huts and anywhere else they could find, Walter and George warily approached a distant figure holding a rifle on sentry duty. As they neared, their step quickened and they joyfully embraced the first non-captive American soldier they had seen in over a year.

In April 1945, with the war all but over, a severely under-weight Walter landed back on home soil at an RAF aerodrome in Surrey for the first time in two years, but it was not to be the joyful homecoming he had pictured during the many months of captivity. Returning to London, he decided to give his parents the surprise of their lives and dialled the number of his home. It would not connect. Several times he tried but each time could not get through. Perplexed, he telephoned a family friend who, upon hearing his voice, became profoundly distressed. Something, Walter sensed, was terribly wrong. Then he was given the awful news: six weeks previously, Walter's mother had taken the traditional half-day Thursday afternoon off from work and had gone home after lunch. Ten minutes later, a German V2 rocket hit the house, destroying it completely. She was found in the rubble alive, but died soon after in the ambulance.

'Here's me looking forward to a wonderful homecoming and it all ended in disaster,' he reflected.

Walter had survived the ordeal of being shot down, nearly drowning in the ocean, being captured, then escaping and heading out in disguise across Germany under the noses of the enemy. His mother, supposedly safe in her living room had been killed just weeks before the end of the war. The awful irony still saddens him to this day.

Taken in by neighbours however, his life took another turn in the form of a pretty young local girl who made him a cake he still remembers to this day. This same girl, now his wife of many years, removes the plates from an excellent lunch she has prepared for Walter and myself. Walter's plate is, I notice, clean.

'You could never throw food away,' Jean told me. 'Not after what he'd been through.'

Postscript

I drove away from my final interview, trying to understand just what it was I had achieved. I had spoken with more than two dozen former pilots, navigators, bomb-aimers, gunners and wireless operators who had flown in deserts, over cities and in the stifling jungles of the South-west Pacific. On each occasion, I was met with complete acceptance in allowing me to dredge up highly personal memories of fear, loss and trauma, often for the first time in decades.

As we spoke, many men seemed to physically transform as the power of recollection worked its magic on their ageing bodies – raising voices, quickening pulses and rekindling fire into dulling eyes – until I felt I was speaking not with men in their eighties, but boys younger than myself who had lived through what they were describing just days, rather than decades, before.

Each interview I conducted was completely different. Some were shy, some were blasé old hands, speaking as if at a dinner party. Some treated it like a stimulating game, becoming more animated and energetic as we went along.

Others found it unsettling, and seemed haunted by the raised ghosts of long-dormant memories. As I said goodbye and turned from their front doorstep, some men wore a look I knew would linger long after my visit, despite the soothing efforts of wives and family members.

Many were astonished by the strength of their own recollection, and more than once I was told that the memories were becoming more vivid as the years went by.

The only common thread with every interview was that, by the end, we were all exhausted.

I had been privileged to be invited as an intimate into a lost and private world, rich in drama and tragedy and in almost every case, the most formative and enduring experiences of a person's life. What I had learned, what I had experienced, albeit vicariously, I cannot accurately measure nor fully appreciate.

But what was it they wanted? I often asked myself. What do these men, these survivors, often bewildered by their own longevity wish above all else to be the legacy of their deeds, sixty years on from the cauldron of their youth? I put it to one pilot directly, and in the brief answer he gave, I felt he spoke for all.

'To be remembered,' he said. 'That's it. Just somctimes to be remembered.'

Acknowledgements

Writing this book was a pure labour of love, a fulfilment of an ambition of many years, which itself stemmed from a life-long obsession with the aircraft of the Second World War and the men who flew them. It took the encouragement of my friend, journalist and writer, Peter Wilmoth to spur me into action, over lunch one day when he was working on his own biography of Bud Tingwell. Peter had a small list of minor technical points he had asked me to clarify concerning Bud's air force days flying photo reconnaissance Spitfires in the Mediterranean. After doing my best to oblige, he looked at me and said, 'you know you should really do a book of your own'. For that one comment, I will be eternally grateful. Peter then introduced me to my publishers, Pan Macmillan, who have been a delight from the word go, and whose patience I have stretched to the limit with a series of elastic deadlines that not once elicited a harsh word.

I must also thank Bud, not only for being part of the book, but for his very generous Foreword.

For reasons of space, I was able to include just over half the number of interviews I conducted in several states over the course of a year. For those men I met, but who I was not able to include I am profoundly sorry. It is in no way a reflection of the time spent together or the value of your war services. In reality, I could have included yours, and a hundred more.

Peter Forbes, fellow aircraft enthusiast and fighter expert was invaluable in helping me contact some of the fighter boys and accompanied me on several interviews offering insights and advice I found most helpful. Peter, I thank you.

Many thanks to Brian Walley, not only for sharing his story with me but also for allowing me to reproduce extracts from the book *Silk and Barbed Wire*, available through Sage Pages (www.sagepages.com.au). Thanks also to the Royal Air Forces Ex-Prisoner of War Association, WA branch.

Thank you also to Tom Hall who kindly allowed me to reproduce an extract from his book *Typhoon Warfare – Reminiscences of a rocket-firing Typhoon pilot*.

The volunteer staff at the Aviation Heritage Museum of Western Australia at Bull Creek in Perth were wonderful to me, allowing me access to their extensive library, and also bending the rules to allow me to crawl around inside their magnificent Lancaster bomber as well as sit in the cockpit of their Spitfire to acquaint myself with the internal layout of both aircraft. I thank them, and highly recommend to anyone with an interest in aircraft to visit this undiscovered gem.

Finally, thank you to the wives and children who went to such great effort to track me down, set up times, give me precise directions and take time out from busy schedules to prepare lunches, make tea and cake and generally make me feel completely at home with their beloved father or husband.